OUT TO WORK

OUT TO WORK

*Migration, Gender, and the
Changing Lives of Rural Women
in Contemporary China*

Arianne M. Gaetano

University of Hawai'i Press
Honolulu

© 2015 University of Hawai'i Press
All rights reserved
Printed in the United States of America

20 19 18 17 16 15   6 5 4 3 2 1

Library of Congress Cataloging-in-Publication Data

Gaetano, Arianne M., author.
   Out to work: migration, gender, and the changing lives of rural women in contemporary
China / Arianne M. Gaetano.
     pages cm
   Includes bibliographical references and index.
   ISBN 978-0-8248-4099-0 (cloth)—ISBN 978-0-8248-4098-3 (pbk.)
   1. Women migrant labor—China—Longitudinal studies.   2. Rural women—China—
Longitudinal studies.   3. Rural-urban migration—China—Longitudinal studies.   I. Title.
   HD6200.G34 2015
   331.40951—dc23

                                             2014031307

University of Hawai'i Press books are printed on
acid-free paper and meet the guidelines for permanence
and durability of the Council on Library Resources.

Designed by George Whipple

Printed by Sheridan Books, Inc.

CONTENTS

Acknowledgments

This book culminates many years of research and writing, during which time I benefited from the intellectual and personal support of many colleagues and friends, and received the financial assistance of numerous organizations. Through these acknowledgments I wish to express my sincere appreciation and gratitude to them.

At Auburn University, the College of Liberal Arts generously provided a non-competitive semester teaching release during the fall semester of 2011 and a competitive summer research award in 2013. My colleagues in the Department of Sociology, Anthropology and Social Work offered steady encouragement; I thank Kelly Alley and Allen Furr especially for their experienced counsel. My (now retired) colleague in Women's Studies, Ruth Crocker, read and commented on the proposal and cheered me on through subsequent stages. Others on campus offered sage advice at key moments of the publishing process: Morris Bian, Paula Bobrowski, Joyce DeVries, Carolyn Fitzgerald, Makiko Mori, and Traci O'Brien.

Fieldwork research for this project, including short and extended sojourns in Beijing and the countryside, extended over ten years and was made possible only with the resources of these entities, to whom I am most grateful: a research fellowship in contemporary China studies from the Center for East and Southeast Asian Studies at Lund University; a research fellowship in migration studies from the Asia Research Institute of the National University of Singapore; a graduate student research grant from the Urban China Research Network; a joint fellowship for study and research from Peking University and the University of Hawai'i; a Haynes Foundation fellowship from the graduate school of the University of Southern California; and a Department of Education foreign language and area studies award administered through the Center for East Asian Studies at the University of Southern California.

I thank Gene Cooper, C. Cindy Fan, Janet Hoskins, and Stanley Rosen for their boundless support and mentoring over the years, which have helped advance my career. I especially thank Cindy for inviting me to participate in a conference panel, and Janet for her detailed feedback on this project and for tracking me down in Singapore and Sweden to discuss my progress. I also thank Charlotte Furth for her warm hospitality. Finally, I am grateful to my undergraduate mentor Jing Wang for first sparking my interest in Chinese language and culture and directing me toward anthropology, and for her friendship.

My research in Beijing was greatly facilitated by the late Bai Nansheng and by Xie Lihua, cofounder of the Migrant Women's Club, who shared their expertise and put me in touch with numerous migrant women workers. I am also extremely grateful to Lu Shaoqing and Zhao Shukai, of the Ministry of Agriculture and the Development Research Council, respectively, who for more than ten years have helped me to better understand this topic, to connect and reconnect with migrant women workers, and to feel welcome in Beijing. I also thank my friends Ding Ning, Jeannie Katsigris, Debbie Lowe, and Zhang Lixin for assisting me to meet and stay in touch with migrant women working in Beijing.

Over these many years my scholarship has been richly enhanced by intellectual exchanges with colleagues in Chinese studies or with expertise on gender and migration in Asia: Rachel Connelly, Mei-ling Ellerman, C. Cindy Fan, Emily Hannum, Tamara Jacka, Ellen R. Judd, Teresa Kuan, Helena Löthman, Cecilia Milwertz, Rachel Murphy, Nicole Newendorp, Eileen Otis, Nicola Piper, Barbara Schulte, Hsiu-hua Shen, Allen Smart, Josephine Smart, Marina Svensson, Tan Shen, Eric Thompson, Cara Wallis, Sunning Wan, Martin K. Whyte, Hairong Yan, Brenda S. A. Yeoh, Hong Zhang, Tiantian Zheng, and Zheng Zhenzhen.

At the University of Hawai'i Press, acquisitions editor Pamela Kelly worked tirelessly to bring this book to fruition and I am indebted to her and also her capable staff. Westchester Publishing Services adeptly managed the production process. Virgina Perrin provided expert copyediting and Amron Gravett prepared the index. I am especially grateful to the three anonymous reviewers selected by the press to review my manuscript, for their careful reading and constructive feedback on earlier versions, which most certainly improved the book, though I alone am responsible for its final content. I also thank Sim Chi Yin and VII Photo Agency for granting permission to reproduce her captivating photo on the cover.

I warmly thank my friends and family members for their unflagging enthusiasm and encouragement for my work. Elizabeth Bowditch, Sara and Michael Kenney, and Gill Murdoch generously provide me with relevant books and videos. My parents, Leonard and Suzanne Gaetano, give their boundless love and support. My spouse, Steve Manos, ensures I have the space, time, and quiet in which to write.

My deepest gratitude is given to the many migrant women met in Beijing over the years who shared with me their stories and experiences, earning my utmost respect for their resilience and humor in the face of hardship. I am most thankful to my key informants, who taught me so much and generously offered me their friendship, and to their families, who welcomed me into their homes with kind hospitality. I dedicate this book to you all.

Parts of Chapter 2 and Chapter 4 are drawn from Arianne M. Gaetano, "Filial Daughters, Modern Women: Migrant Domestic Workers in Post-Mao Beijing," pp. 41–79, in *On the Move: Women and Rural-to-Urban Migration in Contemporary China* (2004), edited by Arianne M. Gaetano and Tamara Jacka, published by Columbia University Press. Portions of Chapter 5 and Chapter 6 expand upon material from Arianne M. Gaetano, "Sexuality in Diasporic Space: Rural-to-Urban Migrant Women Negotiating Gender and Marriage in Contemporary China," *Gender, Place, and Culture* 15 (6) 2008: 629–645, special issue on heterosexuality and migration in Asia edited by Katie Walsh, Hsiu-hua Shen, and Katie Willis. These materials are published here in revised form by permission of the publishers.

Introduction

A New Beginning

I left home. When the car began to move, I didn't shed a tear, because I wanted to go . . . a new beginning. Filled only with a strong yearning for the city, I gave no serious thought to the matter of my employment. My aunt had prepared for me a battered old suitcase. Inside I had packed only some clothes, books, a pen, and two notebooks. I wore a watch, and carried two hundred *yuan* given to me by my mother upon departure. My father didn't quite agree with the work I was setting out to do, yet he didn't oppose me when I insisted that I would go anyway, and said only: "Come back if things don't work out." My mom was pleased with where I was headed, only sad that I wouldn't be able to return home often. No one else knew I was leaving; my brother was at school, so I didn't see him to say goodbye. In the car, speeding along the highway, I turned my head to look out the window at the trees passing by and saw the budding shoots that heralded spring, and then I cried. So quickly did the scenery flash by that I sometimes couldn't clearly make anything out. Still, the car continued rushing toward the endless horizon of that highway. Beyond was the city where I was headed—a strange and unfamiliar place. Perhaps there the sky would not be as deep a blue as in my hometown, and there would not be a quiet path like the one in my village. I did not even know why I wanted to go there.

In this recollection, recorded in her diary, a young woman I will call Qiaolian describes her initial migration in 1997 from her village to Beijing to take up a job as a *baomu*[1] caring for a toddler and doing housework for a three-generation family in exchange for a small salary, room, and board. Qiaolian is a member of China's large "floating population" (*liudong renkou*).[2] Rural women like her are collectively known as the "working sisters" (*dagongmei*), young and unmarried daughters from predominantly agrarian households who make up as much as 33 to 50 percent of China's rural migrant labor force (*nongmingong*), which has steadily grown from between 20 and 30 million in the mid-1980s to over 160 million people in 2012 (Chan 2012).[3] Qiaolian's diary selection neatly conveys the tension in the moment between departure and arrival that is pregnant with possibilities, in which Qiaolian's emotions range from excitement and optimism to homesickness and anxiety, as she anticipates a journey of great significance in her life.

The text provides some clues as to Qiaolian's specific motivations, expectations, and concerns in regard to the imminent journey, which in turn reflect her individual characteristics, family background, as well as the broader social and cultural context of contemporary China. For example, her battered suitcase and meager possessions indicate the family's relative poverty by urban standards at the time, and suggest a motive for going out to work. Her dizziness at the passing scenery attests to the novelty of riding in a car, and further highlights the contrast between the village and the city as well as between herself and her employers—actual and symbolic differences between people and places that are brought to attention as migration creates spaces of traversal and contact. The notebook and writing utensils represent Qiaolian's wish to continue her formal education, which was prematurely cut short due to a combination of poverty and gender discrimination, and hints at a more personal motive for migration. Her father's reluctance stems from his shame at having an unmarried daughter working for strangers and doing menial labor, in violation of norms of gender and social respectability that reflect poorly on the family. Her mother's practical gift of cash bestowed like a dowry, as insurance against uncertainty, belies her worry about her daughter's safety, although her satisfaction at Qiaolian's departure resonates with her daughter's optimistic expectation for a better life. As the car speedily propels her away from the village and the past, toward the city and the future, Qiaolian gives voice to doubt, foreboding the hardships ahead. Indeed, by dint of her origin, gender, age, and marital status, as well as education and occupation, Qiaolian would occupy an inferior and marginal position in the urban labor market and urban society, and thus be quite vulnerable. She would therefore suffer disappointments and setbacks along with rewards in her new life as a migrant woman worker.

In her narrative, Qiaolian is the protagonist who parts with "tradition," symbolized by an idyllic rural setting, and seizes the opportunity to become a subject of history and modernization by embarking on a path toward the distant beckoning city. Her writing thus calls to mind Berman's (1982) description of the _ambivalent experience of modernity,_ wherein a new temporality "objectifies the past and presents horizons of possibilities located far beyond one's present, such that the future becomes something to be desired" (Hirsch 2001: 143). "One can now dream of a different life—more decent, bearable or enjoyable" (Bauman 2001: 122). Predicated on an individuated and self-conscious subjectivity, modernity offers opportunities for self-making and transformation of identity (Felski 1995; Giddens 1991), yet simultaneously "threatens to destroy everything we have, everything we know, everything we are" (Berman 1982: 15). Such a dramatic rupture with the past that enables a hopeful yet uncertain future of one's own making is reflected in Qiaolian's desire for a "new beginning" expressed in the opening passage.

This book is an ethnographic study that focuses on rural Chinese women, including Qiaolian, for whom migration entails not only moving across space but also venturing in new directions in life and reinventing themselves in time. In contemporary China, the association of the city, urban life, and urbanites with dynamic, forward-looking, "modern" culture in contradistinction to the countryside, rural life, and rural inhabitants, considered mired in "traditional" culture and behind the times or "backward," is a powerful ideological construct of place and identity (see, e.g., Chu 2010; Liu 2000; Sun 2009). These symbolic connotations also mark a shift away from the more positive view of peasants as a revolutionary force and the backbone of socialist development under the leadership of Mao Zedong (e.g., Meisner 1999). Among rural Chinese youth in the postreform period, leaving the village to work in the city is widely perceived as an integral part of becoming modern, as well as becoming more mature and increasing your moral worth, and thus migration becomes a search for self-identity and self-transformation. Mobility and modernity have become inextricably linked in the contemporary era of globalization (e.g., Urry 2007). My purpose is to explore how mobility and modernity intersect in the lives of Qiaolian and her peers.

This project is motivated by curiosity about rural migrant women's lives in contemporary China, and the feminist concern of whether or not labor migration benefits them and promotes gender equality. How do they experience migration, and what are the cultural, social, and even political ramifications of their migration experience? This study builds upon a robust literature focused on gender and migration that has emerged over the past few decades.[4] In the 1970s and 1980s, feminist scholars began to illuminate women's roles in migration. Privileging their perspectives has since served as an important corrective to the field of migration studies that had long overlooked women. By the 1990s, with the understanding of gender as a socially constructed, fluid, and relational category, feminist scholars began to explore the gendering of migration. On the whole, the scholarship indicates that migration affects women and men differently and that therefore it "looks different" from the perspective of the individual and female migrant. Moreover, due to the dynamic nature of gender, gendered ideologies and practices may change as individuals encounter shifting economic, political, and social structures through migration (Donato et al. 2006: 6).

Drawing upon these insights, a central goal of this study is to investigate how migration impacts rural Chinese women's identity and their agency or capacity for self-determination. In turn, it aims to illuminate whether or not, and how, migration empowers rural women and fosters positive social change, by transforming gender norms, roles, and relations in ways that promote gender equality. My research contributes to this literature a longitudinal focus on change over the life course of individual women, and across numerous sociocultural and spatial contexts, including the family and intimate relations as well as at work and in the city. Such an approach reflects a reconceptualization of migration within interdisciplinary scholarship, as a sociocultural process (Halfacre and Boyle 1993), which unfolds across space (Silvey 2006) and in time (McHugh 2000), rather than as a one-off event or unidirectional move. It also responds to recent calls by migration scholars to integrate anthropological approaches to personhood and family with migration theory (e.g., Halfacre and Boyle 1993; McHugh 2000).

It is particularly significant that rural Chinese women are participating in this quest, and hence important to better understand their experiences. First, migration to distant cities for work was not an option for most rural women of previous generations. Migration opens up new paths to rural women, including those previously forged only by men; enterprising young women who walk along these roads can have very different futures from previous generations of women. Second, for unmarried women, migration corresponds to a critical juncture of their life course between youth and impending adulthood, signified by marriage and motherhood, and thus has great potential to influence that trajectory. Third, migration enables them to become wage earners, consumers, city-dwellers (albeit temporary), and even migration brokers, new roles that both augment and challenge their primary social identity and roles in the family and household as well as their marginalization in the labor market and urban society. Fourth, migration creates a "state of in-between-ness," which is disorienting yet potentially empowering (Lawson 2000: 174). No longer identifying with the village but also not fully integrated into the urban milieu, migrant women have the task to manage identity "in relation to negotiated meanings of gendered concepts in both their communities of origin and their urban surroundings" (Silvey 2000: 511). Rural women's changing visions of themselves and their futures, gleaned through labor migration, reflect their awareness of other possibilities for being-in-the-world that could be a basis for social change, starting with their own lives. Migration thus engenders profound transformations that have broader social significance as individuals adopt ways of thinking and being that call into question normative discourses and practices and unsettle the status quo of power relations in the domestic and public spheres. Finally, a focus on rural migrant women's experiences and agency is theoretically useful for critiquing the discourses of Chinese modernity that portray rural women as passive embodiments of timeless or backward "tradition" but not as subjects and agents of (their own) history.[5]

My research focuses closely on the life stories of a cohort of young women born between 1976 and 1984 who first migrated from their villages in central and western provinces to Beijing between 1993 and 2000, in their mid-to-late teens, to work in the informal service economy as domestic workers and hotel housekeepers, and documents their lives over an extended period of fieldwork. Multisited research, in key informants' hometowns (sending villages) and in Beijing (destination), along with regular and continuous contact with key informants over several years, allows me to situate migration across social and spatial contexts. I am also able to consider migration's impact on the individual's life trajectory, as time and experience engender shifts in migration goals and meaning, as well as shifts in the options and resources available for individuals to express agency and effect cultural change.

This project originated in eighteen months of dissertation fieldwork conducted from 1998 to 2000, primarily in Beijing, which included interviews with and participant-observation among thirty migrant women domestic workers or hotel housekeepers, two-thirds of whom were under age twenty-five. During a subsequent research period in 2002, I followed up with several of the younger women who were still in Beijing: Qiaolian, Changying, Ruolan, Yaling, Shuqin, Shuchun, Meilan, Peiqi, Rongli, Xiulan, and Lina, and cultivated two additional informants (Xiaofang and Yarui). Since then, with the aid of airmail letters, e-mails and instant messages, cell-phone texts, and annual trips to China from 2006 to 2010, and again in 2012, I have maintained regular and close contact with Changying, Ruolan, Shuqin, Shuchun, and Yarui. I have visited each woman's natal village at least once, and have spent time with their spouses, offspring, siblings, parents, and in-laws. The stories and experiences of these "key informants," with whom I have had extended contact, comprise the heart of this book. In addition, I draw upon interviews or conversations with other migrant women I have met over these many years, including the original group of thirty informants, as well as the friends, covillagers (*tongxiang*),[6] and coworkers of my key informants.

Of the thirty migrant women interviewed between 1998 and 2000, ten were older domestic workers employed by my Beijing friends or neighbors, and were either introduced to me by their employers or met randomly around my residential complex. During that time, I also interviewed fifteen employers, all from the professional class, about their relationships with their domestic workers. Other informants were contacted through the Migrant Women's Club (Dagongmei Zhi Jia) of Beijing, an organization established in 1996 by a small group of urban women activists committed to the alleviation of social inequalities between residents of the countryside and the city and between men and women (Milwertz 2000). I attended numerous Club functions, including the First National Conference on

Migrant Women Workers' Rights and Interests, held in April 1999 (see Jacka 2000). From January to June 2000 I regularly participated in the Club's activities, met frequently with the organizers, staff, and members, and voluntarily offered English-language lessons to interested members. Over this period of time I established rapport with a core group of fifteen members of the Club, all unmarried and under the age of twenty-five, who had experience in domestic service. I interviewed each woman at least once for a few hours outside of scheduled Club meetings.

I met Qiaolian, whom I have already introduced, and Changying, her middle-school classmate, in 1998 when they were working as teachers in informal, illicit schools for migrant children in Beijing.[7] Qiaolian had previously worked in domestic service. During the 1999 Spring Festival, I accompanied these young women to their coastal home villages, about 250 miles from Beijing, to meet their families. Around this time I also became friendly with two sisters from a poor and remote village in north China about five hundred miles from Beijing, which I toured in 2002. Shuqin had worked for a time in 1997 as a chambermaid at a Beijing hotel where my American friend, who introduced us, held a long-term room lease. Her elder sister Shuchun had been a domestic worker for a Beijing family. When I first met them in 1998, the sisters were working together in a small-scale, private apparel factory in Beijing. In late 1999 they joined a custodial services company contracted to a four-star hotel. I spent much time at the hotel, observing them on the job, and at the worker dormitories, hanging out with them and their coworkers. I also interviewed the janitorial company boss and the hotel housekeeping manager. Another American friend in Beijing introduced me to Ruolan, a chambermaid at the hotel where she stayed from 1996 to 1997. From a village just 150 miles from Beijing, Ruolan too had worked previously in domestic service in Beijing. I got to know Ruolan better in 2002 and during several visits to her natal and postmarital homes since 2006. Also in 2002 I met Xiaofang and Yarui, Shuchun's coworkers at the four-star hotel. Xiaofang had previously worked with Shuqin as a chambermaid in 1997. I forged a lasting bond with Yarui; since 2006 I have twice visited her natal village, less than 150 miles from Beijing. I have maintained relationships with all of these key informants for at least a decade, with the exception of Qiaolian and Xiaofang, both of whom I last saw in 2002.

Methodology

The combination of detailed interviews with participant-observation and long-term fieldwork among key informants enables me to provide a "thick description" (Geertz 1973) of migration from the perspective of the migrant, a viewpoint often overlooked in migration studies (Brettell 2000; Kearney 1995). Indeed, acknowledging migrants as social actors is a key contribution of anthropology and ethnographic research methods to migration scholarship (Brettell 2000; Mahler and Pessar 2006; McHugh 2000). Much migration scholarship focuses on macroeconomic structures and systems, or on the individual as a rational (male) economic actor, and considers migrants to be like "iron filings . . . impelled by forces beyond their conscious control . . . denied the creative capacity to innovate and shape the worlds from which and into which they moved" (J. Abu-Lughod 1975: 201). In contrast, I pay attention to agency, by which I refer to each individual's "independent modes of ideation and practice" and "capacity for purposeful action" (O'Hanlon 1988: 196–197).[8] Migration is not simply something that happens to migrants; they are conscious participants. Taking into account their motivations and desires, embodied experiences, and situated meanings of migration dispels facile assumptions and illuminates complexities. For example, similar to Qiaolian, most migrants from rural China are not fleeing desperate poverty but seeking an improved quality of life, the very definition of which evokes nonmonetary symbols, values, and statuses. Ethnographic methods are best suited to documenting subtleties and ascertaining their significance to migration.

A theoretical approach that engages both anthropology and feminist studies highlights the intersection of individual subjectivity and agency with discourses and institutional structures in the lives of rural migrant women in China (e.g., Kabeer 2000; Parker 2005; Wright 1995). Foucault established that agency could not be based on "an unmediated and transparent notion of the subject or identity as the centered author of social practice" (quoted in Hall 1996: 5). Rather, domination is exercised through symbolic production, and social identities are negotiated in dialogue with discursive power, not external to it. In turn, Bourdieu's theory of practice (1977) as taken up by anthropologists like Ortner (1984, 1995, 1996, and 2006), proposes how individuals may unconsciously reproduce cultural discourses according to social position; agency is thus "embedded" in structures (Ortner 1996: 12–13). Accordingly, shifts in social roles incurred through migration, such as when rural daughters become migrant workers, also involve discursive moves that open up new possibilities for identity and agency, and may engender cultural transformations. By highlighting migrant women's own understandings and experiences of migration and modernity, my ethnographic research sheds light on how state projects of modernization and development become individual ones that creatively play out over a woman's lifetime.

Further, feminist scholarship emphasizes that gendered ideologies, institutions, and practices mediate migration (Mahler and Pessar 2006: 33). Thus, migrants can be conceptualized as positioned within multiple and overlapping discourses and structures: at the micro level of the individual; at the meso level as members of households and families as well as social networks, and the gender relations and roles determined therein; and at the macro level of the political economy, including state policies and nationalist ideologies, which are themselves gendered (Brettell 2000; Silvey 2004). To explore the various sites, social positions, and identities that migrants simultaneously occupy, and to understand how they intersect with gender and impact rural migrant women's agency (Brettell and Sargeant 2006; Lawson 2000), I analyze interview transcripts, conversation notes, participant-observation field notes, and migrants' written works (e.g., letters, diaries), and also consult secondary sources.

At the macro level, a dual economy and labor market system, supported by an institutional mechanism of household register (*hukou*) and ideologies that maintain sociospatial class and gender inequalities, together construct young rural women as a cheap and flexible migrant labor force, who must sacrifice their youth for national development. Despite unjust conditions, young women are empowered by the chance to leave home, gain independence, see the world, and change fate. Urban consumer culture, shaped in global capitalism, likewise exploits their rural origins, youthfulness, and femininity and engenders new desires to be satiated by continuous labor (Pun 2003). Yet by capitalizing on these traits, and risking the "migration trap" of perpetual debt (Oishi 2005), young rural women can accrue significant symbolic and social capital.

At the meso level, a division of labor by sex, a patrilineal-patrilocal marriage and family system, and a tradition of son preference conspire to render daughters as temporary members of their natal households. On the one hand, they are susceptible to discrimination; on the other, they are expendable and available to migrate. Gendered social networks channel them into job niches that mimic divisions of labor in the household and reinforce gender stereotypes and inequality. But within these limitations, migrant women gain meaningful experiences, useful knowledge, and important capabilities that generate shifts in identity and social roles, expand their agency, and individually advance gender equality.

At the micro level, biography and personality shape each woman's migration motivations and experiences in myriad and unpredictable ways. I focus on a handful of key informants in an effort to convey each woman's unique history and character and to shed light on processes of change. Each is special in her way; as a group too they are rather exceptional. Their tenacious perseverance, through struggles and hardship, and their sheer ingenuity in recognizing and seizing upon opportunities afforded by migration, ultimately enabled them to achieve a degree of improved social status and social mobility. Yet their relative successes occurred within the context of wider gender and sociospatial inequalities that made their journeys so difficult. My approach is truly an "ethnography of the particular"

(L. Abu-Lughod 1991), which aims to illuminate culture as it is embodied and experienced by individuals, and reproduced or transformed in the context of social relations and interactions. The longitudinal ethnographic focus on a handful of individuals is appropriate to this task, but their stories are not intended to represent those of all migrant women from rural China.

Young rural women exercise agency when they reflect on their lives and reformulate their goals in light of old and new (to them) social rules, values, morals, and identities—including those encountered through migration, and thereby increase their capacity for purposeful action. Social positions and cultural discourses then become resources to be strategically manipulated. The choices these women make among available options variously enable and constrain their autonomy in different contexts, reaffirming the observation that "if systems of power are multiple, then resisting at one level may catch people up at other levels" (L. Abu-Lughod 1990: 53). For example, by playing the role of obedient and diligent "model workers," informants created gender-appropriate workspaces where they could preserve their maidenly reputations. Such an arrangement reproduced patriarchal relations in a new setting even as it allowed them to earn an independent wage. As another example, informants' refusal to marry in the traditional manner shows resistance to patriarchal authority vested in the kinship system. Yet the chance to exercise greater agency in marriage paradoxically entailed their continued subjection, as "migrant women workers," to the authority of employers and to capitalist discipline. These examples highlight the complex interplay of identity, agency, and the individual's life trajectory.

A focus on agency thus avoids a "zero-sum" approach to power as something gained or lost, as well as the polarizing debate in the literature on Chinese women and factory work over migrant women worker's identities as either "filial daughters" (under the authority of patriarchal households) or "rebellious daughters" (Woon 2000). Rather, I heed the call for a nuanced approach to how rural migrant women balance tensions they face simultaneously as "individual actors and in the context of the family and workplace patriarchal structure[s]" (Woon 2000: 162; see also A. Lee 2004), at particular moments of their lives. From this perspective, empowerment is situational, contextual, and also temporal, as it intersects with specific events in the life course. It is individual, though it has the potential to incrementally effect broader cultural and social transformations.

Organization of This Volume

This book is arranged chronologically as well as thematically, so that key informants' lives unfold over successive chapters. Chapter 1 provides the macrohistorical context for the migration of women in China over the past two decades. I briefly sketch China's "reform and opening" and explain how it set the stage for the labor migration of women by rearranging the relationships between rural and urban, women and men, and rural women and the state. I emphasize that the new economic policies of "market socialism" drew upon and intensified institutional and ideological forms of sociospatial (i.e., rural-urban, peasant-worker) class as well as gender difference. This seemed to naturally result in the creation of a cheap workforce of migrant women, disadvantaged in the labor force relative to urban workers and to men, and which has greatly enabled China's rapid accumulation of capital and economic growth. In summary, policy change has steered China in new directions, presenting rural women with new possibilities for their futures and hence to forge new beginnings, albeit under severe constraints and conditions of inequality. Successive chapters explore rural women's migration decisions and journeys and how they faced daunting circumstances by drawing upon an expanding repertoire of material, symbolic, and experiential resources to (re)negotiate identity and challenge patriarchal power in different social contexts and at different moments in their lives.

Chapter 2 presents and analyzes migration from the micro level of the individual and the meso level of the household. I explore rural women's motivations and expectations of migration, explaining how migration subjectively emerged from young women's desires for the new and modern, as well as a sense of filial responsibility to their families and households. Such cultural orientations reflected not only nationalist discourses of development and modernization, but also the patriarchal values of the traditional kinship and family system. Gender division of labor in the household and gender roles in the family shed light on why and how migration is gendered in a particular pattern. One migration story is explored in detail to further illustrate that migration motives are complex, and may vary according to an individual's particular biography and character (Pessar and Mahler 2003). The chapter thus highlights the importance to migration studies of a gender analytic as well as a migrant-centered ethnographic approach, which together present a more clear picture of why and how people migrate than do macro-level economic, demographic, or institutional explanations.

Chapter 3 describes the function and significance of social networks of kin, and covillagers guided by the principle of reciprocity, that facilitate migration by providing material and social support to new migrants, as well as guarding the moral reputations of unmarried women. Young migrant women are both pawns and players in social networks. On the one hand, the social network extends the reach of rural patriarchal power to the city and curtails women's autonomy. On the other hand, migrant women gain interpersonal skills, social status, and social capital, which can parlay into more and better work opportunities and social mobility. Importantly, participation in reciprocity-based social networks through migration marks rural women's foray into a sphere of activity generally associated with men.

Chapter 4 describes migrant women at work, highlighting work conditions, relations with employers and customers/clients, opinions and attitudes about their work, and their efforts to improve their position in the workforce. I also draw upon interviews I conducted in 1999–2000 and 2002 with employers of migrant domestic workers and hotel chambermaids, supplemented by casual conversations with key informants' employers and coworkers during 2006–2010, to explore labor relations and how they have changed over this time. Migrant women faced numerous obstacles and risks in the labor market and workplaces on account of their doubly disadvantaged status as migrants and women, as well as their youthful inexperience. Their efforts to overcome such barriers and dangers demonstrate the fluidity and multiplicity of identity. Importantly, in negotiating new roles and identities through interactions with employers and coworkers, migrant women develop useful skills and accrue resources that empower them in a restrictive labor market, and even more so in their families and rural communities, and in regard to their futures, as I explore in subsequent chapters.

Migrant women's exposure to urban lifestyles and consumer culture through working and living in cosmopolitan Beijing and its impact on their embodied subjectivity and gender identity, as well as on their social status, is the topic of Chapter 5. Migrant women's seemingly frivolous concerns with consumer taste and trends are in fact emblematic of a deeper anxiety about belonging, identity, and social status. Applying knowledge and techniques of consumption to their own bodies and lifestyles allows relatively powerless rural women a degree of control and freedom to make themselves over from "country bumpkins" to "urban sophisticates." Ostensibly superficial makeovers can also have significant social effects, as migrant women parlay their symbolic capital and expertise into social and economic capital. For example, experienced migrant women gain respect of kin and peers back home by providing information and advice. They can also benefit financially by exploiting their youthful bodies and femininity. Yet, their self-transformations are insufficient to fully overcome their marginalization in urban society. Meanwhile, the stresses of migrant life negatively impact on their physical and mental well-being. Also, their sexier images are a source of tension as they conflict with conservative ethics and social mores, and may interfere with filial obligations to family and kin. No longer identifying with the village but not fully integrated into the urban milieu, migrant women symbolically occupy an in-between space, a position of ambivalence, but also one of potential strength and power.

Chapter 6 reflects on the ways that the experience of labor migration impacts the life course, as rural women spend their youth living away from home, and in turn how this transforms traditional courtship, marriage, and family. Different from their parents' generation, young migrant women anticipate romance, engage in extended courtships, and are more selective in choosing a spouse than are their nonmigrant peers. Ultimately, the experience of labor migration empowers rural women to assert themselves in romance and make independent decisions about their own future. Their postmarital lives further depart from tradition as they aspire to provide an even better future not only for themselves but also for their families and, especially, their children, by maintaining jobs and residences in the city. As migrant working wives and mothers, my informants embody both the self-sacrificing "traditional Chinese woman" and the "modern" individualized woman who asserts her own desires and interests. Balancing identities and roles to achieve their goals entails the strategic negotiation of their households, finances, and conjugal and extended kin relations across rural and urban contexts. Their competent performances in turn evidence migrant women's empowerment and capacity to mitigate patriarchal power in both domestic and public spheres.

The Conclusion reflects on the significance of this book to understanding migration, gender, and social change in contemporary China. By offering an agent-centered and gender-aware perspective on migration and modernity as understood "from the ground up" as well as over the long-term, and taking into account how migrants are embedded in social relationships, discourses, and power on multiple levels, this study reveals a complexity that is not captured in official rhetoric and political-economic explanations. Throughout the book, I describe and analyze rural migrant women's experiences in light of the meanings, affects, and understandings they ascribe to migration, on the one hand, and the context in which these take shape, on the other. Their experiences thus articulate with broader sociocultural transformations in China: increasing gender and class inequality; the growth of consumer culture and new forms of social distinction; changing norms of gender and sexuality; and a revolution in marriage and family. I argue that the potency of rural migrant women's agency is evident in how they negotiate social inequality in the home and workplace and how they leverage their migration experiences over their life course. These experiences include enhancing their bargaining power in their families and households, expanding their social networks and public role, fulfilling aspirations for romance and marriage, and improving their own and their families' economic and social status. In these ways they forge new beginnings toward new futures for themselves, potentially for other rural women, and new possibilities for gender equality.

Numerous scholars stress the importance of paying attention to "what differently placed [i.e., in power] people really do say" about modernity (Taylor 2001: 9; see also Felski 1995: 14–15; Mills 1999: 12–15; Rofel 1999: 17–18). Feng Xu (2000: 19) argues that a "bottom-up" study of the lived experience of rural Chinese migrant women can "expose the silences" of a unified nationalist discourse of modernity, not only revealing the inequalities that underlie China's economic miracle but pointing the path toward a more equitable future. By listening to the voices of rural migrant women, who have heretofore been largely ignored or silenced, I endeavor to show how their experiences reflect and contribute to a changing China, as well as how migration becomes a means to change individual lives.

CHAPTER ONE

Rural Women and Migration under Market Socialism

In December 1983, the Beijing Municipal Women's Federation established China's first company to recruit, train, and place domestic workers in urban households: the March 8th Housework Service Company, named for the date of International Women's Day. At its inaugural, the company was heralded by the authorities for "doing something really good for women and children" ("Chaoyang" 1983). The fact that a local branch of the official organization for women, the All-China Women's Federation,[1] was closely involved in the founding of such a company reinforced the notion of domestic service as exclusively women's work. And, although the company did not specify gender in seeking applicants, in practice it was geared toward employment of women.[2] In addition, the company made use of the extensive political networks of the Women's Federation cadres (i.e., civil servants) at county and village levels to recruit young rural women into the occupation (Croll 1986). The association of domestic service with rural migrant women was affirmed in 1986, when the Beijing Labor Bureau, with the approval of the Beijing Municipal Government, designated the proliferating domestic service employment placement centers, now run jointly by the Women's Federation, the Federation of Trade Unions, and street committees, as the sole officially authorized channels for migrant domestic service job seekers.[3] By 1989, 400,000 rural women were reported to be working in domestic service in Beijing (Huang 1992: 99), while as many as 3 million were working in urban households nationally (Dai and Dempsey 1998: 11). As demand increased steadily over the subsequent decades, ever more young women migrated to Beijing. Similar to Qiaolian, introduced in the Introduction, they handily found work as live-in maids or nannies providing round-the-clock childcare, eldercare, food preparation, laundry, cleaning, or other domestic services for urban households.

The national Women's Federation likewise championed affordable domestic service as a means of advancing women's interests ("Fanzhong" 1985). Hired household help would relieve urban working wives and mothers of the dual burden of their reproductive and productive roles, enabling their participation in the (waged) labor force, and thus putting them on more equal footing to men. It would also permit urban women more leisure time in which to increase their household's consumption activities, which in turn would stimulate the market economy (Guo 1994). Simultaneously, domestic service as an occupation was touted as a means to raise rural women's relatively lower social status.[4] This would be achieved primarily by increasing their productive opportunities, providing waged work in the public sphere, which had long been a central tenet of socialist efforts to redress gender inequality.[5] A typical news report titled "Housekeepers Help Others and Better Themselves" (Yang Ji 1994), which espouses the many benefits of the expanding market for domestic service, simultaneously conveys a pervasive urban bias toward rural society and rural denizens: "Family members can devote more time to work, while housekeepers not only make money, but also improve their cultural quality [wenhua suzhi] due to the influence of urban civilization. . . . They understand that a woman should have a life outside of the fields and the kitchen. This awareness will surely help improve the quality of life for women in the rural areas."

As the quotation suggests, migration and employment would expose rural women to modern culture and gender roles, and thus improve their "quality," or suzhi. A nebulous but widespread keyword in contemporary Chinese discourse, suzhi refers to "innate and nurtured physical, psychological, intellectual, moral, and ideological qualities of human bodies and their conduct" (Jacka 2009: 524–525; see also Anagnost 1997). The association of rural migrant women with low suzhi is a powerful discursive trope that marks spatial and gender difference and hierarchy (H. Yan 2003a). Entwined with neoliberal capitalism, quality discourse tends to individualize risk and obscure structural inequality. No longer understood as a function of class to be overcome through mass struggle, as during the era of revolutionary socialism (under Mao Zedong), inequality now appears as the result of each individual's different ability to exercise rational choice and succeed (or fail) at accruing wealth and status (Hoffman 2006; Judd 1994). Quality, or suzhi, discourse arguably elides material poverty with cultural insufficiency, and neatly posits development as the only means to advance individuals and society (H. Yan 2008).

This chapter provides a macrohistorical context for understanding the migration of rural women in China over the past few decades in order to delineate the officially sanctioned discourses, policies, and institutional structures that ultimately impact their agency, whether as resources or as constraints. The chapter describes how the state, through its policies of reform and opening to the global economy, presented rural women with new opportunities for migration and work, but under conditions of sociospatial stratification and gender inequality that circumscribed their agency and made them vulnerable to exploitation and other abuse.

I first describe the ideological frameworks, like *suzhi* discourse, that construct difference and hierarchy. Next I sketch out key state policies and institutions that maintain sociospatial stratification, namely the *hukou* system and the dual labor market. Finally, I consider how these discursive structures intersect with cultural constructions of gender and gender discriminatory practices in the labor market to create a cheap and flexible workforce of young migrant women. As their labor has greatly enabled China's rapid accumulation of capital, maintaining the status quo of inequality is beneficial to achieving the state's target economic growth. Despite these powerful constraints on their agency, young rural women have seized the opportunity provided by postreform market socialism. They have embarked on new paths previously unavailable to rural women, which has had profound consequences for their own futures and for gender identity, roles, and relations more broadly.

Foundations of Sociospatial Inequality

The ideology of rural-urban difference has its origins in the early twentieth century. Prior to that time, China did not have an exact rural-urban divide but rather had a "continuum," which only "changed to a 'gulf' beginning in the early 20th century, as Chinese elites engaged with western ideas of modernity and techniques of spatial planning, administration, and engineering" (Hanchao Lu 2002: 129; see also Stapleton 2000). While urban centers underwent modernization, rural environs were left socially and economically in disarray after the collapse of the Qing dynasty in 1911 (Hanchao Lu 2002). Gradually, "rural" and "urban" came to indicate economic and social difference and hierarchy, rather than merely administrative zones. The rural was regarded as the land of "unenlightened masses"; in contrast, the treaty ports of China's coast and old imperial cultural centers like Beijing were the enviable gateways to foreign lands and centers of translation and exchange of foreign ideas (Hanchao Lu 2002; Faure and Liu 2002).[6] Cohen (1993: 155) argues that the term "peasant" (*nongmin*), with its negative valence, came into use in China at this time, by way of Japanese.

The peasantry became a necessary "other" against which the nation's modernity or degree of civilization and cosmopolitanism were defined and measured.[7] Likewise, literature of the period featured the ubiquitous figure of the suffering "traditional Chinese woman" as a metonym or allegory for the nation itself and its vulnerability to foreign domination.[8] As women as a group were disadvantaged in Chinese society, their plight highlighted the backwardness of the nation-state, and even more so when combined with the poverty of the peasant (Feuerwerker 1998: 245; Larson 1998: 32).[9] Liberating peasants and women from imperialism, capitalism, and feudalism became the clarion call of the socialist revolution and a cornerstone of socialist policy. The consequent social advancement of these formerly oppressed groups has became a measuring stick for modernity and critical to the party-state's claims to legitimacy in leading the nation to a better future through reform and opening.[10]

During the socialist era, a household registration or *hukou* system was implemented that gradually solidified the rural-urban division as a symbolic and social demarcation as well as an economic one, which persists into the present (Whyte 2010).[11] Developed in the 1950s as the state grew concerned with the rapid influx of peasants into cities, the system regulated population movement and resource distribution, and hence slowed urbanization (Chan and Zhang 1999).[12] The schema classified the nation's population into either agricultural or nonagricultural households, which in turn were mapped onto residential distinctions, such that "farmer" (*nongmin*) households became synonymous with rural residency, and "worker" (*gongren*) identity with urban residency, though in fact some urban *hukou* holders were farmers and vice versa. Combined with a Soviet-style centrally planned economy, the *hukou* system organized the allocation of labor, goods, and services (Solinger 1999). Urban residents were assigned to work units—industry, research, defense, or government organs—which were guaranteed "iron rice bowls," providing a lifetime of employment and welfare, including housing, education, medical care, insurance, and pensions to their members. Rural residents were organized into cooperatives and, briefly, into communes that provided the state with quotas of staples, which the state distributed to urban areas at a subsidized price, and were otherwise self-sufficient. Cooperatives had the burden of providing welfare for their members, so the quality of services varied according to the productivity of the entity. With the state, through the work units, the sole distributor of basic goods and services, whether directly or through allocation of subsidies and ration tickets, it was nearly impossible to exist outside the work-unit system in urban areas. Moreover, even overnight stays away from one's place of residence required registering with police authorities. Consequently, the *hukou* system ensured that rural-to-urban migration (and vice versa) was severely restricted, with the exception of periods of national disaster or political upheaval.

The household registration system was more or less fixed. First, registration was inherited. Until 1998, policy declared that *hukou* must be inherited through the maternal line (Cai 2003).[13] Clearly the inheritance policy was originally intended to dissuade entire families from migrating to urban areas, as well as minimize the economic burden on the state of extending benefits to dependent family members of its rural-based urban personnel, such as soldiers, county and township-level cadres, and others (Cheng and Selden 1994). Dependents were most likely to be wives and children, as more men than women were recruited to work in heavy industry, the military, and party ranks. Second, *hukou* transfer was difficult (Chan and Zhang 1999). Among urban workers, transfers between work units required special permission of the work units involved, and was nearly impossible. Even marriage, a traditional pathway to upward social mobility, did not guarantee the transfer of *hukou* from rural to urban (Fan and Huang 1998). Moreover, the maternal inheritance of *hukou* and its implications for the welfare of future offspring was a major disincentive for urban men to wed rural women, as their offspring would inherit a rural *hukou* and thus be denied access to urban public goods, including education (Davin 1998).[14] Generally speaking, opportunities for rural women to acquire urban *hukou* were far fewer than for rural men, and thus they had a disproportionately slimmer chance of social mobility through legitimate *hukou* transfer.

While the difference in standard of living between rural and urban areas during the Maoist era was not large, urban workers, cadres, and intellectuals generally enjoyed a better material life as their basic needs were guaranteed. Rural residents were well aware that urban residents led a more privileged lifestyle: peasants referred to urban residents as "those who eat the public grain" as if to stress that they alone had to toil for their subsistence, and they actively strategized to secure the prized urban *hukou* (see Kipnis 1997: 166–167; Potter and Potter 1983: 303–312). Indeed, *hukou* determined one's material and social prospects, and urban *hukou* became a symbol of social status as well as legal residency (Solinger 1999: 1–14).

Migration and *Hukou* Reform

Under the reform platform inaugurated in 1978, China's leaders pulled away from the Maoist vision of an egalitarian utopia achieved through endless class struggle, and in turn rejected the Stalinist planned economy, agricultural collectivization, and focus on heavy industry that had characterized the previous thirty years. Revolutionary ideology was set aside, and economic performance was used to reestablish the legitimacy of the party (Goldman and MacFarquhar 1999; Gries and Rosen 2004). "Socialism with Chinese characteristics"—market socialism—encapsulates the continuance of Chinese Communist Party rule despite a shift from socialist policies toward market economics and neoliberal capitalism (Zhang and Ong 2008).

The reestablishment of a market economy in the 1980s[15] meant the state could no longer control migration by linking basic goods and services, especially food staples and housing, to local *hukou* registration, because peasants could manage to survive away from their villages by purchasing goods on the market. The re-distribution of collective lands and agricultural responsibility to households also unveiled the surplus labor that collectives had formerly absorbed, while rising agricultural productivity made even more labor redundant. As the state discontinued grain purchase and grain prices fell, it encouraged new forms of income earnings through a policy of "leave the land but not the village." While as many as ten million rural laborers were employed in local industries during the 1980s, most local initiatives, such as the township and village enterprises (TVEs), proved unsustainable, especially in rural areas too remote from urban markets and far from sources of capital investment. The most successful TVEs were located near newly created "Special Economic Zones" (SEZs) of privatized market economies established on China's eastern and southern seaboards and around port cities. These areas, and numerous priority development regions and export-processing corridors established throughout the 1990s, attracted foreign investment through preferential policies favorable to international trade and investment, such as tax write-offs and rent subsidies.

By the early 1980s, migrants plying produce and offering services at open markets had become a common sight in large cities like Beijing (K. Zhou 1996). In response, the state too began to gradually loosen restrictions on migration, allowing peasants to reside temporarily in towns and cities and places specially designated for industrialization and urbanization. As a consequence of reform policies and relaxation of migration restrictions, the household registration system was transformed from an instrument that suppressed migration altogether to a tool for managing migration flows as well as for disciplining migrants, and for orchestrating gradual urbanization (Chan 1994; F. Wang 2004; Wu 2010).

Successive nationwide measures were put in place in the mid-1980s by the Public Security Bureau (i.e., the police) to ensure that migration would be orderly and contained. Primary among them was the requirement that migrants apply, for a fee, for a temporary residence permit at their destination, and renew the permit periodically (Chan and Zhang 1999: 832–833). Furthermore, like all Chinese citizens, migrants were to carry a national personal identity card. In addition, the Ministry of Labor required migrants to arrange for an employment registration card prior to leaving their locality and for a work permit with their employer at their destination, also for a fee. Labor recruitment agencies often required migrants to obtain a certificate of good health. For women, the costs of migration were slightly higher. Under the national family planning regulations,[16] migrant women of childbearing age were to carry a "marriage and fertility permit" and register with the Ministry of Family Planning in their destination to ensure their compliance with the program (Hoy 1999). The fees charged by the various government organs for permits were not standardized and there was little oversight to rein in corruption. Whether due to the high costs of fees or lack of information about the regulations, fewer than half of migrants in 1997 appeared to comply with the temporary residence permit requirements (S. Zhao 2000). Over a decade later, the compliance rate was still only 40 percent (Young 2011). In Chapter 4, I describe the various ruses devised by the sisters Shuqing and Shuchun to avoid paying fees for employment permit renewals, and the consequences when their schemes fail.

Sporadically, Beijing authorities have pushed to enforce temporary residence permit regulations, usually by subjecting migrants to random searches, and rarely by targeting employers of migrant labor. Campaigns to "sanitize" (qingli) the homeless, drifters, beggars, and vagrants from Beijing's streets have usually coincided with visits of foreign dignitaries to Beijing or the intensification of the national anticrime campaigns. During the 2003 SARS public health crisis and the 2008 Beijing Olympics, for example, the movements of migrant workers in and out of Beijing's city center were tightly controlled by the Public Security Bureau, which in 2010 proposed to seal off suburban enclaves occupied by migrants (Jiao 2010). Fear of being detained (in a temporary jail) and fined or repatriated to their villages intimidated migrants to either comply with regulations and renew permits or stay off the streets to avoid detection. For example, in the spring of 2000, Beijing public security officers apprehended three young men, whom I knew, as they cycled from their dormitory to the hotel where they worked as custodians. As they lacked proper permits, they were detained for several days until they could post bail, which they had to borrow from their boss. That same season, I overheard Qiaoling and Changying warn each other not to speak loudly in public places for fear that plainclothes officers might ascertain their nonlocal[17] origins from their accents and demand they show their residence cards, which were not up-to-date.

Fortunately, the state's stance toward rural-to-urban migration underwent a sea change starting in the mid-2000s under the leadership of former President Hu Jintao and former Premier Wen Jiabao. Official attitudes shifted from control to encouragement, and from concern with the costs of migration for cities to concern for migrants' well-being. Migrants were finally recognized to be critical in narrowing the rural-urban income gap, as they redistribute wealth through remittances and apply new knowledge and skills to develop rural areas. In the mid-1990s, municipal governments in large cities like Beijing, concerned about labor unrest among the millions of workers furloughed from bankrupt state-owned enterprises, had passed regulations barring the allocation of job contracts to migrants in nearly one hundred industries and occupations, further limiting their employment options (Wang Huaxin 1998). But in 2003, the State Council ordered that all such discriminatory labor regulations and practices be abolished. At the same time, the Public Security Bureau's system of detention and repatriation of migrants was officially dismantled (in response, in part, to the death of a migrant during a detention in Guangzhou). Migrants were still required to register with the police, but the temporary residence permit fee was waived. Since 2008, the "marriage and fertility certificate" entitles migrant women to receive certain subsidized reproductive health services in the city, so they no longer need return to their place of *hukou* for the mandatory semi-annual health checks (Mao, Shen, and Liu 2008). Minimum wage levels for cities and provinces were issued, trade unions were ordered to open doors to migrant workers, and cooperative pension and social security schemes for migrant workers were established. New regulations and a revised Labor Law of 2008 affirming their labor rights empowered migrant workers to more vocally express their demands (see, for example, C. K. Lee 2007 and Pun and Lu 2010). Various towns and cities began to extend local *hukou* social benefits to qualifying migrant workers, mainly educated and skilled technicians, entrepreneurs, professionals, and investors, according to the needs of the labor market (Chan and Buckingham 2008). Some municipalities began to offer local *hukou* in exchange for home ownership (Li and Li 2010; F. Wang 2011).

Since coming to power in 2012, President Xi Jinping and Premier Li Keqiang have each emphasized the importance of accelerating China's urbanization rate as a means to ensure continued economic growth—articulated as the "China Dream"—by stimulating middle-class consumption ("Building the Dream" 2014). A new urbanization plan circulated in 2014 establishes the goal of increasing the urban population by one hundred million, from about 54 percent urban population in 2014 to 60 percent in 2020 ("Moving on Up" 2014; World Bank 2014). Such a plan would require local-level policies to fully integrate migrant workers into urban society, including raising wages, facilitating access to education and other social welfare, and ultimately dismantling the hierarchy of privilege maintained by the *hukou* system. However, specific details of the plan, including a timeline for implementation, as well as actual outcomes, remain to be seen ("Moving on Up" 2014; World Bank 2014).

Despite these developments, migrants on the whole remain disadvantaged, excluded from the rights and privileges associated with urban citizenship (Chan 2013; Chan and Buckingham 2008; Selden and Wu 2011; F. Wang 2011). Their relatively low levels of education, skills, and work experience, and their dearth of urban social connections, combined with the *hukou*-based job distribution system still practiced in higher-end managerial or state-sector employment, have ensured their relegation to low-skilled jobs that most urbanites eschew. These jobs are known in English as the "3-D" jobs because they are dirty, dangerous, and difficult or degrading (Chan 2010). According to a 2002 survey, 94 percent of rural migrants in Beijing worked in low-end jobs (Guang and Kong 2010). Even the term "migrant worker" (*dagongzhe* is the plural form; *dagongzai* refers to young men and *dagongmei* to young women) implies a distinction in kind: "to work" (*dagong*) connotes casual, manual labor that is distinct from the legitimate "work" (*gongzuo*) of the urban proletariat (*gongren*) (Pun 1999: 3). In the current lexicon of neoliberal individualism and entrepreneurship, *dagong* also implies working for a boss, rather than for oneself, and thus continues to mark inferiority (e.g., Griffiths 2010; Pun and Lu 2010). Despite the rising wages in certain sectors since 2003, migrant workers' earnings overall have not kept pace with inflation and have been outpaced by rising wages of employees with urban *hukou* (Cheng et al. 2013; Selden and Wu 2011). My key informants toiled for years without wage increases, and rarely earned more than the minimum wage (see Chapter 6). Especially in big cities, migrants are denied equal access to affordable housing and health-care services, social security benefits, and public education for their offspring, all of which continue to be tied to the *hukou* system (Chan 2013; Selden and Wu 2011). They are still vulnerable to sporadic police checks targeting undocumented temporary migrants (F. Wang 2011). I discuss impacts of this system on migrant women and their families in future chapters.

Gendering Migration

Thus far in this chapter I have explicated the ideological and institutional bases of sociospatial difference and inequality under market socialism, including the use of *hukou* to manage migration and migrants. In this section I consider how these intersect with cultural constructions of gender and gender discrimination in the labor market to create an easily exploitable and temporary workforce of rural migrant women, who in turn must navigate this complex of symbolic and structural inequality.

The migrant workforce is segmented into culturally determined gender-appropriate categories of work. Arguably, this segregated labor market benefits migrant women by reserving certain jobs for them without competition from men. Young, single, rural women have been the preferred workers in export-oriented light-industrial manufacturing firms (i.e., textiles, apparel, toys, and electronics) of southern and coastal regions (C. K. Lee 1998; Pun 2005). Likewise, rural women have had a virtual monopoly in urban domestic service and hotel and restaurant hospitality, two occupations that I explore in depth in later chapters. However, within these sectors, women are disproportionately concentrated in low-skill, low-wage jobs. Male migrants have more occupational choices and greater earning potential. In large cities like Beijing, male migrants have concentrated in construction and industry, which afford the highest wages, while young rural women have been predominantly employed in the service and retail sectors, where wages are generally lower (Wang Zheng 2000).[18] Further, migrant women workers disproportionately cluster in the private, informal sector, beyond the reach of minimum wage regulations and labor laws, or, in the case of domestic service, completely excluded from them.

Migrant women's rural origins and position as dependents (whether as daughters or wives) rationalize their low wages relative to urban counterparts or male migrants. Moreover, their relative youth and inexperience and their distance from kin reinforce their dependence on employers and make them highly vulnerable to discrimination and sexual harassment. This is especially so for women working in the illicit (or illegal) and hence risky entertainment sector (Zheng 2009) and in live-in domestic service, where employees are easily isolated and rendered invisible from public scrutiny (Mellerman 2008). Employers of Beijing domestic workers and hotel housekeepers justify exploitative labor practices in the name of paternalistic oversight of their "girls." In Chapter 4 I explore how informants dealt with injustice and abuse while working in domestic service and hotel housekeeping especially.

Young women are preferred for service-sector jobs as they are seen to embody vitality, deference, sexuality, and glamour (Hanser 2008; Hooper 1998; Otis 2011; Wang Zheng 2000). Those who turn their youth and femininity into capital for profit are said to "eat spring rice" (*qingchunfan*), a play on the socialist term "iron rice bowl" (*tiefanwan*), which referred to the guaranteed lifetime employment of urban workers (Zhang Zhen 2000). Rural migrant women are especially desirable because they can be worked hard for a few years, then dismissed without incurring long-term investment costs (Tan 2000). Their youth also implies deference to superiors (elders), and an ability to toil long hours at exhausting physical labor. Such qualities lend them a distinct advantage in the labor market against older urban women workers laid off from the restructuring state sector, but they enter the labor market on distinctively inferior footing. Indeed, jobs that involve cleaning dirt and providing services to others evoke historical associations with servility and also gender transgression.[19] Such perceptions may contribute to employers' prejudicial attitudes and exploitative behaviors toward their rural employees, and make workers themselves feel stigmatized and ashamed, as I explain in greater detail in Chapter 4. Rural women meet the demand for youthful and feminine workers in occupations like domestic service and hotel housekeeping because they have few alternatives. As a migrant hotel housekeeper with only an elementary-level education once asked me rhetorically, "What else am I qualified to do?"

The gendering of occupations has ambivalent repercussions for young migrant women, offering opportunity at the expense either of gender parity or equality, or of economic security (Hooper 1998; Wang Zheng 2000; Zhang Zhen 2000). The value placed on such ephemeral characteristics as youth also reinforces their status as temporary workers, which the *hukou* system likewise ensures, and leaves them little choice but to postpone marriage and family formation to continue working, as I demonstrate in Chapter 6. In addition, cultural constructions of gender, marriage, and kinship contribute to the perception of young rural migrant women as secondary wage earners. All Chinese women are expected to marry and, after marriage, take primary responsibility for the domestic sphere, raising children and serving their husbands' family. Further, rural women must marry to secure property and livelihood. Although since 1949 women have a legal right to inheritance, men and marriage customs mediate rural women's actual access to land and, hence, livelihood. As Judd (1994) explains, in rural China, patrilocal postmarital residence patterns create communities comprised of agnatically related men, whose authority is strengthened by common interest and kinship, as well as the state's recognition of their leadership. Thus, in the Maoist era, in order to maintain a stable supply of labor and keep land within brigades, (male) leaders encouraged rural women to seek mates within their work brigades (Lai 1995). Decollectivization in the 1980s disenfranchised women in regard to land allocation and use rights, by formally reinstating the authority of the male household head as landowner (Davin 1998; Summerfield 1994). For example, Bossen (2002: 95–96) reports from the locality she studied in Yunnan that, during the reallocation of collective land to households in the early 1980s, male village heads and team leaders devised regulations to guide land transfers through marriage. The new regulations exhibited a patrilineal bias: married-in daughters would be allocated collective land, but married-in sons in most cases would not. Based on fieldwork in the 1980s, Judd (1994) likewise observed an androcentric bias in land and labor allocation that disadvantaged women and reinforced their dependence on men.

Opportunities for rural women to marry urban men and settle in the cities (i.e., hypergamy) are limited, largely due to the *hukou* system and the class hierarchy it helps maintain that equates such marriages with (men's) downward social mobility. Given the social expectation and economic need for marriage, and the difficultly of finding a mate from the city, most unmarried rural women eventually return to the countryside to settle down. Independent migration and work are thus merely an "episode" in a young women's life course, prior to marriage and motherhood (Davin 1998: 237).[20] Rural migrant women such as my key informants who marry away from home and/or continue to work in the city after marriage challenge such norms, as I explore in Chapter 6.

Normative marriage patterns combined with obstacles in the way of married women's migration and to family settlement in the cities have reinforced a predominant division of labor by gender that is conducive to rapid capital accumulation. While migrants work in cities, their rural households are responsible for providing care for children, the elderly, and the infirm. When there is no longer work for them in the cities, migrants return to their rural households for sustenance and support (Fan 2007; Q. F. Zhang 2011). Within rural households, it is predominantly the unwaged labor of rural mothers and, increasingly, grandmothers, that provides for the social reproduction of the workers (Murphy 2004). In short, policy and institutional measures support patriarchal family and village structures and ensure that rural households serve as economic buffers to maintain the cheap and flexible migrant workforce (Fan 2007).

Meanwhile, migrant labor produces goods and provides services that help urban households to achieve the quintessential middle-class dream of the "good life" (Chen 2001; Hanlong Lu 2000; Li Zhang 2010). The guarantee of a cheap and flexible female rural migrant labor force has been critical to reaching the state's goals of economic growth by encouraging consumption (i.e., satiating demands for affordable goods and services) and by maintaining the urban labor force, particularly urban working mothers, while allowing state decentralization and withdrawal from welfare provisioning. The advantages of maintaining this profitable, informal service-sector labor force likely explain why the state has not endeavored to help rural migrant women expand their employment opportunities, keep their jobs after marriage and childbirth, or settle permanently in cities with their spouses and offspring. Indeed, the status quo of gender inequality is beneficial to economic growth.

Summary

Rural labor migrants are a symptom, and a symbol, of China's latest experiment in constructing a modern nation-state. In the three decades under market socialism, China has achieved rapid economic growth, indicated by an average annual GNP growth rate of between 8 and 10 percent, and people's livelihoods have, on the whole, improved compared with the Maoist era. However, the urban-rural income gap has steadily widened to a ratio greater than 3:1 by the late 2000s (Li and Luo 2010). Diminishing returns to agriculture, decreasing land allocations, a large surplus labor force, and a high tax burden on agricultural households (eliminated in 2003), are key "push" factors that have propelled peasants out of agriculture and villages since the mid-1980s. Meanwhile, a burgeoning nonstate industrial and service sector that includes private and foreign-invested enterprises as well collective and joint-invested firms have generated new employment demand that has thus far been met by a large and cheap labor force "pulled" from the country-side (Selden and Wu 2011).

China's transition should not be seen as simply the inevitable outcome of market forces, as it has been, and continues to be, engineered by a powerful state adapting neoliberal ideas. The state has regulated and managed migration through policy and institutional mechanisms, which in turn reinforce an ideology that rationalizes hierarchy largely along rural-urban lines, as well as by gender difference. State policy and planning are responsible for uneven development in which inland rural areas appear economically sluggish in contrast to the dynamic urban and coastal areas. In addition, being from a "poor and backward" region has taken on a social and moral taint that stains those least able to successfully accumulate capital—those lacking in *suzhi,* and those geographically most remote from the urban centers of modern life (Liu 2000: xi). In this schema, to reside in the countryside, and to be a peasant, implies being temporally "left behind" in the drive toward progress. As rural women are associated with the least productive roles of both farmer and housewife, they are symbolically, socially, and geographically more distant from modernity.

Women's social status has been a benchmark for the modernity of the nation-state (Barlow 1994). Whereas republican nationalism blamed women's relative low status on a combination of class and feudal patriarchy that socialist revolution sought to redress, contemporary nationalist discourse attributes women's relative low status to the underdevelopment of "productive forces" and the "low cultural quality" of rural women in particular, and seeks redress through economic and social modernization. A socialist narrative of women's liberation through collective class struggle under CCP leadership has been neatly replaced by a neoliberal capitalist discourse about market opportunity, individual effort and merit, and consumer desire (Hoffman 2006; Rofel 2007; H. Yan 2003b). However, the narrative of historical progress belies the policies, institutionalized practices, and ideologies that together produce inequality and hierarchy.

The Women's Federation promotion of domestic service is illustrative of the state's contradictory stance regarding "the woman question." On the one hand, it seeks to increase women's productive roles to advance their status, in particular by developing the tertiary sector.[21] Yet, the "gendering" of the service sector as an explicit policy goal undermines the commitment to gender equality. First, many jobs in this sector that culturally are seen as appropriate for women are poorly compensated and poorly (if at all) regulated, offering little by way of benefits and protections. Second, such jobs tend to rely on and reinforce patriarchal ideologies that maintain patterns of gender inequality. Most notably, identifying domestic service as a distinctly women's occupation does not challenge a household division of labor by gender and a gender ideology that associates housework with women and devalues that form of labor.

Further, the marketing of domestic service to rural migrant women is indicative of the unfulfilled promise of revolutionary socialism to smooth over the "antagonistic contradiction" (Mao "On Contradiction" 1965 [1937]) between the rural and urban. It allowed the state's "feminine arm" (i.e., the Women's Federation) to demonstrate an ongoing commitment to achieving gender equality while transferring to households the costs of social reproduction of the workforce. In the cities, this burden falls primarily on rural migrant women workers, whose labor is made cheaper through migration policy and institutional mechanisms. In the rural areas, it falls upon the rural housewife and other female relatives, whose unwaged labor is rendered invisible by patriarchal family and kinship structures.

The state makes contradictory demands of rural women. They are simultaneously encouraged to overcome the burden of history and modernize themselves, raising their *suzhi* by participating in development as migrant workers. Yet formidable obstacles impede their becoming equal subjects of modernization, leaving them in an ambivalent and liminal state of becoming. In this chapter, I explicated discourses of sociospatial and gender inequality, and how they proliferate through institutional structures and practices of the *hukou* system, labor market segregation, and marriage and family. While reform and opening provide rural women new opportunities for self-determination through migration and wage work, the contours of such possibilities have been delimited by a powerful state in league with neoliberal capitalism and rural patriarchy. In subsequent chapters I look at the influence of these powerful social constructs and structures on young rural women's subjectivity, their participation in labor migration, their incorporation into the urban labor market and society, their interactions with employers and urbanites, their consumer behavior and self-images, and even marriage and future family. I explore how rural migrant women negotiate, accommodate, and challenge these constraints or opportunities as they make autonomous choices and exercise agency.

CHAPTER TWO

Dutiful Daughters and Migration Desires

Xingjuan left her Anhui village for Beijing in the early 1980s, when she was just a teenager. The youngest of five children, she was the first to leave the village to migrate for work. In her recollection, she described her decision to migrate as being an exercise of her own volition, requiring firm resolve against initial parental opposition.

> I was fifteen, going on sixteen, when I announced: "I'm also going to Beijing." My father disagreed; I decided for myself. My sister-in-law didn't agree either, saying I was too young. But I had little to do at home. . . . Later I said to my father again: "I want to go out to work, and I won't come back for five years." I had made up my mind. I said, "I'll be back when I'm twenty-two"—I was then seventeen—I said, "In five years I'll come back only once." They still didn't trust me. . . . Then my mother supported me a bit, and saw that I had nothing to do at home, that I didn't have any interest in farming. She urged, "Let her go out to work."

In deciding to migrate, most of my informants initially faced opposition from their parents, as Qiaolian did from her father (see the Introduction). Understandably, parents were concerned for their children's safety and well-being. Tales of unscrupulous employers and the dangers of city life recounted by returning migrants fueled their worries. Yanmei, a Migrant Women's Club member who migrated to Beijing in 1996, at age sixteen, and worked in domestic service, explained: "The elders in my village returning from work in Beijing said the city had lots of tricksters and bad people, people who wouldn't give you your salary or would cheat you. . . . Because of what returning migrants said, my parents worried, and didn't want me to come to Beijing."

Despite potential risks they anticipated, young women were quite persistent in their efforts to win parental support and in their determination to leave the village. Those who succeeded took strength in the knowledge that they had made an autonomous decision, and passionately resolved to stay the course. Rongli, a

Migrant Women's Club member with whom I reconnected in 2002, told me: "My mother and I are very close, like sisters even, so the first month that I was in Beijing, I missed home so much that I often cried, and I wondered why I had ever wanted to make myself suffer so! Later, though, I thought, 'this was the path I myself chose, and there's nothing wrong with that!' "

This chapter analyzes individual rural women's motivations for migration and the influence of gender roles and relations in the household and family on their migration decision making and agency. I argue that constructions of sociospatial and gender difference and hierarchy under market socialism impact subjectivity and agency in ways that empower individual young rural women to choose migration, yet also create particular gendered patterns of migration that reflect and also perpetuate such difference and inequality.

As explained in the Introduction, macro-level political-economic explanations of migration obscure the experience of migrants and the complexities of the migration process, and thus compromise knowledge and misinform policy. Further, in neoclassical and structural (meso-level) analyses of migration, households are assumed to strategize for the optimum balance of resources among family members, including by organizing the migration for waged work of its surplus laborers, as they respond to changes in the political economy (Trager 1988). But feminist attention to the roles of women in migration—whether as "women who wait" or as migrants—has led to criticism of this so-called household strategies approach. This approach fails to account for intrahousehold dynamics and for the possibly competing interests of household members differently positioned by gender and kinship (see, e.g., Fan 2007; D. L. Wolf 1992). Among my informants, as the examples above highlight, rural Chinese daughters frequently decided to migrate over at least initial objections of parents or other household members. While a daughter's migration economically benefited her natal household, the concept of "household strategy" is nonetheless insufficient to fully encompass the many rationales for migration expressed by individuals. A holistic perspective on migration that takes into account gender relations in the household and family, as well as each individual's unique biography and personality, helps avoid gross generalizations or oversimplifications and provides a more balanced understanding of migration processes.

As discussed in Chapter 1, the neoliberal policies of market socialism and the social and economic disparity concomitant with their implementation provided the "push" and "pull" conditions for young women's migration from the countryside to cities and urbanizing economic development zones beginning in the mid-1980s. Subjectively, as I explain below, migration emerged from young rural women's desires for the new and modern, the chance to make something of themselves, and their sense of responsibility to family and household. Such yearnings reflected their internalization of a discourse of modernization and social development that construes rural space and occupants as impediments to progress. These yearnings also reflected the values associated with their social position in the patriarchal family and household, even as these were transformed by market socialism. I first explore here young rural women's subjective longings and their migration decisions. Then I describe how household structure and intrafamily relations also influence migration choices. The final section of this chapter highlights the complexity of young rural women's agency in migration decision making.

Disenchantment of the Rural

Young women's persistent efforts to overcome parental opposition to migration indicate that their decisions to migrate were expressions of individual agency. Although "to escape poverty" or "to earn money" were common knee-jerk responses to the question of "why did you migrate?" further questioning always elicited a variety of motivations (see also Chang 2008; C. K. Lee 1998). The decision to migrate was not just a response to conditions of uneven development and relative poverty. Rather, a host of desires and ambitions—from helping family and community, escaping boredom, or postponing marriage to seeking to acquire new skills or improve education so as to avoid a life of farming, or seeing the world and satisfying curiosity about urban life—factored into their decisions to migrate (see also Jacka 2005, 2006). Such expectations must be understood in the context of their generation's rejection of the increasingly devalued rural identity and yearnings for the trappings of modernity associated with urban consumer lifestyles, which in turn reflect ideological and structural forms of inequality.

In Chapter 1 I traced the historical evolution of a rural-urban distinction and the symbolic category of the peasant "other." China's preeminent (late) sociologist, Fei Xiaotong, eloquently explained the practical logic of peasants' strong spiritual attachment to the land, as manifested in the worship of the Earth god (*Tudi*): "We often say that country people are figuratively as well as literally 'soiled,' (*tuqi*). Although this label may seem disrespectful, the character meaning 'soil' (*tu*) is appropriately used here. Country people cannot do without the soil because their very livelihood is based upon it" (1992 [1946]: 37). When Fei penned his famous essay, urban intellectuals distinguished themselves from their "earthy" (*tu*) rural counterparts. Under socialism, peasants were celebrated for their revolutionary potential, yet were less privileged than urban workers. More recently, neoliberal policies have widened the economic gap between rural and urban areas, and in turn underscored negative connotations of rural folk compared with relatively wealthier urbanites. In the contemporary lexicon, being soiled or earthy is rarely a proud or defensible identity but rather a sign of a lack of civility and culture—that is, of low *suzhi* (quality). In particular, beliefs and behaviors that are out of step with the state's political directives or that threaten the political or social order are considered remnants of a feudal past and trivialized as superstition, and taken as evidence of cultural backwardness or low quality (Kipnis 1997: 167).

Generations of rural youth born in the reform and opening era have absorbed pervasive stereotypes about the cultural inferiority of rural life and people. As discussed in Chapter 1, able-bodied youth have the greatest potential to migrate out of the village due to the great demand for their youthful labor power. It is therefore not surprising that they are most vociferously critical of "traditional" ideas and practices and impatient with fellow villagers whom they perceive to be attached to peasant ways of life. During several Chinese New Year holidays spent in my key informants' natal villages during the late 1990s and the 2000s, I observed many such customs that elicited their negative responses. Some examples from my first visit to the countryside, when I accompanied Qiaolian and her *laoxiang* Changying home to their neighboring villages about 250 miles from Beijing during the Spring Festival in 1999, are illuminating. Throughout my sojourn, these young women made clear distinctions between "traditional" and "modern." They identified local folk beliefs and practices and certain rituals of noncontractual reciprocity (*guanxi*)[1] as "backward" (*luohou*) and contrasted these to rational social relations as well as new technology, scientific methods, and knowledge exhibited by returned migrants.

For example, I was curious about some of the activities I observed among villagers in preparation for the New Year, such as setting up a spirit tablet (to the kitchen god) and sweeping the courtyard before lighting incense in the kitchen, or lighting incense sticks in courtyard entryways to welcome the ancestors or scare away bad spirits. But whenever I asked Qiaolian to explain these happenings to me, she would only shrug her shoulders and dismiss such activities, saying, "I don't know, it's just what the old people do. I detest these feudal superstitions." Soon after arriving in the village, I learned that my gift to a little girl of a plush toy rabbit, the zodiac symbol of the Lunar New Year, had unwittingly triggered some lineage contention in this two-surname village. Qiaolian's relatives felt slighted by my gift to a member of the other lineage and complained, which caused Qiaolian's mother such deep distress that she cried and fretted over the matter for hours. Qiaolian reluctantly intervened, explaining the situation to me and suggesting the remedy of distributing additional gifts to the children of her family's lineage. Qiaolian was extremely embarrassed and apologized for what she called "backward" behavior and preoccupation with kin-based loyalties that she felt reflected the "low quality" of certain villagers.

The association of peasant culture with the beliefs and habits of the so-called feudal past reinforces a sense that it impedes the progress of the nation-state, civilization, and modernity. Consequently, migration appears a means to modernize places and populations, by improving human capital, generating wealth, and fostering development. Those who lack the opportunity or inclination to migrate, mainly the elderly and married women with young children, appear conservative and unproductive compared with youth who can and do migrate. Objectifying certain villagers as backward and identifying others as progressive creates a social hierarchy that privileges youth and those who leave over the elderly and those who stay.

Together with Qiaolian and Changying, fellow villagers of all ages took pride in demonstrating to me the many ways in which the area was modernizing with the help of migrant remittances. On a walk through the village that drew people out of their homes and into the lanes, I was shown renovated traditional-style residential courtyards decorated with ceramic tile mosaics, newly built concrete houses that towered over older brick-and-mud constructions, and a proud farmer's shiny new red tractor. Certain villagers were singled out and proudly introduced to me. In addition to two (male) students learning English who held aspirations of passing the college entrance exams, I was introduced to the county school's English teacher, Qiaolian's high-school-educated father and uncle, several returned migrants, and the villages' few secondary-school graduates who wanted to practice their rudimentary English with me. Villagers gave me tours of new enterprises established by returning migrants who had been exposed to scientific technology and acquired new skills while working outside the village. Half a day was spent touring greenhouses with Changying's (male) relative, who had invested the savings from his thirteen years as a construction worker in the city into new hothouse technology for a profitable tomato cultivation business.

On New Year's Eve in the village, I shared in the excitement of eating a meal of dumplings prepared earlier in the day while watching CCTV's annual gala variety show, which in the 1990s attracted a massive viewer audience each year. Watching television had been made possible in Qiaolian's village only in the mid-1990s, with the introduction of electricity. At the time of my visit, the village had just one telephone from a line extending from the main road. The TV program demonstrated the power of media to influence culture. Indeed, most of rural China is tuned in to radio and television programs that objectify rural life and present back to villages images of peasant character that reflect the stereotypes of urban producers (Ballew 2001).

Another evening, Qiaolian and I were invited to the house of a neighbor, a returned migrant, who had purchased a karaoke/VCD machine with his earnings. A large group of villagers gathered around the TV, and Qiaolian and a few other young people took turns crooning Hong Kong and Guangdong pop tunes. The older women in the audience, many of whom wore the "peasant" garb of head-scarves over their hair, giggled through hands that modestly covered their mouths, at once amused and scandalized by the soft-porn video images of gyrating and scantily clad "foreign" (mainly Asian) dancers that accompanied the song lyrics. These new forms of media and technology, and the computers and Internet that would soon follow, enabled national and even global culture to penetrate this village before it had even one paved road. Yet, the images of urban and global modernity contrasted starkly with the bare and rough interiors of the rural homes into which they were projected, revealing the substantial distance between reality and the imagined future.

Although proud of the influx of modern consumer goods and boastful of the achievements of its college students and returned migrants, villagers worried about the momentous task still ahead of raising their "low level of cultural quality." They accepted the official and popular pronouncements about rural cultural inferiority, but villagers disputed the cause of this condition. Like the Fujian villagers studied by Chu (2010), they attributed it to structural inequality, the result of material shortcomings rather than innate characteristics or inherent weakness. As Beijing domestic worker Rongli clearly understood: "In the countryside, our cultural level is limited, for there are few books and magazines to read." Improving cultural quality requires investment in human capital—the requisite education and technical skills thought necessary to succeed in the competitive market economy. Education is a Confucian virtue and, historically, it was a primary means of social mobility; under Maoist socialism, college graduates were generally guaranteed urban residency and employment (Kipnis 2001; Unger 1982). In the market economy, in response to growing demand for a skilled workforce, education is infused with new value, both economic and symbolic.[2]

Along with industrialization, the rise of the so-called knowledge economy further contributes to the devaluation of rural China and of agricultural labor in particular. In classical Confucian doctrine, agricultural work epitomized manual labor (*wu*), and was opposed to mental labor (*wen*), which was associated with high culture and civilization, but they were perceived to be complements (Bray 1997). Under socialism, agriculture was venerated and intellectuals were sent into rural areas to learn from the peasants. Today, the drive for economic growth and global competitiveness has placed a premium on education and expertise rather than the political dedication of the prototypical factory or farm worker celebrated during the Maoist era. Agriculture in China is not technologically complex, and its location in the relatively underdeveloped countryside contrasts to work in modern factories or high-rise offices. Indeed, the state recognizes that illiteracy and low levels of education cannot generate the cultural and economic capital necessary for development, and thus promotes educational expansion and reform (Kipnis 2011; Postiglione 2006b).

It is little wonder then that young people are keen to avoid a future in agriculture. Moreover, as my informants emphasized to me repeatedly, farming is "extremely *hard,* physically exerting labor." During my visit to her natal home in 2007, Yarui noted that women of the village (of her mother's generation) sneer at the suggestion that factory or clerical work might be equally difficult: " 'Just let those [urban] women try standing bent over crops all day!' they say." The physical hardships of agricultural work might be less objectionable if agriculture were profitable. Receiving little fiscal outlay from the central government, local government has been dependent on peasants for their own salaries and budgets; the rural tax burden rose steadily during the 1990s until the agricultural tax was abolished in 2003. Further, grain prices steadily declined in the face of world market competition following China's entry into the WTO.

Other reasons for agriculture's declining appeal were identified by a study of the evolution of Chen Village (Chan, Madsen, and Unger 1992) in Guangdong during the 1980s, replicated in later years throughout rural areas. Researchers found that distinctions of gender, class, and spatial location intersected to shape villagers' perceptions of rural life and peasant identity, and consequently their negative attitudes toward farming. Chen Village's spatial proximity to Hong Kong and to a newly constructed Special Economic Zone (SEZ) provided an opportunity for working-age men to earn relatively high wages by working in construction or in factories in these urbanizing areas. Village women substituted for the men, leading in the short term to a feminization of agricultural work. Gradually, Chen Village women also found lucrative employment, mainly in the nearby township enterprises, in turn leaving agricultural work in the village in the hands of recent in-migrants from poorer areas. Nearly all Chen Villagers opted out of agriculture when other choices were available. After Chen Village's transition from rural backwater to a satellite town in a SEZ, agriculture became devalued not only because villagers could avail themselves of more lucrative sources of income, but also because villagers grew more consciously selective of their choice of work.

Significantly, agriculture's declining appeal to Chen Villagers was concomitant with the entry into the fields of increasingly marginalized groups: women, the aged, and migrants from poorer villages. Agriculture's prestige plummeted due to a symbolic association with emasculation and class debasement, and not just its high material cost and low remuneration. Others have likewise observed that the devaluation of agriculture and the feminization of farm work go hand in hand (Fan 2000). In rural China by the mid-1990s, a general pattern of division of labor had appeared whereby women, children, and the elderly remained in the village to undertake farming, childrearing, and housework, as well as sideline enterprises (such as raising livestock), while a majority of men left the village to work off the farm, as seasonal or casual laborers (Jacka 1997). Certainly demand for male labor in "masculine" jobs like mining and construction in part determined this division of labor. But local state actors, who are usually men, also had much input into labor allocation in village agriculture and industry (e.g., TVEs) (Judd 1994; Kipnis 1997). A further explanation for the declining prestige of agriculture involves its new association with the domestic sphere, as I explain below.

In addition, among women, laboring in the fields is undesirable as it conflicts with both indigenous and global cultural prescriptions of femininity and beauty (see also Chapter 5). In late imperial China, elites associated femininity with confinement to the "inner" quarters, and thus equated beauty with whiter and softer skin, as darker skin and rough hands were signs of laboring "outside," and hence a marker of lower class. Indeed, women refer to laboring in the field with the expression "being burnt by the sun," making the connection between agriculture, dark skin, and status explicit. The class implications of darkened skin were evident among the Shandong peasants studied by Kipnis (1997) in the 1990s, where families with discretionary income kept their daughters from farm work, for fear that blackened skin resulting from daily exposure to the elements would ruin their daughters' marriage chances.

Young rural women's aversion to agricultural work today may be interpreted as a reversal of the "gender neutrality" (M. M. Yang 1999) promoted by the Maoist state in favor of alternate visions of femininity.[3] Chinese women today are bombarded with advertising images that promote a global ideal of beauty and femininity, which is based on a white, Western image (e.g., white skin, double eyelids, and light-colored hair). Evans (2000) argues that these images associate the rural peasant with increasingly racialized projections of physique (i.e., "dirty" or "black") that imply moral and qualitative inferiority (see also Schein 1994). The "modern" woman is thus constructed in contradistinction to images of "subordination and exclusion, most notably of the rural, uneducated, and poor" (Evans 2000: 238). Avoiding farm work is thus essential to a cosmopolitan feminine appearance; rural life is anathema to modern womanhood. (In Chapter 5 I explore how urban consumer culture experienced through working in Beijing profoundly impacted migrant women's self-awareness of their bodies and sexualities.)

An amusing incident during a visit to Yarui's natal home in June 2008 emphasized the gulf between the desexualized femininity of the Mao era and contemporary hyperfemininity. Yarui's mother and father live in a traditional residence consisting of rooms arranged in a square formation with a large open courtyard in the center. Her parents occupied one set of rooms opposite those of their eldest son, his wife, and child; Yarui's elderly grandfather lived on another side of the courtyard. Returning home to prepare lunch after laboring in the fields one hot summer morning, Yarui's mother unselfconsciously tore off her sweaty T-shirt as she walked through the gate into the courtyard, revealing her breasts to everyone seated outside, including me. Slightly embarrassed, Yarui scolded her mother for displaying immodest behavior in front of a guest. Nonplussed, her mother continued to wash her face and arms at the outdoor washbasin. "I'm hot," she explained to me matter-of-factly, and Yarui refrained from further comments.

The devaluation of rural culture, peasant identity, and agricultural labor, and the incompatibility of rural life with modern femininity, imparts rural youth and especially young women with a keen desire to "leave both the farm and the village." Their choice to migrate paradoxically validates those same ideological constructs of sociospatial and gender differences that mark rural denizens as culturally backward and inferior, even as it offers individuals the chance of a better life and new identity. Due to their position in the patriarchal household and family system, young rural women are most readily available to migrate, as I next explain.

Household Division of Labor and Migration

As discussed in Chapter 1, Chinese women are associated with the domestic sphere and the roles of wife and mother, while men are perceived as the primary producers in the household economy. This determines that, overall, fewer women than men migrate, and that among the women who do migrate, most are young and unmarried. The demand for youthful labor is also an important determining factor. Historically, Confucian and neo-Confucian doctrine demarcated gender through differential social and moral spaces of inside (*nei*) and outside (*wai*): inside was coded feminine and associated with women, and outside was coded masculine and associated with men (see Bray 1997; Ko 1994; Mann 1997). This binary also established separate but complementary spheres of social interaction, relegating women to the domestic realm, comprising family, household, relatives, and so on, and according men with status as mediators of public life (Ibid.). Revolutionary socialism "liberated" women from the domestic sphere by mobilizing them into the public sphere of remunerated work. Yet, despite their increased participation in agriculture and industry, women's historical association with the domestic sphere persisted; efforts to socialize domestic chores and thereby eliminate a contradiction that perpetuated gender inequality were largely unsuccessful (see Croll 1974: 62–66; Jacka 1997: 32–35).[4]

In the postreform period, rural women have lost their status as producers that they gained under the policies of socialism. Decollectivization initially made rural women disproportionately redundant in agriculture. They were then exhorted to give up paid work and "return to the home," which solidified a perception that their primary role was in the household (Beaver, Hou, and Wang 1995). The new policies did encourage women to develop home-based businesses, such as orchard cultivation, which enabled them to contribute economically to their households and hence gain greater autonomy and respect (Judd 1994). Yet, ideologically, these forms of labor were simply incorporated into the domestic sphere, where they were seen as natural extensions of women's household role. As Jacka (1997) explains, under revolutionary socialism, the greater emphasis on labor performed outside the household established a clear division and hierarchy between the (formerly complementary) domestic and public spheres, and accorded each with new gender significance. By contrast to waged work in the public sphere, the domestic sphere was perceived as inferior, nonproductive, and feminized. As agricultural labor and home-based enterprises increasingly have become the purview of women, they are rarely considered productive or acknowledged as "work" when compared with off-farm wage work (Henderson et al. 2000). The perception of men's work as public and hence more significant is reflected in rural women's pronouncements that "men are more able" (Judd 1990).

The belief that men are the primary producers and contributors to the family economy is also a function of kinship. In China, young people are raised with a strong sense of filial duty, and children have historically been the primary means of support for the elderly (Fong 2004; Ikels 2004). Sons especially are expected to bear responsibility for care of their parents in old age. The kinship system (of the majority Han Chinese) is patrilineal, so sons are viewed as providing a family with continuity, and their responsibility to their natal households only increases over the life course. Moreover, the dismantling of rural collectives and restructuring of the state-run economic sector undermined China's health-care system (Yip 2010). In the absence of a universal social security program, the rural elderly are increasingly dependent on their offspring for support.[5] Yet the decreasing economic contribution of rural elders, in the context of their limited authority in land distribution matters, has negatively impacted their former high social status in the family.[6] The state has responded to reports of children shirking filial duties with propaganda stressing filial duty as a civic virtue (Ikels 2004). In most of rural China, sons take on the bulk of financial support for their retired rural parents (Jun 2004; Miller 2004). However, rural daughters do play a growing role in parental care, providing emotional and physical support, as the elderly spread the burden of social support among family members (Evans 2008; Fong 2004; H. Zhang 2004). Despite changing social practices, filial ideology remains powerful, and earning cash through migration is one means by which sons in particular can fulfill their filial duty.

The convention of patrilocal marriage, whereby sons "marry in" (*qu*) a "daughter-in-law" (*xifu*), puts greater pressure on men than on women to earn income. Although couples increasingly establish a separate residence upon marriage (an effect of increasing prosperity and changing social mores), they tend to do so in the husband's village. The groom's family is expected to provide bride wealth—cash and consumer goods presented to the new couple at marriage. Economic prosperity has raised brides-to-be and their families' expectations of what they will receive from the groom: the groom's family is now pressured to provide a new residence for the couple at marriage, which requires an outlay of tens of thousands of *yuan* (Kipnis 1997; Liu 2000; Y. Yan 2003). In a survey of migrant workers in enterprises in four cities throughout China, researchers Knight, Song, and Jia (1999) found that more male respondents than women cited pursuit of "higher income" as their motivation for migration, whereas the majority of female respondents chose social reasons, such as "to get life experience." Of course, this finding might simply be a factor of men's greater earning potential. Nonetheless, preparing for future marriage is one expense shouldered disproportionately by young men.

In contrast, the kinship system construes daughters to be temporary and therefore expendable members of the natal household.[7] At marriage, daughters leave their natal households and take on the identity of "daughter-in-law." In fact, marriage for rural women is commonly referred to as finding a "mother-in-law's home" (*popo jia*), reaffirming that a bride's primary responsibility is not to her own parents, but to her in-laws. Relying on a daughter for the maintenance of the household economy could be only a temporary measure until her marriage. Thus, whereas a son's migration may be seen as integral to the household economy and to the continuation of the family, a daughter's migration is more likely considered a means of relieving the natal household of the expense of her daily subsistence rather than providing significant earnings.[8] A daughter's labor—helping in the fields and aiding mothers at household tasks—is, moreover, replaceable in farm families where younger siblings are present to take over household tasks. The consequence of note here is that when women do migrate for work, they are less likely than men to be expected to earn more than their own keep. Shanshan, who migrated to Beijing in 1988 at age eighteen to work in domestic service,[9] put it thus: "I didn't think about making money. Back then, for a young woman in the village, it was just enough to find a stable and safe job."

A corollary of the pivotal position of sons is that they generally receive a greater proportion of household resources compared with daughters, particularly when there is competition for scarce resources. From 1985 to 2005, the cost of rural education increased at the same time that the national government had decreased funding to local schools. During this period, girls received less education than boys, and this was attributed to gender discrimination (Hannum, Wang, and Adams 2010).[10] When families are unable to afford to educate all their children, it is most often daughters who are withdrawn from school, in part because educating someone else's future daughter-in-law is not considered an investment equal to educating a son. Indeed, a common refrain among my informants was that they had dropped out of school, voluntarily or not, to allow younger siblings to attend. Others lost interest, not realizing the importance of education.

Suyin, who came to Beijing in 1996 from an impoverished rural area of north China at age sixteen, describes how the birth of a brother impacted her education, and expresses great regret about having to cut short her own education. She was the middle daughter in a large family that included three elder sisters and one younger sister, and one baby brother. After the birth of Suyin's younger brother, her mother voluntarily underwent sterilization, and was never fined for "excess births" (i.e., over the family planning limit) because an uncle was party secretary of their poor and remote village. But the large number of children and the cost of education strained the family's resources. Suyin recounted with strong emotions how her parents forced her to drop out after just one year of middle school. She cried and pleaded with them to let her stay in school, even physically scuffling with them. Recalling that event years later, Suyin was still angry, although she said she understood that poverty had given her parents no other choice. None of her elder sisters completed middle school either, but only Suyin showed such resentment and stubbornness about quitting. She quipped, "I have the personality of a boy!"

Suyin's characterization of her strong yearning for schooling as inappropriate for a girl also suggests the extent to which young women may be invested in gender norms. Similarly, many young women were proud of how their remittances or their absence from the household would help finance or free up resources for younger siblings' education, and usually siblings included at least one brother. For example, I calculated that sisters Shuqin and Shuchun regularly remitted 25 percent of their salary from 1999 to 2002 to supplement their parents' income from farming. Their earnings were used to pay for their mothers' medical bills and for tuition for a younger brother. Nonetheless, these stories also suggest that young rural women may choose migration because in fact they have nothing to lose, having already lost hope of bettering their lives through education.

Yarui's story is a case in point. She had been a promising student until, at the end of her second year of middle school, she fell ill and was forced to stay at home from school for an entire year. Lying in bed and worrying about missed schoolwork, Yarui grew so despondent that she attempted suicide by overdosing on sleeping pills. She slept for four days and three nights, and no one in her family was the wiser since she was already ill. Even after her recovery, she never completed her studies. Her parents did not value education highly and could not afford to send their three children to school. School fees per child were 1,000CNY annually, one-third of the family's annual income (from farming) of just 10,000CNY. Already behind in school and lacking financial or emotional support to catch up, Yarui chose to migrate to earn money to support her siblings.[11]

The division of labor by gender in rural households as well as the different responsibilities ascribed to men and women by the kinship system shape migration patterns in particular ways. Along with state-supported propaganda about filial duty, these factors limit the opportunities for wives and mothers in rural China to migrate while encouraging the migration of daughters, sons, and husbands. Moreover, young women's desires to migrate are intensified by their liminal position in the family and the life course, as I explain next.

Liminal Stage of Life

During my visit to Qiaolian's natal village, I was struck by an interaction with her neighbors' daughters. The three young girls, aged eight, twelve, and fifteen, were gaily dressed for the holidays in red cotton-padded jackets, their long hair decorated with red ribbons or covered by a red scarf. The youngest was still enrolled in school, but her older sisters had not completed middle school. I asked them what they typically did all day. "Nothing," and then, "we just play," they replied, which my friend and her parents later confirmed. The two eldest girls were typical of many young village women, who would choose to migrate if given the opportunity. "There was nothing to do in my village" or "I was idle" were the most common refrains I heard as informants gave their reasons for migration. A daughter's marginal position relative to sons in the household economy in part explains such responses, for those with younger brothers. For others, such as Tingting, who worked with Shuqin in 2000 as a hotel housekeeper, migration is motivated by boredom with small-town life and eagerness to "find excitement" elsewhere. Yet, taken in a metaphysical sense, such responses are articulations of young women's liminal position at a critical juncture of the life course just prior to marriage.

Following the completion of schooling and prior to settling down, young women are poised between carefree youth and responsible adulthood, which is traditionally conferred upon marriage. For nearly all rural women, opting out of marriage altogether is unthinkable as well as impractical, but it looms large on the horizon because it signifies a certain loss of autonomy and end of idealism, even as it holds promise for the future. The ambivalence about marriage is in part rooted in the unique structure of marriage in rural China, whereby, as Croll argues, young women experience time as "discontinuous" or as a rupture, as one life ends and another begins (1994: 210–211).

Sons take brides in order to continue the family line via offspring. The very terminology "to marry" (*chengjia*), literally "to create a family," reinforces the idea of marriage as being in the interest of procreation. Of course, the emphasis on childbearing is at once a long-established custom and a practical strategy, all the more necessary, in the reform era, to provide social insurance in old age and reproduce laborers for the household. For the most part, rural marriage has been seen to be primarily for the formation of a stable nuclear family and only secondarily for individual emotional or sexual fulfillment, although this is gradually changing (Y. Yan 2003; see Chapter 6). Indeed, most rural couples bear children shortly after marriage. Moreover, for young brides, childbearing may be a strategic choice; a new bride's position in her new household is liminal and insecure until she bears a child, particularly a son, which becomes the basis for her own "uterine family" (M. Wolf 1972).[12]

Given that marriage implies spatial relocation and a new identity as a member of a new family, and possibly in a new household, it is no wonder that many young women view marriage both with trepidation and anticipation. In fact, most young women imagine limitless possibilities for their future, only to be largely disappointed by reality (Croll 1994). New brides married far from home may find themselves unable to get along with their in-laws, or be homesick (Tan and Short 2004). Moreover, young rural women who fail to achieve social mobility through marriage, even though they have avoided becoming a farmer's wife, may feel keen disappointment. In extreme forms, rural women may express disillusionment with love and marriage through suicide. Although China has 21 percent of the world's population, it is responsible for 44 percent of the world's reported suicides, and 56 percent of women's suicides globally (Phillips, Li, and Zhang 2002). Globally, more men than women die by suicide, but the reverse is true in China. Nearly 20 percent of deaths among rural women ages fifteen to thirty-five are the result of suicide (Phillips, Li, and Zhang 2002). While the roots of such high suicide rates are still being investigated and debated, evidence indicates that young rural women's frustration with their inability to change the course of their lives is a factor. Facing an uncertain future after marriage, young women may thus seize upon migration as the last chance for autonomy and independence, resulting perhaps in some sense of continuity between youth and adulthood.

To the many young rural women who complain of boredom and uselessness, migration promises some diversion and even adventure or a chance to become productive. As I suggest above, feelings of restlessness may be tied to a young women's life course and mixed attitudes toward a future married life. In addition, the position of daughters as temporary members of their natal households, combined with gender roles and expectations, means that young women are generally not expected to be primary contributors to household income either through agricultural or off-farm work, but instead are appreciated for becoming self-sufficient, saving for their own dowry, or providing supplemental income to the household. Thus, young women's desires and opportunities to migrate are shaped within the context of household and family gender roles and relations, which in turn are changing under market socialism. Young women's decisions to migrate should not be seen as outright rebellious against "traditional" roles and identities associated with belonging to households and kin groups—that is, as dutiful daughters and (future) virtuous wives and good mothers. However, migration has consequences for rural women, their families, and rural society as it infuses new meaning to these gender identities, as I will explore in subsequent chapters. Importantly, the decision to migrate demonstrates young rural women's efforts to take control of the present, and instills them with a sense of purpose and direction, which I explore next.

"To Make Something of Oneself"

Many rural youth aspire to compensate for insufficient *suzhi* by expanding their horizons through migration and work. They commonly articulate their goals for migration using vague catchphrases like "self-development," "improving quality," and "challenging oneself." As what one *does* rather than who one *is* (i.e., one's family, class, or political background) has come to define identity in contemporary China, "going out to work" has become the only way for rural youth to fully realize their human potential. No wonder then that migration is now considered a rite of passage into adulthood for rural youth.

Symbolically, the city is a dynamic space of growth and advancement. Migration to the city offers the opportunity to increase productivity, to raise quality, and otherwise improve one's self-worth, as one's value has become measured by economic success. As Tingting optimistically intoned of Beijing: "As long as you have ability, you'll find a way [to succeed]." The attraction of cities in part reflects the disenchantment with the rural, which has been identified in official rhetoric and policy as a place that lags behind and must be brought up to speed with the more advanced cities. As Rongli indicated, "Beijing is much, much better than our village, where nothing has changed these past five years, though there have been a few changes in the town."

As the primary focus of the reform and opening policies, cities have vastly outpaced towns and villages in terms of growth of income, infrastructure, and communication technology (see Whyte 2010). Rural citizens may fully understand that uneven development results from calculated policy decisions, yet they nonetheless ascribe to neoliberal notions of development as based on individual opportunity and responsibility. As twenty-four-year-old Liping, a domestic worker and Migrant Women's Club member, clarified for me in 2000: "In the past, if you stayed doing farm work you lived pretty good and had no need to go out. But now things [e.g., grain] have gotten very cheap and the prices are not fair [to the producers]. But if you go out to work, your household will be stronger, so in recent years many people have gone out to work."

The flip side of the neoliberal belief in the market as a space of open and free competition is that failure to find success in the city suggests a character flaw or moral failing of the individual. An encounter in 1999 with Qiaolian's cousin and two of her middle school classmates conveyed to me the unfortunate repercussions of this interpretation. These young women, who were Qiaolian's age, lamented that low wages and unsteady work forced them to return home from the provincial capital where they had migrated for work. Returning to the village should have implied their readiness to settle down and get married, but their attitude was one of resignation and defeat. After visiting with them, Qiaolian herself was despondent. She vowed, as she would repeatedly, that she would not return to her village until she had "really accomplished something." Her words encapsulate the pressures on rural youth to propel themselves and their families into a better life. Young rural women are especially keen to prove their worth and change their fate before it is determined for them through marriage. At the same time, each individual's decision to migrate is unique. Even as agency is shaped by gender, which is conditioned by broader historical, political, and social trends, it is also shaped by individual histories and backgrounds (Pessar and Mahler 2003). To fully understand Qiaolian's decision to migrate, it is also necessary to consider her personality and her biography.

As she journeyed to Beijing for the first time, Qiaolian carried the weight of her family's history. The contents of her suitcase described in the Introduction— "books, a pen, and two notebooks"—symbolized a source of shame, her low quality, signifying her low level of education, which in turn signified a deeper shame—having been born a girl. Three years before, her father had terminated his support for her dream of a high school education, as he thought that it was not useful for his daughter to be so educated at the expense of her younger brother. At that time, the family could ill afford tuition for both children. Compared to her brother, Qiaolian was the more promising scholar, who was more motivated and more likely to pass the high school entrance exam, but her father instead pinned his hopes on his son.

Although Qiaolian did manage to earn a vocational teaching degree (*zhong-zhuan*), it only qualified her to teach in rural schools, and fell short of her goal to "really make something of herself." Those lofty educational aims were inspired by her late maternal grandmother, who, Qiaolian recorded in her diary, "would stand over and fan me on hot summer nights while I did my school homework," and tell stories of the family's ignoble history—like the time when poverty drove the grandmother into the streets to beg for food, which was considered shameful.[13] Qiaolian wrote: "I was probably the most attentive of all the listeners in my grandmother's entire life . . . I was her hope. I press on diligently to meet her high expectations of me."

Qiaolian's educational aspirations were also a means to get a well-paid job, so she could help out her parents financially, and give them respite from a lifetime of toil on the land: "My father always blames himself for having no ability, but I have never thought that. I've always cared deeply for my good parents, whose lives have been so full of hardship. The money for my education was earned by their manual labor on the land, toiling day in and out and never leaving this land, so that their kids could one day leave it."

Thus, the items in Qiaolian's suitcase also symbolized her ambitions: to retrieve her lost educational opportunity in the city, to work hard and earn money, and thereby to erase the shame of her own, and her family's, past "worthlessness." In a desperate act of survival, Qiaolian's grandmother ventured out of her (husband's) village during pre-liberation, wartorn times, with nothing to her name, to beg on the streets. Qiaolian's mother left her natal home only on her wedding day. Carrying only a spare outfit made of homespun cotton, she walked to a nearby village where she would become a farmer's wife and live with her mother-in-law (see Conclusion). Qiaolian left home in a car sent by her wealthier city employers, carrying a sense of debt to her parents and her own aspirations to achieve glory for herself in honor of them and especially her grandmother.

Summary

In contemporary China, rural youth are discursively inscribed in a moral geography and teleology of modernity such that leaving the countryside is mandatory to modernizing oneself, one's family, one's village, and the nation. The migration of young rural women conveniently meets the needs of the state for a youthful, relatively cheap, and flexible labor force for the accumulation of capital (see Chapter 1). Yet migration cannot be accurately explained as solely an involuntary response to the demands of the developmental state. Participation in migration has become an essential rite of passage for individuals to cultivate their talents and exercise their prerogatives, and for youth to become adults. Migration represents an especially meaningful odyssey of exploration and personal growth never before possible for young rural women.

Cultural constructions of gender based on separate spheres, gendered divisions of labor, and a patrilineal-patrilocal marriage and family system, together with state ideologies and policies that buttress them, influence women's motives and opportunities for migration. In particular, women's migration decisions tend to be based on noneconomic considerations and are formulated in the context of their liminal position in the household and family, as well as in the life course. At the same time, each individual migrant's desires, identities, and experiences are unique. The importance of a gender analytic as well as a migrant-centered ethnographic approach to migration studies cannot be overstated. Together they present a clearer picture of why and how people migrate than do macro-level economic, demographic, or institutional explanations. They illuminate how the state's postreform agenda dovetails with individuals' aspirations and identities to create new possibilities.

Recognizing the motivations and expectations propelling young women out of the village to the city is also key to understanding their *ambivalent* attitudes toward migration and work and toward their futures, which I explore in subsequent chapters. On the one hand, choosing to migrate allows them to express and pursue their dreams and is therefore empowering. On the other hand, beyond the village young rural women inevitably encounter much hardship and heartbreak, leaving many expectations unfulfilled. In the next chapter, I explore how gendered social networks facilitate young rural women's migration pathways and job prospects, but also constrain their newfound autonomy from their households and rural community by enforcing social norms. Paradoxically, social networking generates social capital that improves young women's status in the family and rural society even as cultural ideas of gender difference and inequality endure.

CHAPTER THREE

Gendered Social Networks and Migration Pathways

In 2002, after living and working in Beijing for five years, Shuqin bragged of her prowess as a skillful migration broker:

> I've helped six or seven [girls from my village] already, and more want to come [to Beijing]. But I have to check out their background first. If their reputations are good, I'll help them, but not otherwise. [I find out] whether the family is stingy, whether the kids are naughty or steal stuff, whether other villagers say bad stuff about them or look down on them. It doesn't matter if the household is rich or not; it's about what the rest of the village thinks of them.
>
> I helped two girls find work in an apparel factory in Beijing. Not long after they arrived, about two months, one started skipping work! There was a man who lived in another room in the same courtyard and flirted with one of the girls—the pretty one. He bought her clothes and took her out on dates. When she "saw the money, her eyes opened wide"; she just saw he could support her and so she stopped going to work. She spent nights with him, and didn't come back to the room [at night]! I didn't know what they were up to, but she was out every night with him. I couldn't control her.
>
> Her dad had told me that although his daughter and I were the same age, he knew that I had more experience, and that he would like me to keep an eye out for her, and make sure nothing happened to her. So I wrote a letter to her father that said: "You know your own daughter well. She's an adult; I can't tell her what to do. She does what she wants to do. If this isn't O.K., I'll send her back to you." After the New Year, our boss fired her, because she often stayed out all night and didn't show up for work. She went back to the village, and didn't come out again.

As explained in Chapter 2, gender roles and relations in the household and the patrilineal-patrilocal marriage and family system position young rural men and women differently in regard to migration. For young men, migration is seen

46

to be an extension of their masculine roles and identities, as they have primary responsibility to make money and find a bride (Griffiths 2010). For young women, migration is seen as a respite between schooling and marriage, perhaps a postponement of the marital decision, and possibly an opportunity to forge a better future, whether through expanding choices of marriage partners or education and work opportunities. Given the insecurity characteristic of this liminal stage of life, many young rural women put great faith in the transformational potential of migration. Yet in pursuing their desires by choosing to migrate, they engage in behavior considered unconventional and even inappropriate for unmarried women, and thus risk negative repercussions to themselves and their families.

Young women minimize such risks in part by turning to social networks comprised of relatives and covillagers for assistance with their migration journey and search for work. Relying on social networks based on kinship and native place assuages parental concerns for their daughter's physical safety and virtuous reputation. Social networks involve cultivating *guanxi:* interpersonal relationships governed by the principal of reciprocal exchange. In rural China, the art of *guanxi* building in the public arena is considered mainly a male purview; because it "involves mixing with a wide assortment of people in society, it is not good for a woman's social reputation" (M. M. Yang 1994: 79). Therefore, rural women's participation in *guanxi* building and social networking through migration is especially noteworthy.

The literature on internal and transnational migration indicates that migrants everywhere utilize such social networks to facilitate their migration. Local social networks expedite migration by providing access to information (e.g., destinations, jobs, housing), material support (e.g., loans, housing), and survival knowledge after arriving in the city, as well as companionship. In essence, social networks are a kind of social capital that accrue material benefits by lowering the risks and also the costs of migration. In China, the lack of institutional support for migrants, at least until the late 2000s, and the expense of formal linkages such as employment agencies, which levy fees and are often shady operations, reinforce informal migrant networks. Along with rural households, these networks subsidize the social reproduction of a migrant workforce by providing services to them that the state does not (see Chapter 1). Indeed, scholars of *guanxi* in China have cogently argued that social networks and reciprocal relationships are central to the reproduction of social life in both rural (e.g., Kipnis 1997; Liu 2000; Y. Yan 1996) and urban China (e.g., Wank 2000; M. M. Yang 1994), and have tangible and subversive effects because they challenge state claims to hegemony. They thus provide symbolic as well as social capital. Yet in the eyes of the postreform Chinese state, certain social relationships formed outside of formal institutions are not "modern" and rational but rather remnants of the feudal past. Adapting noncontractual social ties to new contexts showcases migrants' ingenuity despite their exclusion from formal structures of employment and welfare, yet also may mark them as "backward."

This chapter investigates young rural women's *guanxi* building through social networking: how it facilitates their migration journey and search for employment as well as how it impacts their identity and agency. Contracting with social networks may be regarded as a "bargain with patriarchy" (Kandiyoti 1988), which enables rural women to migrate but compromises their autonomy. For example, the opening quotation suggests that Shuqin was effective at helping *tongxiang* (e.g., fellow villagers) find work in Beijing because she upheld normative gender prescriptions, which secured parents' trust and the interest of employers, who expected disciplined and diligent workers. Shuqin thus helped widen the boundaries of the possible for herself and her rural sisters, but paradoxically enforced restrictive gender prescriptions of morality that underscore patriarchal forms of power. In particular, she censured her covillager for (presumably) engaging in premarital sexual relations, and reaffirmed parents' control over their daughter's sexuality and courtship. Further, as social networks are usually sex-segregated, they tend to channel migrant women into gender-appropriate jobs (Fan 2004), and thus perpetuate gender inequality in the labor market (described in Chapter 1). Yet, by developing social networks and thus participating in the public sphere, young migrant women accrue significant social and symbolic capital for themselves and their families. Below I describe the characteristics and functions of informants' social networks in journeying to the city and securing housing and jobs. I also consider how their social networks change over time. Throughout, I analyze how these networks may be at once constraints on young women's autonomy and resources for empowerment.

Autonomous Migrants

In general, few migrant women migrated on their own or pursued job opportunities independent of informal social networks. Those who did so usually found jobs by attending officially sponsored employment fairs in their county, such as those organized in conjunction with the Women's Federation that targeted recruitment of domestic workers. One who found work and then dared to travel independently was Rongli, introduced in Chapter 2. She responded to an advertisement in the county newspaper recruiting domestic workers, which was sponsored by the local labor bureau and the Beijing Women's Federation. Before leaving home, Rongli cautiously prepared for every possible emergency, including failure to be hired in Beijing: "Going out to be a domestic worker, I also worried that I would be cheated. Then what would I do? So that day that I went out I took some money, including enough for the return fare and three days' living expenses. This money came from my parents, because I'd only done house chores and worked on the family plot. If something happened, I would only stay in Beijing one day, visit Tiananmen Square, and then go home."

Importantly, those few young women who found jobs independent of social networks gained important skills of self-presentation and communication. Yanmei, introduced in Chapter 2, found her first job in Beijing in 1996 through family contacts, but switched jobs in 1997 using a domestic service placement agency operated by the Beijing Women's Federation. In 2000, she explained the procedure to me:

> At first, it was me who negotiated with the employer. Those people there [i.e., the company personnel], they don't go out and find an employer to talk to you. It's you who seeks out the employers. You must rely on yourself. Like, if the employer looks down on you, you must convince them [they can] rely on your ability. They asked me if I could do certain chores. Then we signed the contract. I was really nervous. It's your first time seeing each other. Employers are really nervous too. You try to see what they are like, see if they seem O.K.

Likewise, Rongli explained how she cautiously assessed her potential employers and work environment prior to agreeing to the job. She intended to care for an elderly person rather than a newborn, because overprotective parents might be too hasty to blame their domestic worker should their child be harmed. She also preferred to work with the elderly because of her positive experiences with her own grandparents.

> Doing domestic service, entering a household, it's like entering a mini society: you must deal with interpersonal relations (*guanxi*). . . . Before I signed the [work] contract, I checked out the situation; if I didn't like what I saw I could always return home, right? So I asked whether the household had any sick people, [and] how many people? They said [there was] only an old couple, two people, nothing complicated, so I figured it was O.K. Also, my grandpa had been so good to me, so I'm good with elderly. Some domestic workers' situation is complex, they maybe have to care for sick people, or for children, and the burden of childcare is the greatest.

These official channels of recruitment were neither systematized nor extensive, and because they charged fees for services, were not cost effective for most migrants. Migrants were also wary of such organizations, having heard widespread rumors (many of them true) about being cheated out of the application fee or otherwise deceived. Leafing through a newspaper one day in my Beijing apartment in 2002, Shuchun pointed out which job advertisements she suspected were out to "trick people." Private, for-profit agencies especially seemed untrustworthy and risky. The lack of formal labor recruitment pathways and the relative higher costs of utilizing formal channels pushed most rural women into dependence on kin and peer-based local social networks.

Bargaining with Patriarchy

In China, as in many other global contexts, the departure of unmarried daughters from rural villages concerned parents and other elders, as migration seemed to challenge their traditional authority in matters of young women's sexuality and marriage (see Mills 1999; D. L. Wolf 1992). Given the centrality of marriage to the life course, and the expectation of female purity, parents and daughters alike wished to maintain a young woman's good reputation, so as not to jeopardize her marriage prospects. Yet because migration connoted moral impropriety, it threatened to sully a daughter's reputation and hence the family's good name.

Historically, itinerant women were considered morally suspect and lacking in feminine virtue, as they had transgressed neo-Confucian ideals of gender that assigned genteel women to the domestic sphere. According to this worldview, women's domestic activities were also moral acts, and thus work performed in the inner quarters was equated with feminine virtue and elite status, while activities that took women outside this realm were comparatively less virtuous or "womanly" and indicated lower social status. Often poverty or family tragedy, such as widowhood, was the catalyst impelling a woman to leave her home and enter servitude, and so women's migration was also associated with economic deprivation and the lower classes (Mann 1997: 30–44).

With the advent of socialism, a new society provided women who "went out to work" a subjectivity and identity as "liberated women" that they could proudly embrace (Rofel 1999). The revolution changed "the context and the rewards associated with" women's labor outside the domestic sphere (Hershatter 2000: 83). Specifically, it provided rural women "the basic conditions of existence, as well as possibilities for recognition and glory" (93). However, socialist liberation did not completely nullify working-class women's sense of shame about their poverty, migration, and work—their transgression of patriarchal gender norms (Rofel 1999: 67). Historically constituted memories and inherited traditions, including neo-Confucian prescriptions about gender and morality, continued to resonate with some women who "went out to work," even after 1949.[1]

Under market socialism, this gendered construction of virtue has become embedded in a moral discourse on wealth and conspicuous consumption (Liu 2000). Official support for increased consumer spending has been tempered by popular outrage against corruption and official condemnation of excessive consumption outside the parameters of law and order. Such ambivalence toward wealth has been linked with gendered discourse on virtue, not least because some of the highest paid jobs for female migrants in the city involve the commercialization of female sexuality, as in the entertainment sector (T. Zheng 2009). In this sense, the bodies and characters of young migrant women have been blamed for the challenges to social mores wrought by liberalizing consumption habits, particularly of "deep-pocketed" middle-class men, challenges that threaten the stability of the nuclear household and the official construction of womanhood, the "virtuous wife and good mother" (Sun 2009).

More pernicious than the association of migrant women with commercialized sex, the commoditization of girls and women under capitalism poses the real danger of allowing them to fall prey to traffickers who dupe them into marriage or prostitution.[2] In Yanmei's view: "At home there are a lot of women who have been sold, especially from Sichuan and Anhui. I know some. They are adults, thirty-something, who are unmarried [men] and can't get a wife through other means, so they purchase one. There are lots and lots. They sell [i.e., traffic] people like they sell commodities."

For all these reasons, beginning in the early 1980s, rural elites were scandalized by the first exodus of unmarried daughters from the village, and lamented it would make the village "look bad" (Gong 1998: 60). Only as more women from any one village or county participated in migration did criticism about the corruptive influence of wealth abate, and local officials even facilitated young women's migration when they realized the value of their remittances (Gong 1998: 60). As a domestic worker who came to Beijing from Anhui in 1989 with her husband noted with concern: "Before I got married, I didn't know anything about going out to work. Not like today, everyone goes out. Even young [single] women just do as they please. They don't listen to their parents." Nevertheless, young rural women considering migration had to weigh the consequences of being associated with such negative stereotypes about morals and money, and devise ways to balance their aspirations for migration with the need to protect their good reputations. As Shanshan (introduced in Chapter 2) explained: "When I went out to work, my family didn't really support me. They worried that a girl who went out would ruin her reputation, so I told them that I wasn't 'chasing money,' I was just going out to work in a safe place."

Young rural women intending to migrate to the city risked violating gender norms associated with rural patriarchy as well as the official construction of womanhood, both of which reinforced as primary rural women's roles as (future) wives and mothers, and the role of migrant-worker as secondary. Such social constructions of gender, as I emphasized in Chapter 1, benefit the state's agenda of development through capital accumulation by rationalizing women's labor as flexible and cheap. But by making compromises with the patriarchal authority of both family and state, and turning to social networks, young rural women were able to act on their migration decisions.

Functions of Social Networks

Youth in China's countryside learn about work opportunities and city life mainly from relatives, covillagers, or school friends who have migration experience. Xingjuan (introduced in Chapter 2) told me, "I didn't know anything about Beijing. I learned about Beijing from my elder brother's wife. She went to Beijing and said how everything there was so great." Social networks thus function primarily as a resource for information.

Further, by facilitating their migration journeys and job searches in a secure manner, social networks provide the chance for young women to actualize their own ambitions with the approval and support of their families and local communities. Generally someone familiar—who is older and already established in Beijing—could be trusted to safely escort a young woman to the city and arrange for short-term lodging there, to provide an introduction to a prospective employer, and be generally accountable for her personal safety and moral integrity. I quote Xingjuan again here: "I had no way to go out, not knowing anyone. But then my mother sent some gifts to that old lady, who then took me out to work. Her daughter was my primary school classmate. In her employer's household there was a dormitory, like those ones they used to have at universities in Beijing especially for domestic workers. I lived with her there for more than a month. Later she found me a position helping a couple care for their infant."

In keeping with local practices of cultivating social relationships (*guanxi*), a gift establishes an obligation to reciprocate. Here, the older woman is made accountable to Xingjuan's mother for ensuring the young woman's safe arrival and care in Beijing. This example suggests ways in which the logistics of the migration journey may be a result of negotiations between young women and their concerned parents. Indeed, a daughter's migration may depend upon her family having established *guanxi* networks with kin and covillagers to facilitate migration and also to protect her from harmful gossip that could sully her reputation.

Utilizing kinship networks and cultural notions of reciprocity is also an effective response to potential physical dangers faced by young women during the migration journey. By traveling with a familiar escort, such as a covillager, male kin, or even a county Women's Federation official, most young women accommodated concerns for personal safety as well as social reputations on their journey to Beijing. As Shanshan said: "[In my village] some of the heads of households whose thinking was rather 'feudal' said it was bad for girls to go out to work, that it was better for men to go out. But in my case, my older brother was in Beijing, and he went out with me. My mom was worried at first, and I was a little worried about coming so far, but having relatives [in Beijing] helped."

Similarly, Shuqin and Shuchun's father was instrumental in facilitating the migration journeys of his daughters to Beijing. In 1997, Shuqin's father entrusted his sixteen-year-old daughter to *laoxiang* (i.e., acquaintances originally from the village), a married couple who had lived in Beijing for twenty years, to travel to Beijing, where they helped Shuqin find a job. For the rest of the year, Shuqin worked as a hotel chambermaid until bankruptcy led management to lay off all the migrant employees without severance. (However, the Beijing staff kept their jobs as the hotel fought out its battles in court.) Meanwhile, her father had also moved to Beijing so he could be near his daughter, finding work as a security guard for a compound that housed a school and a small garment factory. He soon secured work for Shuqin operating a sewing machine making apparel at a factory in the compound, which was run by a Beijing husband-and-wife team. Early in 1998, when he returned home for the New Year, he escorted Shuchun to Beijing to join her sister at the same factory. Reassured that the two girls together would care for one another, he returned home.

In addition to providing logistical support with the migration journey and job search, social networks were also an important source of support to young women in the city. Small informal communities comprised of kin, school classmates, or covillagers form in the city to provide care and assistance to all their members. Such groups provide emotional sustenance for young migrant women away from home for perhaps the first time in their lives. Suyin (introduced in Chapter 2) told me that each night for the first week that she was in Beijing, she was kept company by her elder sister, who was already working in Beijing. Suyin provided the same companionship for their younger sister when she in turn came out to work in Beijing.

Shuqin and Shuchun were grateful to the existence of such a social network when they met with emergencies in Beijing. In 1999, while working in the apparel factory, Shuqin's appendix nearly ruptured, requiring costly emergency surgery that, as a migrant, she would have to pay for out-of-pocket. Her desperate sister pleaded with their boss for help, but he offered only one month's advance salary and would not even allow the sisters to cash out the security deposits he had collected from them to use for the operation.[3] Shuchun spent a frantic few hours calling their relatives and covillagers throughout the city until she had raised 3,500CNY cash, the cost of the appendectomy surgery that she had directly negotiated with a surgeon down from his asking fee of 5,000CNY. The sisters repaid their debts over the next eighteen months at the rate of 100CNY each per month, about 25 percent of their income.

Importantly, such social networks serve to extend the reach of rural patriarchal authority into the cities, regulating gender and enforcing standards of sexuality and morality expected of village daughters. For example, Xingjuan expressed the following disdain for her *laoxiang* and coworker, whose similar background would certainly have been the grounds for solidarity had she not been judged of low moral quality due to a lust for money: "My employer's household had two domestic workers, one to cook, and I took care of the baby. That one who did their cooking was also from Anhui, and we were about the same age. But her motive in coming out to work was just to make money."

As illustrated by Shuqin's letter to her *tongxiang*'s father back home, the mere threat of rumors and gossip about a young woman's wayward character or behavior flowing back home serves as an indirect mode of patriarchal control over young migrant women.

Producing Social Capital

Reciprocal relationships (*guanxi*) are most effectively cemented by moral obligations (*renqing*) and an emotional component (*ganqing*). The filial sentiment shared by children and their elders is the ultimate source of human relations in China (Fong 2004; Kipnis 1997). Young rural women are thus motivated in their capacity as dutiful as well as loving daughters to choose particular migration pathways that renew and strengthen their family's social networks. However, engaging in *guanxi* on behalf of family may exact a sacrifice of individual autonomy, as it enmeshes a young woman in ongoing obligations without clear and direct benefit.

Indeed, reciprocal relationships can mask class inequality and labor exploitation (see also Chapter 4). For example, Migrant Women's Club member Xiulan found her first job in 1998 when educational administrators from Beijing visited an elementary school they funded in her hometown. Through her sister, who happened to be a teacher in the school, Xiulan was offered a job providing childcare as a live-in domestic worker for the household of one Beijing educator. Xiulan worked for the family for two years, staying long after she realized that her monthly salary of just 200CNY was far below the going rate for domestic service. However, she did not immediately quit because she felt indebted to her employer on behalf of her sister, whose job necessitated maintaining a good relationship with all the administrators. During the two years that Xiulan worked in domestic service, she successfully passed the examination for the *zhongzhuan* (i.e., vocational or technical degree), and then set her sights on self-study for the *dazhuan* (i.e., college associate's degree). But her employers would not concede to her request for designated study time, nor would they allow her to leave their employ. When they found out that Xiulan was looking for a new job, they tried to prevent her from leaving the house! When I first met Xiulan in spring 2000, she had just left their employ and was starting a job in sales for a small privately run company. When I reconnected with her in Beijing in 2002 she was still working in sales and sharing a flat with another young migrant woman whom she had met at the Club.

Another Migrant Women's Club member with whom I spent much time in 2000 had a similar experience. In 1993, Yaling became the domestic worker for the household of a retired cadre (public official) at the behest of her father, a lower-ranking cadre. Yaling interpreted the opportunity as an expression of her father's support for her ambitions: "My dad wanted me to go out and get life experience." Yet to preserve the social relationship between the two men, she endured ridiculously low wages in her new position: "I earned 50 or 60 *yuan* per month. It was low. Back then domestic workers were earning about 300 *yuan* a month. Over three years my salary was raised to 100 *yuan*. . . . Whatever humiliation I suffered, I didn't speak up."

Participation in social networks likewise compromised Shuqin's and Shuchun's autonomy even as it enabled them to leave their impoverished village and earn independent wages. From a young age the sisters were put to work, making hand-woven carpets at home for a village enterprise. In the early 1990s, the family rented out their property and moved to the nearby township, where their father had found work in a government office, although he was not considered a civil servant (cadre). He then used his expanding social network to seek out better work opportunities for his four children. Shuchun was hired as the assistant to the township Women's Federation cadre in charge of family planning. Shuqin was dispatched to a factory that produced machine-sewn cloth sacks in the prefectural city. But her father came to fetch her home when, after six months of work, she still hadn't received any payment. Next, her father found her a job in the county town as a waitress in a restaurant owned by his acquaintance. Shuqin disliked the job and fought frequently with the chef, whom she said called her clumsy and sloppy. But when she tried to quit, her father scolded her and forced her to continue, for the sake of his reputation, or "face" (*mianzi*),[4] and his relationship with her employer. Long after their father returned to the countryside, having seen to their employment in the apparel factory in Beijing, the two sisters remained indebted to his *guanxi*-based social network.

But with experience and time spent in the city, young rural women can expand their family's social networks and opportunities to accrue social capital through reciprocal exchanges. Indeed, a daughter's migration can be considered an investment in *guanxi* building for the family, and also benefits her directly. Importantly, seasoned migrants are expected to become facilitators themselves, enabling the migration of younger kin and covillagers. Young migrant women gain social status and feel proud as they are recognized as the "go-to" person who has social connections beyond the village. For example, on a visit with me back to her natal village in 2002, several parents beseeched Shuqin to help their daughters get to Beijing and find work. She responded with a mixture of satisfaction at her enhanced social standing and annoyance: "You just can't help everyone, and not everyone has the capability to do well in Beijing. Nor can I do much as I make so little money myself. But if I don't help, they will say I'm selfish." Material as well as social benefits result from assisting others to migrate and find work. Shuqin and Shuchun, as well as their parents, often received gifts from families whose daughters they had helped settle in Beijing. Thus, a daughter's migration helps her family accrue symbolic and social capital, with potentially positive benefits for their material and social well-being. However, *guanxi* making is a time-consuming, enervating, and emotionally fraught undertaking.

As hotel housekeeper Tingting once intoned, "If you don't help fellow villagers, they will gossip about you back in the village." Concern with maintaining a good reputation and fear of slander, including of a sexual bent, also compels young rural women to participate in *guanxi* production by facilitating others' migration. *Guanxi* is thus a cultural practice that indirectly enforces young women's membership in the rural community, with attendant benefits and drawbacks to their agency.

Gradually, young migrant women may develop their own social networks beyond kin and covillagers by befriending other migrants, such as coworkers met in the city, and even urban colleagues, clients, or employers. Relationships forged in the city and on the job with other migrants are often critical to finding better jobs or housing. My key informants forged close friendships with peers met in Beijing that bore fruit in concrete ways. For example, Shuqin and Xiaofang worked together in hotel housekeeping in 1998; in 2001, Shuqin paired up with Xiaofang in wholesale retail; in 2002, Shuchun helped Xiaofang find work again as a hotel housekeeper. Yarui met Shuchun (and also Xiaofang) on the job in 2002, and they remained fast friends over the years. Yarui was responsible for introducing Shuchun to a Beijing bachelor, whom she married in 2009 (see Chapter 6). Likewise,

Changying relied on an extensive network of fellow teachers of migrant children to find new teaching positions over the years.

The restrictive work environment, work conditions, and labor relationship of domestic service, which I describe in Chapter 4, leaves domestic workers largely unable to cultivate social networks in the city. Yet domestic workers are sometimes rewarded for their loyal service with help finding a new job when their period of service ends. Shanshan, for example, had cared for an elderly lady and her husband for four years. In gratitude, their middle-aged daughter helped Shanshan become a manager of a street stall that sold cigarettes and liquor after her services to the family were no longer required. Stories similar to these are chronicled in Chapter 5.

Hotel housekeepers, whose work lives I describe in Chapter 4, had multiple pathways for social networking and building *guanxi*. In addition to currying favors from their bosses and supervisors, they paid close attention to coworkers, especially those with more experience, and also clients, from whom they could gain useful information, advice, and potential job opportunities. For example, between 2000 and 2002, Shuchun cultivated a close relationship with her coworker at a four-star hotel's spa and sauna. Shuchun admired this twenty-five-year-old Beijing high school graduate who was studying part-time toward a college degree in traditional Chinese medicine, and deferentially called her "Elder Sister." Her coworker in turn seemed to genuinely take pity on Shuchun, who was severely overworked, and let her take catnaps behind the counter when guests were few. She also shared with Shuchun the sales promotions and freebies that she received in her capacity as a "regular" employee (i.e., having local urban *hukou*). When Shuchun quit the job, her friend provided support and advice, and also offered a place to sleep. In the years after Shuchun left the four-star hotel, the two women remained in close touch. At the same time, both Shuchun and Yarui became acquainted with several middle-aged Beijing women who had health club memberships at the hotel (where Yarui also worked in 2002). They addressed the older women as "Auntie" and confided in them. One even proposed that Yarui quit her job and work as her domestic worker. Yarui trusted the woman to be a decent and even generous employer, and so gave the offer much consideration. But ultimately she declined, for she did not want to lose even the limited freedom of her job, which at least gave her a few hours each day to herself.

An additional function of social networks, which I describe further in Chapter 6, is to facilitate matchmaking, particularly between rural women and urban men. Some of my informants met their future spouses by way of their Beijing employer. Through marriage, and hypergamy in particular, a young woman can expand her natal family's influence far beyond the village.

As the examples above illustrate, young migrant women learn how to manage complex human relations in the public sphere through the maintenance and construction of social networks based on reciprocal exchange. Their roles in facilitating the migration of kin and covillagers, as well as expanding rural social networks into the city, reap symbolic capital, as they and their families gain face and status within the community. They also increase their potential for amassing social capital in the form of *guanxi,* leading to material benefits such as better jobs.

Summary

This chapter has illustrated that social networks forged with the principle of reciprocity are integral to the migration process. Relying on them is a practical strategy for young rural women constrained by a dearth of formal channels for migration and job recruitment. It is also personally and culturally meaningful to them as it connects young migrant women to their families and communities, and expresses their filial devotion. Further, participation in *guanxi* making through migration is also empowering to individuals and to rural women generally: It allows them to accrue symbolic and social capital for themselves and their families and significantly broadens their agency into the public sphere in ways traditionally associated only with men.

Yet, social networks and *guanxi* building are integral to the reproduction of gender roles and identities, namely the filial daughter, and thus may reinforce rural patriarchal ideology and power, such as by remotely controlling young women's sexuality. Also, obligations to members of a social network who have helped secure a migrant woman's employment may severely constrain her freedom to protest labor exploitation by changing employers. Moreover, as Fan (2004) has observed, gendered social networks of female kin and covillagers that facilitate the migration of rural women from China's countryside also contribute to the homogenization of women's migration experiences. In particular, they channel rural women into gender-specific job niches with limited opportunities for occupational mobility, where their cheap and expendable labor accumulates capital for the developmental state, as outlined in Chapter 1.

The next chapter focuses on the labor relationship between migrant women and their urban employers, and the impact of work on young rural women's subjectivity and agency. Importantly, cultivating a close personal relationship with employers is a strategy deployed by young migrant women to manage the social stigma of their identity as menial workers. However, such relationships also complicate class difference and contribute to labor exploitation.

CHAPTER FOUR

Menial Women and Model Workers

When I arrived at the place where I was to work, I discovered I would be caring for a naughty three-year-old boy, washing clothes, cleaning the house, and cooking meals. Before I'd even set down my worn suitcase, the boy's mother assigned me a long list of tasks. I felt like a bondservant from the old imperial days. . . . My bed was a cot placed in a corner of the living room. Every night the family stayed up late watching TV; I could only wait until they turned off the set to get to sleep, and in the morning I had to quietly rise before they awoke, to prepare their breakfast. . . . One evening, I stood in the kitchen boiling pot after pot of dumplings while they ate at the table. By the time I was finished, there were only a few dumplings left on the table. As I put these into my bowl and headed into the living room, I heard Auntie suggest to her husband, "Why not let her eat yesterday's food?"

When I first met Qiaolian in 1998 in Beijing, she and her *tongxiang* Changying had just started jobs as teachers in an informal (and illicit) primary school for the children of migrant workers.[1] It was quite some time before she acknowledged her past as a domestic worker and invited me to understand her experiences as chronicled in her diary, including the passage excerpted above. Still she would not, or could not, speak to me or to others about that period of her life, as her feelings of humiliation and shame were overpowering.

During the 1990s, the Women's Federation (introduced in Chapter 1) endeavored to erase the stigma associated with employment in domestic service by professionalizing it as a technical occupation.[2] Nonetheless, employers I interviewed in 2000 and 2002 viewed the occupation through older frameworks of servitude or apprenticeship, in which caregivers and housekeepers were incorporated into employer households as "members of the family." This was understandable for a number of reasons. First, privatized household help had all but disappeared under revolutionary socialism.[3] Only elite cadre households were authorized to hire help, who were considered public employees—"servants of the people"—as the state directly or indirectly disbursed their salary and benefits.[4] During the Cultural

Revolution, privatized household service was attacked as a bourgeois practice and class exploitation, and intellectual households were compelled to dismiss their hired hands. No wonder the reemergence of a domestic service market in the 1980s invoked the pre-liberation past.[5]

Second, domestic service has never been a legally recognized occupation involving a formal labor relationship. Even when done for a wage, caregiving and housework are conceived of as emotional labor, rather than work per se, because they are associated with women's family roles and undertaken in the domestic sphere, and hence invisible to the formal economy (Anderson 2000). Moreover, domestic work has not been considered "modern" because it is not fully marketized (Y. Yan 2003). Urban households generally bypass recruiters to hire domestic workers through their own social networks, and working conditions and wages are negotiated informally. Evocative of servitude, devalued as (unproductive) women's work, and arranged informally, domestic service has maintained its stigma, which certainly lowered the self-esteem of rural women like Qiaolian who undertook this occupation, and contributed to some employers' disregard for their domestic worker's humanity.

This chapter explores how incorporation into the informal urban service economy impacted young rural migrant women's subjectivity and agency by focusing on their everyday experience of menial labor. Speaking of rural Chinese women workers in early twentieth-century Shanghai's cotton mills, Emily Honig observed: "daily routine represents the social reality from which their consciousness of themselves as women and as workers eventually emerged" (1986: 135). I document how the social stigma associated with menial jobs, and domestic service in particular, negatively impacted women's self-esteem and social status. Further, the unregulated labor process and informal labor relationship enabled exploitation as it reaffirmed gender, generational, and rural-urban difference and hierarchy between migrant women workers and their employers.

Despite these disadvantages, migrant women workers were not passive victims of exploitation. Although their actual experience of class was complicated by gender, generational, and rural-urban differences, these intersecting identities also opened up space for negotiation with power. Young rural women creatively adapted familiar discourses and identities to the work context to capably manage social stigma and navigate inequitable labor processes and relationships in ways that were both culturally meaningful and personally beneficial. In particular, they brought to bear "traditional" identities as filial daughters and virtuous maidens to justify their "choice" of menial work among limited options. They negotiated the "modern" sphere of capitalist labor exchange by applying kinship-based ethics (*ganqing*) and social norms of reciprocity (*guanxi*). They performed the role of "model worker," exercising self-discipline to prove their capability and negate demeaning stereotypes and to win concessions from employers. When their strategies failed to garner favorable outcomes, they used their positions as temporary workers and migrants in the city to "vote with their feet."

Below, I discuss social stigma, labor process, and labor relations as they pertain first to domestic work and then to hotel housekeeping. Then I turn to a discussion of power, accommodation, and resistance. In the first section, I draw upon interviews with domestic workers and their employers conducted between 1999 and 2000 in Beijing and interviews with members of the Migrant Women's Club with experience in domestic service. The section on hotel housekeeping and office cleaning focuses on the experiences of Shuchun and Shuqin from 2000 to 2010 and Yarui from 2002 to 2010, drawing additionally on interviews with their supervisors conducted in 2002 and 2006, and conversations with their various coworkers throughout the years.

Stressed and Depressed: Labor Process of Domestic Service

As is common among rural-to-urban female migrants in other places and times, young rural Chinese women are channeled into live-in domestic service as a first job in the city, either through gendered social networks or specialized recruitment agencies (e.g., sponsored by the Women's Federation). Although domestic service pays relatively low wages compared to other jobs available to migrant women, not to mention migrant men, it appeals to many newly arrived women migrants in Beijing as a matter of convenience. Live-in domestic service requires relatively little initial capital outlay yet resolves the immediate crisis of finding shelter. Additionally, as domestic work is regarded by workers and employers not as skilled labor, but rather as an extension of a woman's household role, it is wide open to newly arrived young women with no prior work experience or with low educational levels.

Live-in domestic service is hard work that is poorly remunerated. But the aspect of this occupation that most influences workers' self-perceptions is its social stigma, as commonly acknowledged. As mentioned in previous chapters, the stigma associated with domestic work appears to result from its historical association with poverty and gender transgression, compounded by its association with servility. Performing intimate tasks, not for one's immediate kin, but for strangers, despite compensation, is seen as virtual servitude. In emphasizing to me the demeaning quality of domestic work, Xingjuan gave the example of "cleaning dirty diapers" daily. Still others point to the lack of respect and human dignity accorded domestic workers as exacerbating the social stigma of domestic service. A rather extreme example was that told to me by a part-time (live-out) domestic worker, whose employer refused to allow her to clean the toilet with anything other than her bare hand. Fortunately the worker was able to quit her employ immediately, since she had other part-time jobs. Qiaolian experienced a similar indignity, caring for the spoiled child of a working couple who continually blamed her for their son's shenanigans, yet objected if she tried to discipline the child. She was particularly humiliated when she was made to wash the child's feet—considered the dirtiest part of the body and a very intimate act—in front of the adults, who laughed when their naughty son splashed her with dirty tub water.

The overlap of the workplace with living space and the physical proximity of a domestic worker to her employer blur the boundaries between work time and rest time and public and private space, leaving domestic workers particularly vulnerable to exploitation.[6] Live-in domestic workers reside with members of their employer's household, in apartment buildings or in one-story brick houses similar to their homes in the village. Labor Bureau regulations stipulate that domestic workers are supposed to have their own rooms, but most double up in their employer's household with their elderly or youthful charges (Beijing Laodongju 1995, 1999). Only a few of those I interviewed were lucky enough to be housed in "domestic worker quarters" offered by large work units, which might include a private room, or the chance to share a room with peers. Not only because of living arrangements, but also because of the demands of caregiving for infants or for the sick or incapacitated elderly, who demand round-the-clock attention, domestic workers may be called upon at all hours of the day and night. Characteristically, domestic workers frequently complain of being overworked and exhausted. As Xingjuan complained, "I never slept until after ten o'clock at night. Every day I cried and cried."

A typical day for Shanshan, caring for an elderly couple in the 1990s, began earlier than she was accustomed to in the countryside: "In the morning, Beijing people get up earlier, at 6 a.m. I helped them wash their hair, then heated them some milk, and went outside to the courtyard to purchase breakfast and fresh milk." Demands on their time made workers complain of "not having time for myself." At most, domestic workers rest one day a week, but most have no days off unless they request to return for a visit to their village. "They didn't offer [time off], and anyway, I had nowhere to go," Yaling explained. Shanshan elaborated: "Working in someone's house, you are restricted. If they say you can't go out, you can't go out. If you go out, you still have to worry, afraid that they'll get angry when you return."

Moreover, the tasks of a domestic worker are all encompassing and never ending. Most domestic workers take care of housecleaning, laundering, marketing, food preparation, cooking, and dishwashing for the entire household each day, on top of ministering to the special needs of children and elderly and attending to the needs of visitors or guests. In addition, most employers require more of their employees than just the basics of household social reproduction, sometimes making demands simply to display their power over the employee's very person, not just her labor (Anderson 2000). Among the domestic workers I met, running errands, escorting children to and from school, and even helping out in the family businesses were routine demands made by employers. For example, Yaling had to care for a three-generation family of five. The household head demanded an extra meal each night: "When I first started, the workload was very heavy. The [male] household head, at 10 p.m., would need to eat a late-night snack, so I prepared four meals [a day]."

Often domestic workers do not control where they work or for whom they work. Some domestic workers are dispatched by their employer to care for a sick or terminally ill household member confined to a hospital, sleeping in the hospital dormitory or even in the sickroom with their charge and taking orders from their employer, their patient, and the nurses alike.[7] Others are hired as domestic workers only to be employed as full-time workers in their employer's private business. For example, Yanmei worked during the day at the family's dry cleaning business, but also did laundry and cooking for the family as needed. Another domestic worker tended her employer's clothing stall during the daylight hours, and returned to their residence at night to cook and clean. Still others are "lent out" part-time as a favor to their employer's friends, or are casually traded back and forth between related households. (Shuchun's situation for a few months in 1998 was just the opposite. After reporting for work at the apparel factory in Beijing, to join her sister at the sewing machines, the bosses directed her to provide them with full-time care for their newborn baby!)

Domestic workers rarely control the content of their work, nor do they control how they do their work. As they learn their tasks, they are frequently supervised by their employer or a household member, and in turn have to police their own actions, leading Yanmei to conclude: "Working in someone else's home is not like being in your own home. You have to remember that. You have to get used to their home. You must have a sense of propriety when you do things in other peoples' homes." Surveillance by an employer may be a blatant indicator of mistrust. Not a few domestic workers, including Qiaolian (see below) were subjected to having employers inspect their suitcases upon departure from their post.

Given the limited occupations available to migrant women, domestic service is not an unreasonable choice, particularly for a first job. Yet the social stigma of the work, often reinforced by degrading treatment from employers, undermines much of the gains of going out to work. Moreover, an employer's control of the worker's spare time, the lack of privacy, and lack of freedom to manage the process of work can leave workers feeling psychologically "stressed and depressed." For many, domestic work feels akin to indentured servitude or slavery, as Rongli poignantly conveyed: "I felt that I had been sold into someone's home."

The unique features of domestic service—its location in private space, the overlap of work and leisure space and time—make domestic workers particularly vulnerable to exploitation. Though no comprehensive statistics exist to indicate what percentage of domestic workers experience mental or physical abuse, surveys suggest rates could be as high as 65 percent, with verbal abuse predominant (Mellerman 2008; Tang 1998). Extreme cases of physical and sexual abuse of domestic workers have caught media attention and garnered popular outrage. Yet very often such reportage sensationalizes violence and perpetuates stereotypes of rural women; rarely does it offer a critique of the systemic or institutional causes of such tragedies (Sun 2004). Moreover, mundane forms of exploitation are rarely addressed, perhaps because domestic work is not seen in the same light as other occupations.

On paper, China's Labor Law (1994 and 2008) guarantees the rights of all workers, including migrants, whether employed by the formal state, in the joint-venture sector, or in the private and informal sector; in practice, rights are frequently violated. The invisibility of paid domestic work to public scrutiny and its common acceptance as women's work or "domestic chores" rather than skilled work compromise its legal status. In fact, domestic workers are legally considered to be members of their employer's household, rather than bona fide workers. In domestic service, employee-employer relations are treated as interpersonal relations, covered only by the civil code, which is less comprehensive than the Labor Law. No wonder that most rural migrant women doubted that "the law" could protect them: "There is no legal protection for *dagongmei*. [Only] if your relative is an official can you get legal help; otherwise, forget it. It [the law] is not for the people," Migrant Women's Club member Wenling explained to me in 2000.[8]

Although domestic service in Beijing is somewhat regulated by guidelines promulgated by the municipal Labor Bureau and enforced by the domestic service job placement agencies affiliated with the Women's Federation, these are suggestions without teeth, and workers are largely skeptical that companies would or could enforce the regulations. Yanmei reported:

> If little things happen, small things, and you find the Women's Federation directly, they might not care. Like my friend, she had some sort of disagreement with her employer, and so she returned to the company. The com-

pany said, "you and your employer can talk it out and resolve this your-self. You don't need to bother us." They didn't care. They said, "resolve it yourself," and only come to them if you can't resolve it yourself. But we only went to them because we couldn't resolve it ourselves! . . . Those people there [in the company office], their talk is empty and they are irritable. . . . They don't have a very good attitude.

Like a Family: Labor Relations in Domestic Service

Labor performed in the intimate space of the home by daughters, wives, and moth-ers is often described as a labor of love, as it is rarely directly remunerated. As la-bor performed in this intimate space, and often involving caring for infants or elderly, domestic work involves emotional expenditure, even when performed for a wage. In China, the location of domestic work in the employer's household, its legal status, and its popular image all contribute to the construction of the do-mestic worker as "a member of the family," which implicitly produces an affec-tive bond between the worker and her employer's household. Social relations be-tween the domestic worker and her employer emulate those of an extended family by adopting forms of address appropriate to age, generation, and gender. Hence, female employers are addressed as "granny," "auntie," or "elder sister," and male employers as "grandfather," "uncle," or "elder brother." Domestic workers are referred to by their last names, preceded by the diminutive "little" (*xiao*), or as "little sister" (*amei*) or "little girl" (*xiao guniang*).

As fictive kin, employees and employers are assigned ideal roles and behav-iors, and their relationship appears governed by affective ties. For their part, em-ployers often perform emotional labor for their domestic worker, caring about their employee's health and well-being, bestowing her with hand-me-down clothes, and sending her home at holidays with gifts and good wishes for her family. Affective ties ideally compel employers to take an interest in their domestic worker's intel-lectual and moral development, as well as her future.

In return for an employer's care and patronage, employees are obliged to be diligent and honest, respectful and obedient, and loyal, like dutiful daughters. One Beijing employer, Mr. Li, praised his family's former domestic worker, a young woman from Henan, as an exception to most young rural women working in the city at the time of our interview in 2000: "At that time [1989], maids were rela-tively new to Beijing, and they were all from the countryside. They were simple and honest and they didn't have any evil thoughts or habits. When they did their work, they weren't lazy or slow, or quick to quit." In looking back nostalgically on the 1980s, Mr. Li implies that domestic workers grew dishonest, indolent, and unreliable over the long term. Mr. Li's recollection is hardly objective; but it is a commentary on the rapid social changes of the later postreform period that have negatively impacted the urban middle class, including an expanding, more competitive, and hence more volatile, domestic service labor market. By contrast, good domestic workers were those who put the needs of their employers in advance of their own interests. For example, I was to go to a park one day in 2000 with Yanmei and her friend on their day off (Sunday), but only Yanmei showed up to our appointment. Her friend was invited at the last minute to accompany "her family"—her employer's household—on an outing. Without denying that employers and workers can, and occasionally do, become companions, ultimately the needs of employers always came first.

Rural domestic workers' lack of urban household registration made them dependent on maintaining good relations with employers, neighbors, and, especially, representatives of the residential committees who kept the household register books and thereby bestowed on them the right to live with an urban family. And those from poor, remote, mountainous regions in particular might encounter strange habits, new consumer goods, and unfamiliar technologies in the urban environment, which reinforced their dependence on employers for acquiring information about these new things. Yanmei was matter-of-fact about the lifestyle habits she learned as a domestic worker in an apartment block: "In the high-rise, everyone wears slippers, and ordinary clothes, and eats good food everyday, and takes a shower daily. The high-rise is very clean, and everyday you must wipe the tables and mop the floor."

Employer Mrs. Tian tells how her former domestic worker, a nineteen-year-old young woman from a village in Inner Mongolia, was overwhelmed by the vast gap in technology and lifestyle between her home and Beijing, an indication of her "low quality": "Regarding lifestyle habits, she was fine in the house. But I recall most clearly that she couldn't figure out how to lock the door, nor open it; perhaps her home was too out-of-the-way and too remote [i.e., so they didn't require gates or locks]. The simplest of everyday common sense she couldn't understand, so she felt a lot of pressure, and wanted to go home."

Additionally, young domestic workers often lack the pertinent experience and skills of cooking and childrearing, and so on, which their relatively older, and generally married, employers have already mastered. As Mrs. Xia said of her former and well-liked domestic worker, "I didn't care whether she lacked experience. As long as she had love for the child, that's all that mattered. The rest I could teach her." Yet the asymmetrical flow of knowledge from employers to employees further reinforces the former's cultural deficiency and the latter's authority and superiority.

Even where domestic workers have knowledge to contribute, this knowledge is often belittled as unsuited to urban tastes. A common example concerns food preferences. Many migrants to Beijing come from the south—Anhui, Sichuan, and Henan Provinces, for example, where food tends to be spicy and meals tend to include rice. As northerners, Beijingers claim to prefer less spicy food, and eat more noodles and breads. Cuisines from the wealthiest cosmopolitan areas of China, Guangzhou and Shanghai, neither of which are noted for spicy food, are generally accepted as the epitome of gourmet fare. In contemporary parlance, then, cooking "too spicy" cuisine has become a euphemism for poor, low-class fare. Most domestic workers are thus made to adapt to their employers' food tastes.

Clearly, affective ties maintain the structural asymmetry between an employer and her domestic worker (see Hochschild 2012[1983]). Even as fictive kin, employers are still in a position of authority as elders, who can, consciously or not, manipulate emotional bonds to extract more labor power from their employee. In reality, a minority of domestic workers interviewed truly felt "like a member of the family." After four years of loyal service and ongoing connection to her employers, Yaling remarked, "Still, they aren't my own family." Office cleaning and hotel housekeeping offer comparatively greater autonomy for migrant women workers, but are likewise stigmatized, informal, unstable, and poorly remunerated jobs, as I explain next. In the final section I discuss the ways migrant women workers exercise agency within these constraints.

Invisible and Anonymous: Labor Process of Office Cleaners and Hotel Housekeepers

Like domestic workers, those who clean offices or provide housekeeping services to hotels perform menial labor, and thus have relatively low status among other service workers. Often they work for contractors who rotate workers among offices, hotels, and residential complexes. Female employees of such companies may use the term "maid" (*baomu*) to refer to themselves, or are called such by their bosses. However, janitors and hotel chambermaids are considered more "professional" than domestic workers, for several reasons. First, a relatively clear demarcation of work and leisure space and time as well as the emotional distance between workers and bosses contribute to a sense that this is clearly a contractual, capitalist work relationship rather than a form of servitude. Although a few women I knew who had worked previously as live-in domestic workers and later became contractual office and residential cleaners did not distinguish between the two occupations, most cleaners I knew felt that working for a public work unit (*danwei*), rather than belonging to a private household (*jia*), distinguished them as superior to those in domestic service.[9] Second, janitorial work is not feminized per se, and hence is not devalued as "women's work," like domestic service. However, gender does structure the division of tasks within the occupation. As janitors, men tend to occupy higher-paid positions considered "skilled," such as shift supervisor, and undertake tasks classified as "heavy," such as operating floor waxing and polishing equipment. In hotels, male housekeeping staff may enter guestrooms to deliver room service goods and luggage, but chambermaids are almost exclusively female.

In early 2000, sisters Shuchun and Shuqin, with the aid of a former coworker from their apparel factory (a woman whom they referred to respectfully as "master" [shifu]), quit the apparel factory and began working for a cleaning company contracted to a four-star hotel. Interestingly, according to municipal regulations in place at the time, migrant workers were forbidden from being employed as hotel housekeepers (Wang Huaxin 1998: 50). When I asked the hotel's housekeeping manager, who had solicited the contract cleaning company's services, about the ordinance, he at first denied that such regulations existed, but later he admitted to them. He explained that formerly the hotel had been state-owned, and had lost money, in part due to providing urban employees and pensioners with so many benefits. Reorganized as a Sino-foreign joint venture, the enterprise saved on labor costs by outsourcing housekeeping and other hospitality services to the private-sector cleaning company.

Comparing the costs of regular, full-time hotel workers, who must hold an urban household registration, with the costs of the cleaning contractor's migrant labor force left no doubt as to the truth of the supervisor's comment. Urban employees of the hotel were of two types: those "permanent workers" hired in the 1970s or early 1980s, who had subsidized housing and guaranteed (lifelong) employment; and contract workers, who did not have housing benefits but shared with permanent employees other benefits, such as a legal labor contract, health coverage, pension plan, severance pay, end-of-year bonuses, and various perks. Their monthly base income was generally thrice that of migrant workers assigned similar tasks, yet they worked only a forty-hour week, resting on the weekends.

The migrant employees of the cleaning company did not have a formal labor contract, health insurance, guaranteed severance pay, or retirement benefits, and were left out of distribution of bonuses or profit sharing. They were provided rudimentary housing, where they slept in bunk beds, eight to ten per room, in dank and dark basement rooms that smelled of adjacent toilets. New hires were allocated bicycles for the hour-long commute between the dormitory and the hotel, but these were frequently stolen, forcing workers to take a public bus to work at their own expense, or share bikes. The distance between the dorm and the hotel put young women especially in danger of sexual harassment. A man accosted Shuqin when she was bicycling back to the dorm in the dark after a late shift; fortunately she was able to avoid harm. In addition, migrant employees were issued meal coupons valid for twice-daily meals at the employee cafeteria (located in the hotel basement). The company provided uniforms and paid for twice-weekly dry cleaning; employees provided their own cloth shoes. Costs for accommodations, meals, and uniforms were deducted from their monthly salaries.

At the time, migrant workers subsidized the fees for temporary registration and work permits, costing as much as several hundred *yuan* a year, through wage deductions that the company later reimbursed.[10] The cleaning company boss complained of tedious paperwork and slow processing rates by the relevant government bureaus, which sometimes blocked applications due to quota limits. By withholding a portion of employees' pay over the course of several months, the company lessened the risk that a worker would quit before the permits were issued and the fees reimbursed in full. The fees and the collection method together constrained migrants' ability to freely change employers.

Shuchun and Shuqin earned a daily rate of only 15CNY after their clothing, food, lodging, and other expenses were deducted, for an average pay of 400CNY per month, similar to the going rate for a full-time, live-in domestic worker. Occasionally, workers received bonuses, such as at the New Year holiday; or promotional materials (e.g., samples of shampoos or washing powder that the hotel was considering purchasing in bulk) and gifts. However, such bonuses were more infrequent than those awarded regular hotel staff. As one migrant hotel housekeeper summarized: "It's better to be a contract employee of the hotel than of the cleaning company."

Hotel housekeepers work long hours. The early morning and afternoon shifts stretched to ten hours, including a half-hour meal break and mandatory staff meeting, which workers found most odious. The meetings were led by a shift supervisor, usually male, who reviewed individual workers' successes and mistakes, lectured about policies or procedures, if necessary, then distributed the next day's assignments and meal coupons. Cleaners worked seven days of the week, with no scheduled rest days. Shuqin explained, "If you are a dedicated worker, your request for some time off will be granted." But workers did not receive pay for their absences, and were paid overtime only as an incentive to work through the national holidays. Housekeepers worked in shifts; those on the overnight shift rested on cots in rooms near the courtesy desk on each hotel floor, where they might be summoned by guests to bring a thermos of water (for tea) or unlock a room door during the night. Over the course of several days, shift rotation provided a modicum of rest time for each worker.

Hotel cleaners' main duties included washing, waxing, and polishing floors; vacuuming and steam-cleaning carpets; washing windows; and dusting furniture in the hotel's public spaces, mainly the lobby, conference rooms, restaurants, hall-ways, shops, business offices, and washrooms. Not a detail was to be missed: One day in 2002, I observed Xiaofang on her knees on the lobby floor erasing a black scuff mark made by a passing guest's shoes. (Recall from Chapter 3 that Xiaofang joined the hotel in 2002.) The cleaning company workers were often paired up with regular hotel staff to work in the hotel's health club and spa, restaurants, or to assist chambermaids. Whatever the specific task, noted Yarui, who was also hired in 2002 as a cleaner at the four-star hotel, being on one's feet all day was "exhausting"; she complained frequently of pain in her back when bending to vacuum carpets or mop floors. Indeed, years of hotel housekeeping took a toll on Shuchun and Shuqin, who were still in the hotel housekeeping business in 2010. The former underwent surgery for arthritic knees in 2003; the latter began wearing a brace in 2006 to combat lower back pain.

As star-rated, joint-venture hotels in particular attract international tourists and business travelers, they are prime spaces for showcasing China's achievements under market socialism to the world. Due to the ideological association with dirt, backwardness, and low quality, rural migrant workers seemed anachronistic in the modern, global space of the hotel lobby. Hence management trained them to be virtually invisible to clients and in public areas. The cleaning company employees were instructed to be neat in appearance and quiet and unobtrusive in demeanor at work. They were required to shower after each shift, using the communal em-ployee showers in the hotel's basement. They were identifiable by their matching uniforms, which Shuqin deemed "ugly," but were not issued individual name tags like regular hotel staff. They were instructed to keep silent around hotel guests, entering rooms to clean up only after guests had exited. Workers were expressly forbidden to socialize with guests beyond a simple greeting, using the respectful "Sir" and "Madam" to address them, and were instructed to refer guests with ques-tions to the concierge. As a result, the slightest acknowledgment by a guest could make Yarui happy all day; I recall her delight in telling me of being greeted by a friendly German tourist encountered in the lobby's ladies' bathroom.

The plight of the hotel cleaners seems to illustrate the paradox of migrant work-ers generally. Although their labor is essential to wealth accumulation that en-ables China to project a cosmopolitan image to the world, it is unacknowledged in representations of the modernizing and globalizing cities (Cartier 2001; Guang 2003; O'Donnell 1999). Rather, as I explain in Chapter 5, migrant women are highly visible in such representations as emergent consumers as well as sexualized ob-jects of consumer culture.

Professionalism and Personalism: Labor Relations in Office Cleaning and Hotel Housekeeping

In contrast to domestic service, professionalism defined the relationship between the cleaning company workers and management, to an extent. They used "Sir" or "Madam" to address the cleaning company boss and the hotel housekeeping supervisors. Social distance between workers and bosses was maintained, not just linguistically, but also through spatial and bodily protocols. The cleaning company boss's small basement office was separate from employees' facilities (i.e., locker room, showers, and mess hall) located elsewhere in the basement. Workers, with the exception of shift supervisors on duty, had to knock, announce themselves, and wait for permission to enter the office. Despite this display of social distance, in practice management was often informal and familiar with workers. As in domestic service, a family metaphor guided relationships within the cleaning company and between the cleaners and the hotel's housekeeping staff. The bosses were avuncular, and coworkers addressed one another using sibling terminology.

The cleaning company boss stressed the importance of building affective ties with his employees as integral to a new management approach, which he contrasted to the rigid management style of the work units of the 1960s and 1970s. According to the latter, he should have meted out standardized punishments to employees. In contrast, he took time to correct his employees' mistakes by guiding them in the right way, and offered incentives and rewards. He confided to me his belief that most "outsiders," indicating migrant workers, were slow learners because they were not inclined to study, implying that most are lazy. Fortunately, his college degree was in psychology, which was particularly useful in his current position. He felt strongly that it was his responsibility not only to groom his young rural workers for four-star hotel service, but also to foster their overall development and prepare them for modern life. By patiently educating his workers, he was confident of meeting his own goal of raising their "low quality" and thereby helping them make a contribution to society as a whole.

The supervisor's solicitude toward his workers extended beyond the workplace and into the dormitories and their personal lives. Such total responsibility was exhausting, he once confided. For example, on national holidays he organized a party for his homesick workers rather than take his wife on a holiday trip. Through these acts that showcased his kindness and care, the supervisor exacted loyalty, discipline, and productivity from his workers. The cleaning company boss was in fact well liked by most workers, as he was considered reasonable and fair, friendly and solicitous toward his employees, and moreover had a sense of humor. In retrospect (in 2002), Shuqin said of him: "He was good to his employees, and knew how to talk with them. He never yelled directly at anyone, but instead would just tell someone what they had done wrong, and tell them how to correct the problem and then give them a chance to do better. He veiled his criticisms of employees through humor, making us all laugh. Everyone liked him. I learned a lot from him."

The cleaning company boss's flexible management style inculcated migrant workers in neoliberal values of self-management. His avuncular attention to his migrant workers' cultural development, rooted in stereotypes of rural character, underscored the hierarchy of gender, generation, and rural-urban differences, which bolstered his authority. Much literature on labor relations views employer paternalism as just another means of exploiting workers and masking their class position. However, attention to migrant women worker's agency reveals a more complex understanding of class and power. As I explain next, young rural women actively accommodated employers' authority for their own reasons and benefit. They endeavored to be respectable and capable as a means to manage the stigma of menial labor and to disprove stereotypes of rural character. Further, as scholars informed by a Foucauldian view of power as "capillary" and diffused (Fraser 1989) have noted, workers can hold power over their employers by appealing to emotion and manipulating affective ties (see Ozyegin 2001). Indeed, young migrant women accentuated their compliance in order to exact concessions from superiors that led to improved work conditions and benefits.

Strategic Accommodation of Authority: Respectable Maidens and Model Workers

Under the constraints of the dual labor market that were enforced through the *hukou* and ideological constructions of gendered work, young migrant women had few choices other than informal service work. Among limited options, they selected jobs that ensured physical safety and social propriety in their migrant destinations. Many justified their decision to enter domestic service on these grounds. In Suyin's words, "I don't care anymore that domestic work is a low-status job. In my opinion, safety is most important." As her friend Lifang similarly expressed: "When you first go out, getting a job in a home [as a domestic worker] is okay. You can't find any good job, and you have no place [to sleep], unless you go to a little restaurant, but that's so chaotic . . . getting a job with a household is a bit safer."

Domestic service was preferable to other available jobs because it involved gender-appropriate activities (e.g., cooking and caring for children) performed for family members in a gender-appropriate setting (i.e., the household). However, many women hid the truth about the work they did in Beijing from relatives and neighbors back home, to save face. As Yaling understood, "at home, if you say you are a domestic worker, you are seen as inferior to everyone."

In contrast, restaurants, bars, saunas, and nightclubs were considered "unsafe" because they were mixed-sex venues where sexuality was openly marketed to anonymous clientele along with culinary, recreational, or entertainment services (and often including escort services), and thus posed a threat to morality. Shuqin unconsciously demonstrated her internalization of this perception when, filling out an application to become a waitress in a bar, she penned the word "safety" on the response line next to the question "What are your job requirements?" Jobs in these locations could compromise a young woman's virtuous reputation by dint of association. Shuqin acknowledged, "villagers don't know anything. As soon as they hear 'hotel' they think you are working as a prostitute." To avoid such gossip, Shuqin and Shuchun were secretive about their hotel work. Their parents likewise were careful to state only that their daughters worked at a "four-star hotel for foreign guests," which sounded rather prestigious.[11] Young migrant women thus managed the stigma of menial jobs by emphasizing their respectability.

Adhering to the fiction of kinship with employers was another means by which migrant women imbued menial jobs with respectability. Parents implicitly entrusted employers to supervise their daughters' moral development, to closely monitor their social activities and take appropriate disciplinary measures when necessary. Live-in domestic service especially was considered "safe" because employers had oversight of employees both day and night. Employers were uniquely able to use this arrangement to their own advantage, extracting ever more labor power from their employees and preventing them from seeking out better job opportunities. However, explicit parental demands could greatly inconvenience employers, especially when requests led to the sudden departure of their only domestic worker, disrupting the entire household's schedule. Employers told of parents requesting their daughters' presence at home for a family emergency, because they needed help on the farm, to introduce her to a prospective husband, or to break up an unauthorized romance, and feeling prevailed upon to comply.

Similarly, the paternalistic solicitude of the cleaning company supervisor toward his migrant workers assured parents of their daughters' physical and moral well-being. For example, through random dormitory checks and listening to employee gossip, he heard that a certain female employee was spending nights with her boyfriend. He promptly fired her and sent her back to the village, earning the gratitude of her parents. Of course his strict enforcement of norms of sexual propriety conveniently saved the company the expense of handling a pregnant employee or working mother. Although this boss bemoaned labor turnover, he also confessed that he was never unduly inconvenienced by a worker's departure, as "migrant workers are easily replaceable." Shuqin and Shuchun appreciated their supervisor's interventions to ensure their physical safety and social reputations in the mixed-sex environment. They were critical of their coworkers who had become "bad women," exhibiting reckless behavior such as spending the night with male coworkers in the men's dorm room, or with boyfriends elsewhere.

In contrast, the sisters were highly critical of their former boss at the apparel factory for his lack of involvement in employees' personal lives. At the factory, the sisters were continually harassed by a young errand boy. One day, Shuqin and the young man got into a heated argument when he called her by a sexual slur. She angrily slapped him and they might have come to blows if her sister and others had not intervened. The sisters expected their boss to come to their aid and defend their honor, such that they in turn would feel protected and respected. Because the boss did not censure the young man nor mediate in this argument, Shuqin accused him of not being "a good boss" and of having no sense of how to properly conduct interpersonal relations.

Young migrant women labored more willingly for employers they considered attentive and respectful. Suyin described how, in her first few weeks in Beijing, she missed home so much that she was clumsy and absentminded in her job as a domestic worker. Instead of scolding her for this behavior, she recalled, her employer kindly asked what was wrong and was sympathetic. Wenling told of how, newly hired as a domestic worker, she instinctively retreated to her own room when she learned her employers were expecting a visit by relatives. She was so pleased, though, when they called her to meet one of the guests, a CEO of a company from her home province. She articulated that employers show kindness by treating their employees as equals.

Young migrant women also realized that to have a relatively stable work environment, they should try to get along with their employer. An honest, disciplined, and industrious "model worker" could best maintain good relations with employers and take pride in the work itself. Domestic worker Shanshan boasted of her housework skills and ability to please her employer by doing her job competently and with self-discipline.

> The old lady wasn't happy before I came. Before I arrived, for a year she was not very happy, and drove out another domestic worker. Our relationship though was very good. She said the first one went out too much, and didn't know how to do the chores. Rural people who come out, they are different from urban people. Me, from when I was small I did housework, and I was attentive to hygiene. And I could do things carefully. In my hometown I helped my parents cook and wash clothes, so I could do all of those chores.

Model workers like Shanshan clearly create value for their employers. At the same time, Shanshan takes great satisfaction in her superior work ethic and productivity compared with others, whom she stereotypes as having more "rural" habits: being unruly, ignorant, and clumsy. In her ethnography of Filipina domestic workers in Hong Kong, Constable (1997) documented the pleasures of deference and submission to employers' ideals, which she attributed to domestic workers' agency and power over personal body care and behavior. In Chapter 5 I explore further the contradictions of pleasure and power rooted in such corporeal and mental transformations.

Moreover, model workers expected employers to reward their hard work and dedication. Reflecting on her work history from the perspective of 2010, Ruolan attributes her success in life to her industriousness and dedication to every job: "I'm not beautiful, but I'm very capable." In her first job in Beijing as a domestic worker in 1993, her employers did not sufficiently appreciate her ability, in that she was underpaid and exploited. But the next household to hire her appreciated and rewarded her industriousness by sharing their books and knowledge with her. "I learned so much from them," she said of these retired intellectuals. Their daughter, a middle school teacher, provided Ruolan with the course books necessary to study independently for a high school equivalency degree, which she earned while still under their employ.

Hotel housekeepers endeavored to please their supervisors in order to win small concessions, such as extra meal vouchers, permission to switch shifts with coworkers or take time off to return home, and to hire their covillagers and kin. Young women workers relied on flirtation to exact favors of male supervisors. With female bosses, they used other tactics. For example, at the state-run guesthouse in 2002, Shuqin impressed her supervisor by introducing me as a "foreign friend" and treating us to an expensive Western meal—at McDonald's. Shuqin's flattery and face-giving treatment resulted in the supervisor granting Shuqin's next request for a leave of absence.

In domestic service, the emotional labor of ministering to elderly or infants may especially engender strong affective bonds between employers and their domestic workers that are mutually advantageous. For example, Yaling had forged a close bond with the elderly lady of the household where she worked for four years in the mid-1990s, although she did not enjoy such affection from the other household members. She remained in contact with this woman over a long period of time, visiting her from time to time. Their relationship seemed to have transcended class to become truly one of a family, as Yaling explained in 2000: "She and I feel affection for each other (*ganqing*). Like right now, if I didn't have a job, she would help me."

Blow-Ups and Resistance to Authority

Migrant women workers' strategies to preserve their respectability and to prove their capability as model workers in order to gain concessions from employers were not always successful. When employers did not recognize or respond in a timely and fair manner to their efforts, workers responded through indirect protest or direct confrontation. The ultimate show of resistance was usually to "vote with their feet" and quit. Such actions effectively challenged the image of migrant women workers as docile and compliant, even if they did not impact broader structures of inequality in the labor market.

The contradictions of the intimate relationship between employers and employees, particularly in domestic service, could erupt in deeply emotional conflicts. Suyin generally got on very well with the three-generation family she worked for, being particularly attached to the young grandchild. But she was really upset by the incident that resulted when her male cousin came for a visit, and stayed the night in her room, a basement apartment that had a separate entrance from her employer's main apartment. The gatekeeper saw him arrive at night and leave the next morning, and reported this information to her employers. They immediately jumped to the wrong conclusion, and scolded her harshly without stopping to hear her explanation. She recounted: "I was so wronged, so humiliated. They knew me for so long and yet they still mistrusted me?" Upset by the breakdown of mutual trust between her and her employer, Suyin still did not criticize the principle that her employers should closely scrutinize her personal life, including dating activities. Yet, in anger and retaliation, Suyin did take action by not speaking with the family, and boycotted work for the rest of that day.

Employers' strict control of domestic workers' social lives left young women feeling isolated and lonely until they made connections with other migrant women. The most extreme case I heard was of Xingjuan's first domestic service job, in 1985, which she quit after just two months: "[My employer] wouldn't let me go out. I really missed my *laoxiang*, and I wanted to go see them, but she said 'No way. You've been here how long and already you want to go out?' I'd been there just about one month, when one day while I was helping her fetch fresh milk I spotted someone who appeared to be from the countryside. I asked if she was from Anhui, and she said she was! When I found that *laoxiang*, and chatted with her, I felt so much calmer."

As a domestic worker, Shanshan likewise chafed under her employer's continual surveillance. She invented creative excuses to find time and space alone, or to spend with friends from home. "Sometimes when I had nothing to do, I would go out and chat with them. They were from my county. We all knew each other. Some of them ran stalls making snacks; some were resellers (of used goods). I often went there to chat with them. I didn't have actual days off, but if there was something I wanted to do, I could say, 'I've got something to do' or 'I'm going to mail a letter,' and then I would have about two hours. Whenever I wasn't busy, I would go."

Similarly, although hotel housekeepers appeared submissive and attentive when interacting with their supervisors, in fact they took a number of risks while on the job in order to circumvent management and make their daily routine more tolerable. Some tactics were individual, such as pilfering small items like shampoos and sewing kits from the hotel rooms for their own use. Other tactics relied on cooperation among workers. One common scenario involved making telephone calls to friends from hotel rooms, which was explicitly forbidden behavior, while a coworker patrolled the hallway as a lookout, in case the supervisor were to catch them in the act. Coworkers also tolerated hosting one another's friends and relatives in the worker dormitory for short-term stays, which was likewise against the company rules.

Workers at the four-star hotel between 1999 and 2001 engaged in a spontaneous protest of the state's temporary-residence permit regulations. Rather than pay the fee to reregister for a new permit each year, the housekeepers one by one adopted the practice of altering their previous years' temporary-resident permits and work permits. Both the cleaning company and hotel housekeeping supervisors tacitly agreed to such a practice, pretending not to notice the forgeries. Interestingly, this was an example of how *guanxi*—here, reciprocity between workers and supervisors—could be used to evade state regulations (in this case by withholding fees from the Public Security Bureau, a government agency). Through such small acts of resistance or "weapons of the weak" (Scott 1985), domestic workers and hotel housekeepers alike reinterpreted their worth, claiming the benefits and treatment they felt they deserved.

Unfortunately, in March of 2001, Shuchun's forged permit was rejected, and she was ordered by her boss to shell out the fee for a one-year renewal, at a cost of 700 *yuan* to be deducted from her monthly pay. She strongly objected that such a request was unreasonable, because although the renewal would extend the permit for one year, once the cleaning company's contract with the hotel ended, her permit would be invalid. (It so happened that the housekeepers had learned that the contract would expire in June.) The cleaning company boss refused to authorize the tampered permit, and issued the ultimatum: "If you don't pay, you can leave." Unwilling to pay, her pride wounded, Shuchun chose to quit. "Voting with her feet" was the only way for Shuchun to protest the unfairness of the government regulations and her boss's complicity in enforcing them. Although her resignation did not lead to systematic change, it restored her sense of justice and dignity, and showed that she was in no way docile.

In retrospect, Shuchun admitted: "The boss was good to me, but at that time, I felt very hurt." Even after quitting, she was disappointed by the loss of good feeling between herself and the boss whom she had come to respect and trust. She said that although she was tempted at the time to express her outrage, she refrained from humiliating her (male) boss by verbally attacking him. She did this out of respect for her *shifu*—a former forewoman at the apparel factory where she and Shuqin had previously worked, who had facilitated the sister's employment under him. Shuchun's silence exemplifies how asymmetrical social relationships based on reciprocity can limit migrant women's agency, as explained in Chapter 3.

Similarly, Qiaolian's stint as a domestic worker did not last long; after barely three months on the job she gave her notice, in a dramatic confrontation with the mistress who accused her of negligence in her work. Her journal entry captures the intensity of her feelings of injustice:

> I was furious. I declared, "I quit! Find somebody else. I'll give you a week to find a replacement for me, then I'm going." . . . Uncle pleaded, "My wife really doesn't want you to go. She says you work really hard and well. We've already had several domestic workers quit on us, and if others hear you are leaving too, well, it wouldn't sound good." I nodded, and thought to myself, "You folks are so concerned for your 'face,' but give me no respect. Why can't you just treat your employees fairly? You say that worker was lazy, the other was a glutton, but you never look to yourselves [for the reasons they quit]."

On the eve of her departure from their employ, Qiaolian was subjected to one last humiliation:

> I gathered together my things back into the same old suitcase I arrived with two months before, and sat in the living room to watch TV. . . . The mistress emerged from the bedroom, looking ill at ease. She looked at me suspiciously and said, "A pair of my old shoes is missing from the sun porch. If you wanted them, just take them, but why not let me know?" She gave me a penetrating look. . . . I thought, "She has accused me of theft!" I told myself, "Don't pick a fight with her. You are leaving in the morning for good." But if I didn't set her straight, she'd believe I'd stolen her shoes. . . . When her husband arrived home, I heard her telling him about the shoes. I stood up and threw open my suitcase, shouting, "Take a look! You'll see there's nothing of yours. You are too much! Although I'm from the countryside, I still have self-respect. Don't you have any decency?!"

Powerful emotions can be catalysts for decisive action and a source of resistance (Barbalet 1998; Jasper 1998). In talking back to her employer and making good on her threat to quit, Qiaolian displayed her strong will and sense of justice, characteristics that may have been fortified by the very experiences that she protested. By appealing to the employers' lack of decency (*xiuyang,* often translated as "cultivation," is a virtue associated with Confucian ethics) and superficial concern with status, she placed herself on higher moral ground, inverting the dominant view that migrant workers have low cultural quality. Qiaolian's story, on the one hand, underscores rural migrant women's economic and social vulnerability. On the other hand, it illustrates how migrant women draw upon a wellspring of emotions, values, identities, and beliefs to express their agency and to protest and even subvert the power structure.

Summary

This chapter has explored the incorporation of young rural women as cheap and expendable workers into the informal service economy. Their menial jobs demand long hours of labor and are stigmatized, poorly remunerated, devoid of benefits, and highly insecure. Social constructions of difference along the lines of place, gender, and generation, as well as the fictive kinship relationship, complicates the power relationship between employers and migrant women workers. On the one hand, such differences naturalize or rationalize migrant women workers' subordinate class position and increases their vulnerability. On the other hand, migrant women's actual experience of menial work, their "practical class relationship" (Ortner 2006), is not simply one of oppression or submission. Attention to agency reveals that migrant women sacrifice autonomy and accede to employers' paternalistic authority in exchange for personal safety and their virtuous reputation in the workspace. They strive to meet employers' expectations as model workers in order to curry favors and counter derogatory stereotypes about themselves. When such strategies backfire, they protest or resist by quitting, and are not stereotypically docile women workers.

In the next chapter I explore how exposure to modern consumer culture changed young rural women's self-perceptions and awareness of their bodies, femininity, and sexuality. Participation in consumer culture enabled young migrant women to present themselves as more cosmopolitan, thus opening the door to cultural citizenship in urban society (Ong 1999). However, this mode of entrée to urban society, in lieu of attaining urban *hukou,* put migrant women at risk of alienating rural kin and distancing themselves from their rural communities.

CHAPTER FIVE

From Country Bumpkins to Urban Sophisticates

Peiqi: Yes, yes, those girls who have just come from the countryside are truly peasants.

Qinyin: Yes, they are very naïve.

Peiqi: They arrive in this big city and they don't understand anything.

Qinyin: Right. But when you come out, you don't stop reflecting. For example, at first you accept a low salary because at home you did household work and you didn't even get one penny. But after you get to Beijing and you live in this environment, and you gradually meet other people, you begin to compare yourself with others in this occupation, and you realize they are making more money. So [her] point of comparison shifts. At first she compared herself to people at home; gradually she will compare herself with other people, including her superiors, and find areas where she is dissatisfied.

In this quotation, two experienced domestic workers express a widely shared opinion that time and experience transform migrant women from dupes to savvy opportunists. They concurred that long sojourns in Beijing and exposure to new people, situations, and ideas had made them more worldly and self-reflexive. They grew cognizant of wage inequality specifically, and of wealth disparity generally, as well as of their own shortcomings. Such awareness made them smugly critical of villagers who had never migrated or who were newcomers to the city, and nostalgic and contemptuous toward their formerly "naïve" selves. Nearly all my informants felt changed by migration. Some expressed embarrassment at how "stupid" or "innocent" they were when they first came out to work; others stressed how "smart" and "confident" they had since become. As they interacted with more experienced migrants and middle-class urbanites, as well as the imagined cosmopolitan bodies and lifestyles of global consumer culture on display in urban space, their frames of reference shifted. Consciously and subconsciously, they adopted new perspectives and desires and adjusted their migration goals and strategies accordingly.

In this chapter, I investigate in turn the processes, characteristics, and consequences of young rural women's changing self-perceptions and identities. I demonstrate how, in everyday encounters with urban society and consumer culture, migrant women were made to feel like cultural inferiors and social outsiders. These women's bodily indicators of difference—speech, deportment, or appearance—were marked as backward and deficient, unsuited to urban cosmopolitanism. Internalizing their "otherness" and inadequacy, migrant women endeavored to raise their quality and thus shed their image as "country bumpkins." Through participation in consumer practices of tourism and shopping, investments in technical training and adult education, and experimentation with more liberal market discourses of femininity and sexuality, young migrant women re-presented themselves as urban sophisticates. Such efforts brought migrant women workers pleasure and boosted their confidence and capacity to blend into urban society, but at the same time challenged their ability to fulfill the moral and social obligations expected of daughters and members of rural communities. Although some migrant women successfully parlayed their acquired symbolic capital into economic and social capital, including better job prospects and raised social status in their households, structural barriers to urban citizenship and full inclusion into urban society persisted. As a consequence, young migrant women workers metaphorically occupied a transitional space in between country and city.

Country Bumpkins

In the city, migrants experience the prejudice and discrimination of urban society as well as anonymous institutions. Liping conveyed shock at her encounter with rude mistreatment: "Some Beijing people are a bit intimidating. For example, on the bus, they'll say: 'Look at this outsider! The bus is so crowded, what are you doing here?' It's like we're dirty; no one wants us near!" Signs of difference are indicated by rural migrant workers' bodies and extend to language, demeanor, and habits. For example, male migrant construction workers are easily recognized when they trek between sites, as they move in large groups, wear helmets and disheveled clothes, and carry heavy tools and rucksacks containing bedrolls. Likewise, migrant women workers may be easily identified by the uniforms typically required of blue-collar workers, distinct from the more formal dress of urban professionals. Off-duty, migrants' attire is simple and functional; they prefer to save or remit earnings to support their families than waste meager earnings on fashion. Also, young rural women typically have long hair, a marker of feminine modesty, tied back with a hair band, rather than the short cuts or long flowing styles that are popular in the city.

Migrants may also sound different from urban counterparts. They learn standard Chinese (Putonghua) in school, but typically speak with their covillagers in local dialect.[1] Certainly they do not speak with the distinctive Beijing accent. As Yaling notes: "When you are going to market, everyone has a bad attitude toward you. They hear by your accent that you have just come out." When together in groups, migrants new to the city tend to speak unselfconsciously and thus loudly, oblivious to the judgmental scrutiny of others as they break the code of silence and anonymity typical of urban spaces.

As explained in the previous chapter, employers were especially eager to point out migrant workers' shortcomings and impart instructions as to how to overcome them. For example, the cleaning company supervisor said he endeavored to correct his migrant employees' "hick" (*tu*) speech and appearance, so they would fit in better to urban society. Recall from Chapter 2 that in the contemporary lexicon, being called *tu,* or "rustic," is rarely something to be proud of, but rather a means by which people distinguish themselves from inferiors. Indeed, some employers attributed differences in appearance, demeanor, or habits to rural people's "nature," reinforcing harmful stereotypes of peasants as innately lazy or clumsy. Ms. Xia described her former employee as follows: "She was a rather good domestic worker, except that she was a bit coarse, being from the countryside. For example, she often burned clothes when she was ironing. She broke things. If she scalded herself once pouring the soup, she would scald herself the next time too."

From the perspective of employers, raising their employee's quality meant instilling work discipline and deference—traits that would serve to increase labor output, as an interview with a representative of a domestic service employment agency made clear (and see Chapter 4): "[Rural women] just do as they please. If there's something going on back home, they simply quit. They have no sense of responsibility, no discipline. This is because their quality is low. They do as they please, with no thought for the employment contract." Employer Ms. Song implied that rural women workers are fortunate because they reap intangible benefits from their work. She explained that exposure to urban lifestyles through domestic service imparted modern, middle-class values to rural women: "In Beijing, [my nanny] has much more ability to interact with Beijing households and lifestyles. She says that when she goes home, she also tries to practice good hygiene and cleanliness, to improve her family's living conditions, and I think that in the future she'll do more to improve her child's education."

On the one hand, the implication articulated by Ms. Song that migrant women gain culture from selling their labor cheaply lends support for the argument advanced in Chapter 4 that "quality" discourse obfuscates real relations of class and structures of inequality. On the other hand, "quality" discourse engendered new forms of identity and agency that brought rural migrant women pleasure and boosted their self-esteem. For example, speaking to me in 2002, hotel housekeeper Xiaofang recollected with great nostalgia a job she held for two years in Beijing in the late 1990s, as a waitress in a coffeehouse on a university campus, which mostly served foreign students. She explained that she most appreciated learning from her coworkers how to dress better and be less "rustic" (*tu*). Further, she liked the campus routines, especially the nighttime "lights out" policy, which she said improved her quality—by teaching her time-management and self-discipline. Importantly, the job was not difficult, the pay was relatively high (700CNY per month), and Xiaofang was allowed access to the university library. Although she ultimately quit because her coworkers, especially those from Beijing, harassed her by "talking behind her back" and being "snobbish," such unpleasantness did not dampen her personal satisfaction at having successfully transformed herself under their influence.

Indeed, a report based on interviews with domestic workers in Beijing found that exposure to urban lifestyles taught young rural women standardized speech, to speak at lower decibels, to pay more attention to personal hygiene, and to generally accept urban values (Meng 1995). Likewise, my informants internalized their "otherness" and, with one notable exception, strove to emulate the speech, habits, and "look" associated with modern culture. Engaging in consumer practices of tourism, shopping, and fashion transformed their embodied identities.

Pleasurable Pastimes

As a historic city and the nation's capital, as well as a booming metropolis, Beijing offers both cultural edification and entertainment. Migrant women workers made use of public spaces and institutions to escape the daily drudgery of menial labor without spending their hard-earned money. As Rongli explained: "Working for one year, sometimes I was in a daze, feeling that every day was the same, extremely dull. Look, there I was, a young woman, feeling I was wasting my talent. Afterwards though, I gave myself a goal: in one year I would tour Beijing city, do things I wanted to do. Like, if I wanted to read I would just go to the library."

Given Beijing's complex urban infrastructure, navigating one's way around the capital could be eye opening and also confidence building. Peiqi and Qinyin entertained me with stories of their humorous escapades getting lost while riding bicycles in Beijing's ancient alleyways. Qinyin shared with me her strategy for navigating the city on her bicycle: Commit a few key routes to memory and never deviate from them!

On their few days off during the year, almost every migrant worker I met eagerly planned to explore Beijing's parks, temple fairs, or scenic and historic sites, often taking advantage of the discounted entry fees at holidays. Touring the city, young women could forget the stigma and oppressive conditions of their jobs, subvert the restrictions on their movement in public spaces of Beijing, and proclaim their equal right with Beijing citizens to enjoy public space. In her spare time, Rongli made the acquaintance of several Beijing elders, and from them learned how to participate in authentic Beijing culture. "Beijing is also an immigrant city, but among five people there will be two or three real old-time Beijingers.... One elderly Beijing man told me that Beijing people like to drink a particular drink a certain way, so I went to the Moslem Temple and bought myself a bowl of it, swished it around in my mouth, and felt so happy."

Rongli was no stranger to public humiliation and discrimination. Once, while browsing in a bookstore, a clerk cornered her and demanded proof of identification, as if implying that a migrant worker (apparently identifiable from her appearance or her accent) would not be buying books, only stealing them. Visiting historic and scenic sites, talking to Beijing elders, and learning about the capital's history legitimized her right to place in Beijing as a fellow citizen of the nation, and somewhat compensated for those moments of exclusion. In fact, as the nation's capital, Beijing had a unique ability to stir up migrants' emotions, as she makes clear: "People ask me, why did I come to Beijing? I say, because there is no Tiananmen Square in my hometown! It gave me a great impression in my youth. Beijing is China's cultural center, its political heart, so coming out is a way of experiencing it and gaining knowledge. If you don't come out of the village, you won't gain such an appreciation."

For most young migrants to Beijing, a trip to tour Tiananmen and perhaps a photograph of the visit was mandatory. Mixing with Beijing families and foreign sightseers, migrants too were transformed into worldly travelers. A memento from Beijing shown to villagers at home might present an image of a successful and exciting life, despite the reality of one's laboring existence. In fact, to return home without first visiting this most important cultural symbol was tantamount to forfeiting face, a significant loss of opportunity to accrue cultural capital, as this sister's letter home suggests: "Although working here is a bit tiring, it's still better than being at home, because as long as you work, you'll be rewarded.... Since we've been here we've not even seen Tiananmen: if we went back now what would we have to say for ourselves?" (Zhao Chonglin 1996).

Window-shopping while strolling along the famous street Wangfujing was another means for migrant women to indulge their fantasies of modern living that belied their roles as lowly service workers. By bargaining hard in the wholesale markets for knockoffs of famous brand clothing or accessories, they could emulate middle-class lifestyles relatively inexpensively. On a shopping trip in 2002, I accompanied two of Yarui's friends, former domestic workers working in sales, to an outdoor wet market where they gleefully bought two live baby chicks, which they said would brighten their lives and keep them company (for a short spell)! Such a gratuitous purchase put these young women on par with middle-class Beijing pet owners, if only briefly. During the same visit to Beijing, I caught up with Shuchun, who after quitting the cleaning company contracted to the four-star hotel had found a light industrial job assembling cassette tapes. She showed me how she had used her earnings to decorate her otherwise cramped and dreary living space with pretty potted plants, inspirational posters, and a colorful bedspread and tablecloth.[2]

Migrant women invested several months' pay in up-to-date technology like pagers, which were popular in the late 1990s, and cell phones, which were ubiquitous by 2006, as status symbols and as practical communication tools (see also Wallis 2013). Indeed, such instruments helped young women keep in touch with friends and family, and served to alleviate loneliness and isolation, as well as facilitate job searches and even romances. They could also be used subversively in the workplace. In the late 1990s, domestic worker Rongli used her beeper to keep in contact with her friends and circumvent the strict rules of (landline) telephone use established by her employer. While working in the light assembly job in 2002, Shuchun bought a cell phone so that her sister and friends could leave her voicemail messages during her long ten-hour workdays, as the factory supervisor did not allow employees to receive or make any telephone calls while on the job. Of course, employers also made use of such technology to keep track of employees and keep them on call.

Partaking of leisure pursuits in public space alongside urban residents, migrant women carved out a rightful space for themselves in the city and crafted identities as consummate consumers and worldly travelers, subverting widespread stereotypes of impoverished and uncultured peasants. They were also exposed to liberal market discourses of gender and sexuality such as those promoted by the beauty industry through ubiquitous advertising—on billboards and buses, in stores and on television.

Fashioning a New Identity

Describing to me her fresh-from-the-countryside domestic worker, Ms. Xia emphasized her masculine characteristics, such as strength and roughness, and lack of femininity: "She liked fetching the replacement propane tanks [for the cook stove] from downstairs. She enjoyed heavy work like that, but not delicate tasks. If I asked her to patch up a rip in my child's clothes, she wouldn't be willing."

As discussed in Chapter 1, market reforms and globalization in China have ushered in modern consumer culture that has significantly altered social constructions of gender and sexuality. After the revolution, women and men were proclaimed equal: women were assigned to formerly masculine fields of study (e.g., science) and occupations (e.g., bus driver), and celebrated in these roles as "iron women." By outward appearance too women were indistinguishable from men: both sexes dressed in simple, solid-color pantsuits ("Mao suits"), and women kept their hair short under their "Mao caps." In public, sexuality and sexual desire were repressed: brothels, taverns, and other entertainment venues were nationalized and sanitized. In the postreform era, gender essentialism, along with gender discrimination, has reemerged in force. Consumer culture aims to recover and enhance women's "essential" femininity. Rural women's apparent lack of femininity not only indicates their relatively low purchasing power but also marks them as throwbacks to an earlier era, out of step with modernity and out of touch with their true nature.

Whether from other migrants, urbanites, or media images, migrant women learned techniques to alter their appearance to erase the visual markers of their difference and inferiority, and better fit in to their new surroundings. Many cut or styled their hair within months of arrival in Beijing, as long, straight hair is perceived as an identifiable marker of the "traditional" village girl. They used their limited earnings to invest in upgrading their wardrobes with more fashionable clothing and footwear, and to purchase moisturizers and skin lightening creams in the hopes of having softer, whiter skin associated with wealth and status (see Chapter 2), thus erasing traces of their rusticity. For example, one afternoon in 2000, I visited Qiaolian and Changying at the elementary school where they taught. They invited me to join them in the converted classroom that served as their living quarters. As the other girls, who sported short, stylish haircuts, combed Qiaolian's freshly washed hair and smoothed moisturizer on her cheeks, they teased her for having dark, "black" skin and long hair, playfully calling her "rustic" (tu).

Migrants learned techniques for remodeling their appearances from each other and also employers. Indeed, employers like the contract cleaning company supervisor (introduced in Chapter 4) judged job applicants largely on the basis of their figures and looks, being of the opinion that appearances were what mainly distinguished peasants from urbanites. In hiring decisions, he favored taller, thinner, and lighter-skinned applicants; presumably, short, stocky dark-skinned applicants too closely resembled stereotypical peasants to be easily transformed into productive workers. Under his influence, he boasted, young rural women like Shuqin and Shuchun grew more citified, and implicitly more feminine. One evening in his office in 2000, after the sisters has finished their shift and changed out of their uniforms into skirts and blouses, and styled their hair, Shuchun sought her boss's approval. "Don't I look like a city woman now?" she asked. "No," he replied in a teasing tone, and pointed to her heavy, thick-soled shoes, implying that high heels were necessary for a complete makeover.

Over the years, I watched as informants underwent makeovers to varying degrees, generally adapting trendier and hence more feminine appearances. For example, upon returning to Beijing first in 2002 after a hiatus of two years, I marveled at Qiaolian. Her hair was shorter and stylishly cut; she wore a colorful, tastefully cut trench coat and calf-high leather boots, and otherwise looked much like any other young woman in Beijing. Likewise, I could no longer find any trace of the sisters Shuqin and Shuchun I had first met in 1998. Each wore tight-fitting jeans with sleeveless print blouses, and sported high-heeled shoes and imitation designer handbags. Their signature long hair was gone: Shuqin wore hers layered and short while her sister's hair had been color-highlighted. Both had applied lipstick and eyeliner. During the same visit to Beijing, Shuchun and I shopped together for push-up bras and nail polish, and she asked me for tips about shaving legs and bleaching facial hair. By the time I met up with the sisters several years later, in 2006, I was hardly surprised by an invitation to join Shuchun for a manicure at her "regular" spa!

A few informants maintained their androgynous and youthful ways, showing resistance to pressure to change. Compared with her fellow hotel housekeepers—Shuqin, Shuchun, and Xiaofang—Yarui dressed rather "traditionally" and conservatively, and had values to match her appearance. During an outing to a Beijing park together in 2002, Yarui remained silent while Shuqin displayed her knowledge of global athletic brands by commenting on my Reebok sneakers, and Xiaofang showed off her new denim jacket, which was embossed with a Betty Boop logo. Yarui then expressed disdain for behaviors on display that day in the park, including a couple canoodling on a bench and a woman exposing her bare shoulders, which she perceived to be indecent in public. On another occasion she and Shuqin shared a self-conscious laugh as they recited a host of etiquette rules taught by their elders and aimed at guarding young women's chaste reputations, like avoiding sitting with one's legs spread wide apart or sitting on the bed with unrelated single men. These observations and conversations indicated that young rural women's embrace of urban consumer culture challenged relatively conservative gender norms that underwrote patriarchal control of rural women's sexuality, as I explore later in this chapter.

From a feminist perspective, young rural women's general acceptance of a new look is unsettling because it reinforces notions of gender essentialism that are used to rationalize gender inequality, as well as a global hierarchy of race that fetishizes whiteness. Yet, young migrant women also experienced the pleasure and power of exercising control over their bodies and self-images. They gained self-confidence from knowing how to blend into urban society and deflect overt discrimination. Further, many set their sights on developing their human capital—"quality"— through technical training or higher education, with the aim of increasing their earning potential.

Developing Human Capital

Beijing offered numerous opportunities for migrant workers to acquire new skills and qualifications that might lead to better job prospects. It seemed nearly every migrant worker I met in Beijing had at some point enrolled in some course of study, making studious use of leisure time in the evenings or on weekends, or while in between jobs. As domestic worker Wenling remarked: "Beijing offers educational opportunities that I can't find at home." Like most young rural women, Wenling came to Beijing intending only to work. After watching a television report about a young doctor who established medical clinics in poor areas, she was inspired to do the same in her hometown, and so she decided to learn Chinese medicine. However, as Wenling had not completed compulsory education (nine years through middle school), she was not qualified to study for a technical degree (*zhongzhuan*) in Chinese traditional medicine. Other domestic workers and hotel housekeepers I knew in Beijing were enrolled in private courses training to become stylists, cosmetologists, typists and word processors, tailors, bakers, and travel agents or tour guides. Those with middle school or higher levels of education, like Qiaolian and Changying, aimed to sit for the national high school equivalency exams, so they could embark on an advanced course of study resulting in a college degree (*dazhuan*), similar to an associate's degree.

Of course, balancing menial jobs with schooling was extremely challenging, and investments in continuing education did not necessarily pay off. In 1999 Suyin was studying typing part-time, while working as a full-time, live-in domestic worker. She was grateful to her employer for giving her the time off to study and for the generous offer of use of her employer's son's computer for her practice: "Auntie [her employer] is willing to help me. As long as I have no other tasks at hand, I can study." But in fact she rarely had such time; she was frequently called upon to do household work, and the son often monopolized the computer to prepare for his high school entrance exams. Similarly, while working as a hotel and office cleaner in 2000, Shuqin invested 1,000CNY to learn data entry at a training center, but found she could not easily arrange her shifts in order to make time to visit the school to practice on the computer. However, Ruolan managed to save up 5,000CNY over five years (1993–1997) working as a domestic worker to support herself for six months in Beijing, renting cheap rooms shared with friends, during which time she took classes to learn typing and word processing. Though she was fired just one week after starting the first clerical job she held, and retreated back to hotel housekeeping, eventually she did transition successfully to clerical work. Although it paid no more than housekeeping, clerical work was less physically demanding and not as stigmatizing.

Likewise, while many rural migrant women attempted to earn *dazhuan* degrees, only a few actually succeeded. In China, there are two paths to attaining such degrees. The first involves studying for the nationwide test (*chengren gaokao*), consisting of five subjects, which is considered quite difficult. Ultimately that degree is less prestigious than a degree earned through fifteen courses at night school, whose prerequisite is an easier test (*gaodeng zixue gaokao*), but whose course of study is obviously more arduous and expensive. Domestic workers Peiqi, Rongli, and Meilan all had the requisite basic (compulsory nine years) education to aim for a *dazhuan*. In all cases, their employer's support for their course of study was key to their success.

Peiqi was an exceptional model domestic worker who turned a close relationship with her employers to her own advantage. When I met her in 1999, she had been in Beijing for seven years, during which time she worked continuously for one family, caring for an elderly couple. At first her employers were supportive of her attending night classes, and she earned a technical degree in accounting. Yet when she announced her intention to pursue a college degree program, her employers objected strongly. She then offered to quit their service, but they were even more displeased. Peiqi said she understood their predicament: They felt she was irreplaceable, as only she could understand their habits and preferences. Eventually the two parties were able to strike a compromise: Peiqi's employers allowed her to work at their daughter's work unit, a government press, doing odd jobs. In exchange, Peiqi continued to live with them and provide (unpaid) help with the evening meal, and helped to supervise her replacement, a covillager Peiqi found for the family through her own social network.

When we reconnected in 2002, Peiqi had successfully earned the college degree and had found employment as an accountant for a tech company in Beijing's "Silicon Valley." Rongli was still working as a live-in domestic worker in 2002, but had just passed the basic computing skills test and was completing a preparatory course in oral English, in anticipation of the English written and oral exams. She expected to have the degree in hand by the end of the year, and planned to find work as an English-speaking tour guide. Meilan was also still living in the household where she had long been a domestic worker, but was working in that family's business, doing data entry and learning how to design Web pages, while preparing for the computer skills exam.

Despite the obstacles in their way, migrant women workers put great stock in acquiring new knowledge that they hope to apply in the future. Many dream of setting up a business in their home county, such as a tailoring practice or hair salon, or opening a school. Their efforts to improve their quality reflect the desire to become more than menial laborers or outsiders. For example, while working in domestic service in the late 1990s, Peiqi was stopped in downtown Beijing by a police officer on foot patrol. The officer was probably suspicious of Peiqi's companion, her younger brother, who was carrying a suitcase and looked to be a recently arrived migrant (which in fact he was). At that time, all migrants were required to carry their national identity card, a temporary residence card, and a work permit. Although neither she nor her brother had the proper permits, Peiqi managed to talk their way out of a fine (or, worse, detention and repatriation), by explaining that she was a migrant worker and that her brother was only visiting on holiday. Telling me about her brush with danger, she determined: "Next time, I will deny I am a migrant working in Beijing. Instead I will say I am a college student!" Thus Peiqi expressed a confidence gleaned from her new identity as an educated person and her conviction that such a person of quality would not be subjected to discriminatory treatment.

Setting new goals of acquiring technical skills or academic credentials, regardless of outcomes, helps to boost young women's self-esteem, enabling them to assert themselves in urban space. Yet modest gains in cultural or human capital alone could not significantly alter migrant women's socioeconomic standing or secure them a permanent foothold in the city. To maximize their earnings, improve their working conditions, and move out of menial occupations, migrant women have relied mainly upon their social networks, their youthful femininity and sexuality, and their ingenuity and persistence.

From Menial to Managerial

Lateral mobility, including remaining in the same line of work but switching employers or moving among various service occupations, has been a basic strategy to improve a worker's lot. A primary strategy for "trading up" in employment is to share job information with covillagers or other migrant women in the city. Thus, the popular image of domestic workers is one that unflatteringly depicts their fickleness for employers and high rate of turnover. Indeed, to discourage excessive turnover among domestic workers, placement agencies began to levy fines for switching employers. Migrant women were able to gain greater control over their work conditions, if not actually to increase their earnings, by exchanging a live-in domestic service position for part-time, hourly cleaning work, or for another menial job like hotel housekeeping.

Shuchun and her sister Shuqin were adept at seeking new opportunities through their ever-expanding network of *tongxiang* and coworkers. I have already mentioned how they found work as hotel and office cleaners by following a lead from their *shifu*—a former forewoman at their previous job in the apparel factory. In 2002, Shuchun took up a light industrial assembly job that she learned about from another former coworker at the apparel factory. Meanwhile, Shuqin had quit the janitorial company and had teamed up with Xiaofang, whom she had worked with as a hotel chambermaid from 1997 to 1998. Together, the two women operated a wholesale market stall, earning 1,000CNY each in monthly commissions, until their boss sold the space to a developer.

Eventually, Shuchun and Shuqin returned to hotel housekeeping for the long term. Conditions of light assembly factory work—sitting on a stool for ten hours a day, seven days a week—had taken a terrible toll on Shuchun's health. In 2003 she developed an arthritic knee that required expensive surgery costing 3,000CNY (about half a year's wages) and several months' rest to heal. Uninsured and unable to afford surgery in Beijing, she was forced to quit her job and return home for hospitalization and the long recovery under the care of her mother.[3] Back in Beijing a year later, Shuchun returned to work as a chambermaid because it was easier on her knees. Over the next few years, she remained in hotel housekeeping, but switched employers a few times, as she learned of better opportunities. Due to her arthritis, Shuchun carefully considered each job's work conditions as well as the salary. When we reconnected in 2006, Shuchun was working at a private hotel that catered mainly to out-of-town businessmen on company trips. Although her monthly salary of 700CNY was considered low, she was satisfied with the relatively light workload (i.e., not so many rooms to clean daily), the regular 8 a.m. to 6 p.m. workdays, and two rest days each week. Six months later, however, she switched to a private hotel in downtown Beijing that catered to international budget travelers. This job paid slightly higher wages than the previous one, gave bonuses for overtime and holiday hours, provided a clean and safe dormitory (in the attic of the hotel itself), and had still a lighter workload. She remained at this hotel, with occasional stints at other hotels in the same chain, for the next several years. By 2010, she had earned the rank of shift supervisor, a significant accomplishment that meant she would no longer be required to make beds or clean rooms.

The sisters also found jobs by responding directly to posted job vacancies. In 2004, Shuqin responded to a help wanted announcement and was hired as a chambermaid at a state-run guesthouse whose clients were mostly Party officials on government business in the capital. After nearly two years on the job, she was promoted to shift supervisor. In 2006, I visited her at work and was invited into her "office," located in the linen and toiletries storage room. She spent much of each day seated at her desk using the computer to update the cleaning schedule according to room occupancy or vacancy. Then, in 2007, she applied for a management position at another state-owned hotel, and was granted an interview that coincided with my annual visit. To prepare for it, she consulted with her sister, who carefully selected for her a professional-looking outfit: high heels, black pants, and a white blouse. Shuqin took a taxi to the interview site. Typically, job applicants would show documentation of their previous work experience to potential employers. Then they might be hired on a trial basis, working without pay for a period of about three days, until they could demonstrate proficiency in the post to the satisfaction of the employer.[4] By confidently overstating her past work experience in the interview and proving her mettle during the trial period, Shuqin earned a promotion to housekeeping staff manager, with a relatively decent salary of 1,200CNY monthly and a regular six-day workweek with set hours.

In 2010, Shuqin's salary increased substantially, to 2,200CNY monthly, when she was hired as a guest relations manager at yet another state-owned hotel, which was affiliated with a prestigious university. Her responsibilities included organizing banquets and overseeing catered events at the hotel's restaurant, which kept her extremely busy. The work conditions were exhausting: she had only one guaranteed rest day per month and was always "on call." Often her work kept her up so late that she slept at the hotel overnight. Nonetheless, Shuqin clearly took pride in her position, modeling for me her stylish and professional "uniform": black dress pants, a blouse, and black patent leather high heels, along with her company-provided cell phone, which she used constantly.

The extent of the two sisters' combined work experience was evident in their vast knowledge of hotel ratings, guest profiles, and housekeeping wages and work conditions in Beijing's many hotels. While riding in a taxi going from one district of the city to another, or while walking with them downtown, the sisters would point out to me numerous hotels where they or someone they knew had worked, and elaborate on details of salaries and work conditions. Their broad social networks and familiarity with hotels bred over time, along with their sheer ingenuity and diligence, helped the sisters make incremental gains within this sector of the service economy.

Due to the lack of prestige accorded hotel housekeeping, the sisters maintained mixed attitudes toward their occupational niche. When she was working in light industrial assembly in 2002, Shuchun was disdainful of hotel housekeeping, claiming that, "it's not for young people but only for old women to do that cleaning work."

Her perspective reflected a gender ideology that devalues jobs associated with servitude and with women's domestic roles (explained in Chapter 1). But ultimately she determined that, despite its lower wages, hotel housekeeping was less tiring and easier on her knees than factory work, and thus more desirable. Also, she grew to appreciate working in a privately operated hotel that attracted an international tourist clientele. In 2010 she was thrilled to be dispatched to another branch of the hotel, in Shanghai, to provide assistance during the World Expo. In contrast, her sister Shuqin preferred to work in state-owned guesthouses, which provided a modicum of stability and legitimacy compared with most privately run businesses.

The young migrant women I interviewed aspired to move out of manual labor to supervisory and managerial positions, and ideally to leave menial jobs altogether for more prestigious occupations. Some pursued semi-skilled occupations such as hair stylist, cosmetologist, baker, travel agent, or tailor, which could develop into entrepreneurial ventures. Those with academic qualifications sought out more prestigious clerical work, where they might sit in a modern office at a desk with a computer. Such jobs represented occupational mobility, even if they paid no more than menial work, because they were neither stigmatized nor considered unskilled. For example, Ruolan emphasized in 2002 that her work behind a restaurant counter where she tabulated customers' bills and expedited orders distinguished her from a mere waitress. Migration expanded young rural women's imagined possibilities for themselves and incited them to embark on the path of individual self-development. Their efforts did not substantively challenge the structural or ideological foundations of gender or rural-urban inequality. However, they did empower rural women to renegotiate patriarchal authority of kin and rural community, as I explore below.

Money and Virtue

In order to achieve a more up-to-date look and participate in the pleasures of shopping or tourism, young migrant women necessarily diverted money that would otherwise be sent to their parents to be used for household expenditures. As Xingjuan recollected: "I earned some money, bought some clothes, and saw a bit of the world. . . . Sometimes I would send a little money home. I sometimes would also buy makeup." To afford technical training or higher education often required that they withhold remittances completely. Recall from Chapter 3 that a migrant daughter's remittances to her family, together with her respectability, which maintains the family's "face," are symbolic expressions of her filial affection (*ganqing*) and moral obligations (*renqing*). These are crucial for sustaining *guanxi*—the reciprocal bonds of social relationships (Chu 2010). By concentrating resources on their individual desires and aspirations, young migrant women challenged the patriarchal authority exercised through normative gender expectations about virtue and filial duty that had previously guided their behavior.

For example, during her first few years in Beijing in the late 1990s, Xiaofang sent most of her earnings as a domestic worker to her parents, to help with her mother's medical debts. But in 2001 she informed them that she would send less home and instead use her earnings to earn a certificate in cosmetology, a profession her conservative parents objected to as unseemly. In China, beauty salons are synonymous with prostitution because many beauty (or massage) parlors offer illicit sexual services in addition to legitimate personal care services (e.g., hair and makeup) (see Hyde 2007). Disguising brothels as beauty (or massage) parlors serves to circumvent laws that criminalize prostitution. Time spent in the urban environment significantly loosened young rural women's observance of social mores. Some young women chose to capitalize on their youthful bodies and femininity and pursue more lucrative work in entertainment or even sexual services (see T. Zheng 2009). Others merely questioned the rationale for patriarchal control.

Likewise, a few years into her job as a domestic worker, Rongli found herself struggling to assert her own desire for autonomy against concern about safety and reputation:

> Now I'm in domestic work, and there are a lot of restrictions, like it's not convenient to make phone calls. At first I didn't really understand. Moreover, at the house I work in now, [my employer] doesn't want me to make friends. It's best if I don't socialize much. However, she lets me receive calls from my parents and encourages me to call them. She says I'm a young girl, and I still don't understand the ways of the world. What if I encountered some bad guys, what then? She has a point, but I don't wholly agree, because one can grow up and mature, and can know how to discern peoples' characters. Like the Chinese saying, "with time you can see a person's true nature."

Similarly, in retrospect, Shanshan was critical of her former concern about moral propriety, which kept her from seeking out jobs with higher pay or trying her hand in petty trade.

> When I came out I was naïve. I didn't think much about how to make a lot of money. For example, going to work in a restaurant washing dishes and so on, that work can net more pay, but it's too unsafe. . . . So even when the wages were high I wasn't willing. I just stayed in their [her employer's]

house. I felt that I could be safe in their house. . . . [However,] each year I became more and more mature, and then I decided to do business for myself; I didn't want to work for others.

During my visit to Beijing in 2002, Shuchun and Shuqin voiced their concern and frustration about Yarui's conservative thinking. Shuqin said of her: "She has no survival skills and cares too much about face when she should be thinking about saving money." Earlier that year, Shuchun and Yarui had shared a dark and dank windowless rented room in the migrant enclave. But Shuchun complained that the dampness augmented pain in her arthritic knees, which had become worse since she started work at the factory. She secured a larger, drier room in a nearby location, and entreated Yarui to move in with her, so they each would save money while keeping each other company. Yarui was between a rock and a hard place. Her landlords, who occupied the main rooms of the house, were connected to her relatives, and her own parents were thus opposed to their daughter relocating to live among strangers.[5] From the sisters' perspective, Yarui was caught in the web of reciprocal obligations (*guanxi*) between herself and her parents, and her parents and the landlord, to her own detriment.

In contrast, the sisters had learned to successfully balance their ethical responsibilities to kin and community, on the one hand, with autonomous desires to save more money in order to live a little better, on the other. For their first few years as migrant workers, Shuqin and Shuchun sent regular cash remittances to their parents, totaling about one-quarter of their annual income. Their remittances were used for their mother's medical expenses and to pay off the family's debts. They also subsidized their older brother's migration to Beijing and on to Shenzhen, and their youngest brother's driver education course and licensing fees. Once their brothers had begun earning money, the sisters withheld regular remittances, and instead sent or brought gifts home at the New Year.

Shuqin explained how she carefully planned the exact cash amounts she would bestow on each relative's household on her New Year visits home. She took great pains to meet their expectations while staying within her constrained means to indulge their imaginations about her wealth. "I can't afford to give much money, because I barely make a living myself. Yet if I don't give them enough, they will say bad things like I am stingy or that I am a failure. But if I give too much, I will go broke, and they still won't be satisfied. It's really frustrating. That's why I didn't want to go back home; that's why my sister and brother don't go home every year. If it weren't for my parents, I wouldn't give those relatives anything!"

Due to the association of migration and consumption with sexual license, and a double standard holding only women to the ideal of purity, returned migrant women were cautious in asserting their symbolic and material capital. That other villagers may judge harshly young women who frittered away their money on superficial appearances and status goods was evident from migrant women's emphasis on their own frugality and contempt for profligate spenders. While families expected daughters to give generously, conspicuous displays of consumption could inspire gossip about the source of her riches that could call a daughter's virtue into question. Thus Shuqin complained to me of her dilemma while packing her bag in anticipation of a visit home: "If I dress too poorly, they will gossip that my life in Beijing is hard. But if I dress too fashionably, they will be jealous and gossip about where my money comes from!"

Yet the admiration and respect of kin and villagers was well worth the (literal) price to be paid for receiving such attention and accolades. Younger village girls would note with envy (and later mimic) returned migrant women's fashion style, as I observed when I accompanied Shuqin to her natal home in 2002. In my field notes I noted: "Interestingly, the women in this village are aware of how they are regarded by urbanites, and joke about themselves being *tu*. They tell me I am 'citified' because I wash my hands after each trip to the outhouse. And they teased Shuqin, who insisted on hygienic beautification practices like washing the dust out of her hair each night, and who stood out with her high-heeled patent leather boots, cashmere sweater, and a leather jacket. They said she was 'more *tu* (rustic) than ever before!'" Shuqin clearly enjoyed their teasing.

Their banter indicated their recognition of and respect for Shuqin's new wealth and skills, as when her *saozi* (her father's brother's son's wife) had to remind her to "speak in the hometown dialect." It also indicated their affection and their acceptance of her reintegration to the local community.

Migrant women parlayed their symbolic capital as knowledgeable consumers of urban space into social capital in various ways. As I explained in Chapter 3, migrant women serve as agents of migration who lead others to the city and help them find work, which significantly raised their social stature among villagers and peers. While migrants are outsiders in the city, the insights they gain through firsthand experience of the urban environment are invaluable to villagers who have never migrated, for whom they appear to be insiders to Beijing's secrets. For instance, when an official from the county town near Shuqin's natal village was sent on a trip to Beijing, she was called upon to meet him at the bus station and to help him navigate the city. She later boasted of her accomplishment: "He couldn't have figured out his way out of the station. He's nearly illiterate!" In this example, the symbolic capital gleaned through migration and familiarity with Beijing's geography momentarily altered typical gender and generational hierarchy.

Young migrant women were admired for their drive to acquire technical training and advance their education through migration, including by parents who may have cut short their daughters' education in the past. Indeed, Qiaolian's father admitted to me during my visit to the village in 1999 that he deeply regretted having cut short his daughter's education, preventing her from attending high school. As it turned out, Qiaolian's younger brother was not studious and failed the high school entry exam. Their father was therefore especially proud of Qiaolian's ambition, which led her from domestic service to teaching children of migrants and independent study toward the *dazhuan* degree. Similarly, Peiqi felt personal triumph that her pursuit of the *dazhuan* degree compensated for schooling that had been abruptly forfeited in order that her younger brother could afford to attend school. Recollecting her father's orders from long ago that she terminate her compulsory schooling, she sighed with regret: "Otherwise, I'd be in college now." But since embarking on the *dazhuan* degree course of study, she felt some satisfaction in hearing villagers praise her and use her successes as a model for young boys to emulate. Embarrassed, but with pride, she recounted: "One of my father's old army buddies compared his son to me, and scolded him in my father's presence, saying: 'Why can't you go out to work like Peiqi?'"

Migrant workers in China are increasingly recognized for their contribution to rural development by bringing material wealth and new technology, skills, and knowledge—including insight about how to consume, back home. Such exchanges strengthen traditional community forged on reciprocity-based social networks. The allocation of migrant resources back to the village is also a gendered process. In rural Chinese families, young boys' education and training may be the favored investment of their migrant sisters' remittances, although recent evidence suggests the rural gender gap in education is slowly closing (Hannum, Wang, and Adams 2010; H. Zhang 2007). While both migrant men and women alike contribute to their family's social status, the sexual double standard puts particular pressure on young rural women to follow conservative rules of moral and sexual behavior. Yet when young migrant women successfully manage these restrictions and "perform modernity" (Mills 1999) for kin and villagers back home, they can earn substantial social status and social capital from the public acknowledgment of their earning power and their symbolic capital.

Summary

This chapter has focused on migrant women's reflexive absorption of urban and global consumer culture, and its impact on their embodied subjectivities. Seemingly frivolous concerns with fashion and tourism are in fact emblematic of deeper anxiety about belonging, identity, and social status. Applying new consumer tastes and techniques allows relatively powerless rural migrant women a degree of control and freedom to transform themselves from "country bumpkins" to urban sophisticates. Investments in modern looks and lifestyles, and especially in technical training and higher education, are also a means for migrant women to improve their "quality" (*suzhi*), a symbolic form of capital that could reap tangible rewards by generating social and economic capital.

Quality discourse wielded by those in positions of power and internalized by subordinates may be a tool of domination, but it can also be a powerful resource for migrant women workers to deploy to criticize their employers or others in positions of authority, or to voice demands for equal opportunity for self-development. As Qiaolian suggested to me in 2002:

> Since I came out of the village to Beijing, since I've been living here several years, economically I haven't improved much, though I still feel that this has been a good experience. I used to think Beijing offered so many opportunities. I could freely [work], that we would all be equal, that my labor would be equal to everyone else's labor. But later I discovered, to the contrary, it wasn't anything like what I imagined. . . . I thought, given that they [urbanites] were superior to me . . . that their character and their "quality" would match their educational credentials. But in fact, although their educational levels were high, their character and their ethics are not necessarily superior. This was a big revelation to me.

For Qiaolian, migration provided the opportunity to pursue her dreams of higher education. In the process she gained worldly insight that led her to question the assumed superiority of the more educated urbanites. Rural migrant women's increased participation in consumer culture likewise upsets strict social mores that undergird patriarchal authority in the family and village.

Rural migrant women profit from their symbolic capital at an individual level, but such achievement is insufficient to overcome the structural and ideological basis of their marginalization in Beijing society. In fact, by objectifying and remaking themselves, young migrant women tacitly validate the ideologies of rural-urban difference that rationalize the continued exclusion of migrants from urban citizenship. They also validate the neoliberal discourse that puts the onus for social change on individuals rather than on society.

CHAPTER SIX

Migrant Working Wives and Mothers

In my hometown, before I got married, there were no opportunities for "freely chosen love matches." Everyone would go through someone else's introduction to meet a partner. After the introduction, the couple would meet a few times over a year or two, sometimes even less time, just three months, and then get married. This kind of marriage is "first marry then develop feelings." In my hometown, if you choose a partner yourself, your parents will object. They want to go through someone else, to find their child someone whom they think is dependable. I was somewhat unlike other rural young women, because I found myself in a different environment . . . Beijing. (Ruolan, from a conversation we held in 2007.)

This chapter considers how migration transforms traditional patterns of courtship, marriage, and family formation as well as intergenerational relations, and the implications for gender roles and identity, women's agency, and patriarchal power. The first two sections of this chapter explore the ways that migration raised young rural women's expectations of marriage and future spouses and liberalized practices of dating and courtship. In the second half of this chapter, I describe and analyze the postmarital experiences of the five key informants with whom I have sustained prolonged contact: Changying, Ruolan, Shuqin, Shuchun, and Yarui.

Generally, migration in China correlates to later age at marriage (Zheng et al. 2001). As migrants spend their youth working away from home, they inadvertently delay marriage and family formation. Migration could also be a conscious strategy to postpone marriage, about which many young rural women feel ambivalent, or to avoid or terminate an unwanted engagement, or to springboard into a higher economic and social status through "marrying up" or hypergamy (see Chapter 1; Fan and Huang 1998; Jacka 2006). Certainly migration raises young rural women's expectations of the future, and hence their view of the ideal spouse (Beynon 2004). Further, although marriage remains the goal as a social norm and culturally meaningful practice, as well as an economic necessity, migration provides the time, space, and means to explore many options.

In contrast to their parents' generation, as Ruolan implies in the quotation above (and see Parish and Whyte 1978), young migrant women anticipate romance and engage in extended courtships, and they are more selective and autonomous in choosing a spouse than their nonmigrant peers. Ultimately, the experience of labor migration empowers rural women to assert themselves in the matter of marriage and take charge of their own futures, and thus contributes to the redistribution of patriarchal power in the rural family. However, their expanded choices and greater capacity to express agency have not freed them of all constraints of gender and class.

Continuing on the path of migrant workers even after marriage or childbirth enabled my key informants to craft new identities as working wives and mothers, to renegotiate traditional gender role expectations of them as daughters and daughters-in-law, and to fulfill their desires for conjugal intimacy, autonomy, and social mobility. However, economic and social disadvantages that include employment instability, prohibitive housing costs, and barriers of access to affordable health care for themselves as well as education for their offspring made their balance of work and family roles highly precarious. The enduring class division between migrants and urbanites, a result of the two-tier employment and social welfare scheme created by the *hukou* system, as well as gender inequality and discrimination, severely challenged their ability to realize the dream of a better life.

Conjuring Mr. Right

Most young migrant women gave no thought to marriage before going out to work, but they could not indefinitely avoid the weighty issue. Marriage is nearly universal in China (Jones 2010). As elsewhere, it is the prerequisite for family formation and continuity, and for taking up the gender and kinship roles and identities that mark adulthood. Marriage is especially important for rural women's future well-being, as it is the primary means by which women secure land and livelihood (see Chapter 1). Given the *hukou* system and sociospatial class inequality, as well as gender discrimination in employment, single migrant women have not been able to independently support themselves into middle age through wage work. Further, in the absence of a universal social security system, children remain essential to the long-term care and support of the elderly. Remaining single and childless, in the countryside or in the city, is impractical as well as culturally unacceptable (see also Evans 2008; Ma and Cheng 2005).

In rural China throughout the 1980s and 1990s, women typically felt pressure to marry around age twenty, the legal age of marriage for women, and most bore a child within the first two years of marriage (see Chan, Madsen, and Unger 1992;

Greenhalgh 1993). An older domestic worker's marriage in the early 1990s conformed to this traditional pattern: "We grew up in one village together. Everyone finds spouses in the village or nearby; it's convenient. We got married and after a year I had a child."

By convention, women marry men a few years older than themselves and, compared to men, have a shorter period of time in which they are considered marriageable. Thus, pressure on women to marry increases with age (Gaetano 2010; To 2013). Yet rural women who migrate for work inadvertently postpone marriage, in part because marriage, and most certainly childbearing, would terminate employment.

For example, after becoming engaged in 1995 at age twenty to a *tongxiang* enlisted in the army, domestic worker Shanshan reassured her concerned Beijing employer: "I won't get married until I'm twenty-five. I'm too young." Although Shanshan really did think her peers were settling down too early in life, her decision about when to marry was also due to her own assumption that, after marriage, she would move to her husband's village to raise children and care for her in-laws, taking up the primary gender roles of wife and mother. So, in order to keep working at her job in Beijing, Shanshan voluntarily delayed her wedding for a few more years.

I met only one domestic worker, Xingjuan, who after marriage continued to work for her same employer on a live-in basis from Monday through Friday, spending weekends with her husband, a petty trader, in a rented flat on Beijing's outskirts. However, her husband objected to the arrangement, and it seemed likely not to last.

For most migrant women workers, continuing employment after marriage is anyway difficult because employers favored young and single women workers, and routinely dismissed pregnant workers who might otherwise negatively impact productivity or profit, demanding maternity leave or special benefits, as explained in Chapter 1. Together, conventions of patrilineal-patrilocal marriage and gender divisions of labor, neoliberal and gender-discriminatory employment practices, and the *hukou* system reinforce rural women's status as temporary migrant workers who experience job turnover at marriage.

The tendency for migrant women to delay marriage is a phenomenon that has received the attention of scholars and policymakers in China and internationally. Many experts are sympathetic to the potential psychological as well as social consequences of rural women aging out of the marriage market and facing ostracism should they remain unwed (see Ma and Cheng 2005; Tan 2000). Others stress the potential crisis to public health or social morality posed by a large population of unmarried women working away from home. In particular, single migrant women have been linked to increasing rates of premarital sex and abortion (Zheng et al.

2001) and are considered to be at greater risk for spread of STDs and HIV compared to nonmigrants or migrant men (Yang and Xia 2008). Popular discourse stereotypes young women from the countryside as predatory "third parties" (*disanzhe*) or mistresses, and blames them for marital infidelity and rising divorce rates among urban couples (Rofel 2007; Sun 2004; Zhao Weijie 1995). Such prejudice compounds young migrant women's vulnerability in urban society as it rationalizes surveillance and control over their behaviors and bodies. It also augments their vulnerability to harmful gossip that could jeopardize their reputations and hence their futures. Such perceptions belie broader anxieties about gender and social change as more liberal and individualized notions of sexual freedom encouraged by the market and consumerism compete with older, parochial orientations that tether sexuality to monogamous marriage and family planning for the benefit of the nation (see Hyde 2007).

At the First National Conference on Migrant Women Workers' Rights and Interests in 1999, a former domestic worker turned social activist voiced her opinion that marriage was the number one problem facing migrant women. She expressed her concern that many would never marry, ending up dejected and socially scorned "old maids."

> I was among the first cohort of domestic workers who went out [in the 1980s], and many of them are still "floating" around in Shenzhen, [although they are] over thirty years old. Ultimately they'll have nothing: no home, no business, no sons, and no daughters. What will their lives be like in a few more years? You figure, in the past, aging single women in the city would still have employment, a place to live, and social security when they were old. I don't think in another ten years they'll all have settled down or have a place to go. Thus, I conclude that going out to work is a good dream that will turn into a nightmare.

As the speaker correctly noted (and see Chapter 1), the shift from the planned economy to the postreform mixed-market economy broke the "iron rice bowl" of basic economic security provided by the state's work units to urban households, and by the collectives to farm households. In its place, a so-called spring rice bowl exploits a youthful labor force that has limited security, as even urban welfare schemes are increasingly privatized. For young migrant workers, who were never entitled to urban public welfare, future economic security especially depends on traditional supports of family and household, to which marriage is central.

Marriage is a particularly vexing issue for migrant women, because the choice of spouse is also a decision about the future, in which location figures prominently

(Beynon 2004). Exposure to the city and urban lifestyles raises young rural women's expectations of how and thus where they desire to live. Consequently, migration alters their vision of the ideal spouse, who would be critical to fulfilling their aspirations for bourgeois modernity. The traditional rule of thumb for matchmaking in China was "matching doors and windows," bringing together couples from the same social strata. In contrast, most rural migrant women have no interest in marrying a peasant or farmer (see also Beynon 2004; Ma and Cheng 2005).

My informants generally had two criteria about the kind of partner they would be willing to marry, which I label "conditions" and "feelings," following Farrer's (2002) typology based on research on youth sexuality in postreform Shanghai. Literally, "conditions" refers to the man's household economic and social situation, such as *hukou,* property and assets, occupation, whether his parents are still living and what sort of care they might require of a daughter-in-law, and how many of his siblings are unmarried and hence would require financial support. A man with good conditions could best fulfill the primary role of family provider, of "being responsible and dependable for a lifetime," in Ruolan's words. Thus, they generally ruled out rural men lacking migration and nonagricultural work experience. They looked favorably on those with savings and/or some marketable skill or technical ability, such as garnered through migration and off-farm work. For example, in 2000, I recorded the following in my field notes: "Domestic worker Liping tells me and her friend Peiqi that although she is engaged to someone back in her village, she doesn't have much to do with him now that she's working in Beijing and he's only in the provincial city. Peiqi asks her whether she 'minds' that her boyfriend 'isn't out working,' thus implying that in her eyes, he was not well suited to her friend."

Most agreed that urban men of means would be out of their sights. As explained in Chapter 1, a long-standing policy that children must inherit the *hukou* of their mother rendered such marriages implausible and undesirable for urban families. Even after the policy was lifted in 1998, such marriages continued to be negatively associated with an urban family's status decline. However improbable, young rural women were nonetheless keen to marry into an urban family on the assumption that it would improve their standard of living. As I recorded in my field notes:

Domestic worker Suyin had no plans to return to the village. She definitely did not want to become the wife of a peasant. She pitied her eldest sister who had married uxorilocally to a *laoxiang,* and was stuck in their impoverished hometown farming the family plot.[1] She hoped to marry like her second eldest sister, to a farmer from a village that had been administratively incorporated into Beijing, and who thus had been granted Beijing *hukou*. She showed me a picture of this sister, her husband and son, standing in front of a solidly constructed house.

In addition, many informants said they considered a man's personality and wanted someone who shared their ambitions for upward social and economic mobility. Thus, in 2002, Yarui considered as a potential partner a former army soldier who worked as a security guard at the same hotel where she was a chambermaid, and who was taking courses for college credit. She said she figured he had good "quality," referring to his bright future prospects as a college-degree holder. She had also heard from his coworkers that he was a good person, both honest and upright, which further attracted her interest.

At the same time, informants spoke of finding a bosom friend (*zhiji*) with whom they could have an easy rapport and fall in love, and who would be caring (see also Ma and Cheng 2005). Most also wanted someone who was good looking. Their emphasis on "feelings" and physical attraction reflects the resurgence in the postreform period of modern notions of romance and love (Farrer 2002; Honig and Hershatter 1988; Y. Yan 2003). By contrast, under revolutionary socialism, youth were expected to show primary loyalty to the state and devote their passions to socialist construction (Croll 1981). Excessive public displays of romantic affection were criticized as bourgeois and individualistic. The state closely regulated sexuality and marriage through its public institutions. For example, university students were forbidden to marry before graduation. Workers required approval of their work unit to register a marriage. Political affiliation and class background of a future spouse's family were an important consideration in matchmaking (Parish and Whyte 1978). The shift to a market economy in the postreform period created the conditions and space for youth to experiment with new ideas and practices like modern love, as I explain in greater detail below.

For many young rural women, migration became an excuse to delay marriage not only in order to have more time to earn money and experience city life, but also to explore possibilities for making a better match than would be possible otherwise. However, as a young woman began to age out of the marriage market, the pool of desirable potential partners began to dry up. Liping humorously described the plight of aging single migrant women like herself: "It's tough for us *dagongmei*. If we look for a man when we're twenty to twenty-two, we can find one who is good looking and has good conditions. When we are twenty-two to twenty-four or so, we can find one who is good looking, but he'll be poor. And when we're even older, we can find a man whose economic situation is good, but he won't be good looking!" Her jest belied a palpable anxiety shared by single migrant women that, by postponing marriage too long, they risked settling for much less than they desired, or never marrying.

Under such pressures, many migrant women simply kept thoughts of marriage from their minds and lived only in the present—"going with the flow," in one oft-repeated phrase—into their late twenties or even early thirties. Meanwhile, it was not uncommon for young women to refuse parental requests to return home, which signaled readiness to settle down. Meirong, a high-school graduate from a small town in western China who worked with Shuchun from 2006 to 2010, explained to me how her parents dealt with their only daughter being still single at age twenty-seven, having worked in Beijing already eight years (as of 2010): "Sure, my parents are worried about me being single and in my late twenties. But I'm independent; I don't need their money. So, there's nothing they can do about it." Clearly, migration significantly decreases parental influence in selection of spouses and timing of courtship, as well as daughters' dating behavior, as the following section illuminates further.

Changing Courtship and Marriage

As Ruolan indicated in the opening quote, rural youth generally rely on intermediaries, whether family, friends, or even professional go-betweens, to facilitate marriage introductions. These practices coexist with the modern ideal of romantic love. Singles choose "freely" from among potential partners deemed acceptable by parents, usually someone from their own village or county, with whom they expect to develop romantic feelings (Whyte 1990; Y. Yan 2003). Time spent in the city not only changed young women's visions of the ideal mate but also provided the space and opportunity to meet potential partners spontaneously and independently of parents or other intermediaries. Most would be unsuccessful in pursuing romance away from home, and would ultimately follow the more traditional route. But a growing and significant minority, including my key informants, found their future spouse on their own, in the city.

For example, Ruolan met her future husband by chance in 1994, about one year after her arrival in Beijing, when she was still a youthful seventeen. He worked as a cook in a restaurant where she was regularly sent to purchase take-out meals for the family who employed her as a domestic worker. They not only had migration experience in common, but were also from the same province, albeit different counties. At age twenty-four, Changying likewise met her future husband while she and her *laoxiang* Qiaolian were working as teachers at a makeshift elementary school for migrant children, in 2000. He was a migrant construction worker from a different province, with an unusually large family of five brothers who lost their father at an early age.

In addition, the city provided the space and resources conducive to fostering modern dating culture, as couples could meet in public with less concern for gossip, find private venues to get to know each other better, and enjoy a plethora of entertainments together (see Hirsch and Wardlow 2006). Ruolan explains how urban space and consumer culture allowed her to have an extended courtship with her fiancé:

> After being unable to continue my education, I went to Beijing in 1993. The people I met there were open-minded and progressive in their thoughts. In Beijing, I met [her husband], and thus began our romance; we married in 1998. In the interim few years, we took our time to get to know each other, meeting on our days off, going to the park, eating meals together. Now sometimes my husband teases me, "You tested me out for five years before marrying me, how cruel!" In the village, there are very few couples like us. If, after you are introduced, you go out on a lot of dates, you'll attract gossip of your kin. Anyway, the countryside doesn't have the conditions for "freely chosen love matches."

In 2007, after nearly a decade of marriage, Ruolan blushed with pleased embarrassment when she showed me a yellowed photo of the couple posed together at a scenic spot in Beijing, which was taken during their courtship period.

These changes in selecting prospective marital partners and conducting courtship undermine parental authority in marriage. Parents generally frown upon matches made outside local village- and kin-based social networks and those that entail a child's relocation far from home, such as to a distant province.[2] A daughter is more vulnerable to abuse or ostracism in her new household and community without protective networks of natal kin nearby (Ma and Cheng 2005; Tan and Short 2004). Moreover, a daughter married far from her natal home is less able to minister personally to her aging parents. In rural China, married rural daughters are increasingly an important source of physical care and emotional support to their own parents, as well as to their in-laws (Miller 2004; H. Zhang 2004). In addition, freely chosen love marriages are clearly made between individuals rather than between two families (Y. Yan 2003). Such couples are less likely to co-reside with (the husband's) parents, preferring to establish a nuclear household of their own (Y. Yan 2002). The trend of freely chosen marriage concomitant with migration and marketization thus has broader implications for intergenerational relations as well as rural women's agency in marriage and family, as I elaborate upon in the Conclusion.

Not a few young women who are already engaged at the time they migrate out of the village might find themselves in a position like that of Xiazi, the protagonist in Li Hong's 1997 documentary *Out of Phoenix Bridge*. After working for a while as a domestic worker in Beijing, Xiazi decides to break off her engagement to a man from her village. But because a marriage broker had officially negotiated the match and because an engagement gift had already been received, and spent, by her parents, Xiazi's decision humiliated and angered her family, causing her great distress. Liping, discussed above, had similar thoughts about breaking off her engagement. Peiqi and other migrant friends sagely advised her to avoid returning to her hometown for a few years, until her fiancé and his family would lose hope of ever consummating the engagement. Such stalling techniques saved the face or reputation of all parties involved, and thus were an effective means for a young woman to follow her heart and still fulfill her obligation to her natal family. Tellingly, none of my informants who freely chose their spouses while working in Beijing exchanged the customary betrothal money and gifts that formalize an engagement and symbolically bind the two families, and otherwise complicate a couple's autonomy from parents. Nonetheless, all of my informants sought and ultimately overcame resistance to win their parents' approval of their independently brokered marriages.

Pursuing romantic liaisons beyond the conventional boundaries established by geography and local social networks, and without formal rituals of engagement, involves certain risks, as young rural women themselves recognized. Feelings were often insufficient glue to bind partners across differences in conditions, often exacerbated by migration. For example, twenty-three-year-old hotel housekeeper Xiaofang had a promising relationship with a former middle school classmate, a high school graduate enrolled in an army college in Guangdong. A future with her boyfriend would be a comfortable life, as he would be assigned to a government position as a cadre (civil servant), eligible for transfer of *hukou* to a city. But since 1997, when he went to Guangdong to study and she came to Beijing to work alongside Shuqin as a hotel chambermaid, Xiaofang had developed doubts about his commitment to her. A lapse in communication caused her to worry that he had found someone else, someone with more skills or education who "better complemented" him, and, by 2002, she had resigned herself to the relationship's end. Ultimately, according to Shuqin, she returned home to marry someone introduced to her by kin.

Likewise, Yarui's first boyfriend (the hotel security guard) proved to be disloyal to her. In despair, she insisted that she wanted to return to her village to marry the traditional way. "If you have no ability to make money, there's no point in desiring it, because it's beyond your reach," was the lesson she had learned in trying to marry up. But, her time in the city had decreased her chances to attract marriage proposals back home, not only as the pool of eligible bachelors dried up, but also due to harmful rumors about her chastity. Thus, even in her heartbreak, she still yearned to marry far from her home, away from villagers whom she called "gossipy and critical," who would insult her if she were to choose a partner not properly introduced to her—as was the case with her ex-boyfriend. They would accuse her, she said, of "having run off with somebody," insinuating that she had needed to elope, to disguise "immoral" behavior (i.e., premarital sex resulting in a pregnancy).

My informants were particularly distressed by the threat of malicious rumors about their chastity, and took pains not to incur gossip, as it would mar their own reputations and be disrespectful of parents. In rural China, premarital sex and cohabitation are increasingly common, but mainly occur among committed couples, in a context where engagement, involving exchange of money and gifts, is a binding social contract (Friedman 2000; Y. Yan 2003). Due to the persistence of a sexual double standard that places disproportionate value on female chastity, young women must be strategic about losing virginity (Zhou Xiao 1989). Premarital sex may prompt or hasten a commitment to marriage; indeed, parents (especially mothers) may collude in their son's deflowering of a future bride (Y. Yan 2002; Zhou Xiao 1989). But sexual intercourse that does not lead to marriage, if discovered, can place a young woman at risk of rejection by prospective spouses.

The situation among most rural migrants in the cities is similar (Zheng et al. 2001). Ruolan, Changying, Yarui, Shuchun, and Shuqin, all of whom met their husbands in Beijing, engaged in premarital sex and cohabitation with their future husbands. For example, Ruolan and her fiancé lived together in Beijing for a year before officially registering their marriage and holding a wedding ceremony in his village during the 1999 Lunar New Year holiday. Even after officially registering their marriage, cohabitating migrant women typically referred to their status as merely "engaged" until they could hold a wedding ceremony. This is a ritual event that bestows social legitimacy to marriage and gives symbolic expression to the mutual affection and obligations between the couple and their parents. Eloping or foregoing the ceremony would be interpreted as unfilial. Indeed, to protect her parents' good name and prevent their loss of face, Shuqin hid from them for months the fact that she was cohabiting with her legally registered spouse, until the couple could afford to hold a wedding banquet in her village.

For the most part, my informants were careful to officially register the marriage before incurring pregnancy. Single motherhood in China is socially unacceptable, economically impractical, and legally complex, as children born to unwed mothers are not entitled to *hukou* registration. Family planning regulations (see Chapter 1) require married migrant women of childbearing age to undergo semi-annual fertility checks and receive official permission to give birth. Due to concern for the social and legal consequences of bearing a child without first securing a marriage license and permission to have a child, Yarui terminated a first pregnancy with the man who would eventually become her legal husband. Her freedom to experiment with premarital sex was sharply curtailed by state controls over marriage and fertility.

Among themselves, the migrant women I interviewed held contradictory views of proper conduct in dating and courtship. In 2000, Changying, her fiancé, Qiaolian, and another *tongxiang* pooled resources to start their own private school for migrant children in a Beijing suburb. When the enterprise failed, relations between the two school friends soured. When I last saw Qiaolian in 2002, she expressed disapproval of Changying's fiancé, whom she felt drove a wedge between the two women, in part by misjudging Qiaolian's relationship to the school's landlord, a divorced Beijing man in his forties, from whom Qiaolian had sought to recover their initial investment. When I met up with Changying in 2006, she explained how, motivated by her own sense of protective responsibility, she had strongly cautioned Qiaolian not to ruin her good reputation by getting involved with a bad sort. Changying reported that Qiaolian had since returned home and married a schoolteacher from the nearby county town. Her attempts to restore their friendship were coolly rebuffed. I also tried to renew contact with Qiaolian, but letters I sent to her parents' address received no response. While undoubtedly a number of factors severed the friendship between Changying and Qiaolian, their own uncertainties about permissible dating and courtship behavior in the unfamiliar and unsupervised setting of Beijing was surely one exacerbating influence.

Several factors make marriages between rural women and urban men less common than marriages between rural-to-urban migrants. One obstacle is the practice, long upheld by policy, of awarding offspring the same *hukou* as their mothers (see Chapter 1). Although the state decreed in 1998 that a child could inherit either parent's household registration, large cities like Beijing were slow to implement the change.[3] A related obstacle is the discrimination against rural brides by urban families, who view such marriages as a form of downward social mobility and also as a risky venture. Brides from the countryside are commonly suspected of mercenary intentions, such as fleeing the marriage after collecting bridal gifts or otherwise cheating the family. Such prejudices reflect a general anxiety about social order and distrust of *waidiren;* living away from their place of *hukou* registration, migrants were virtually untraceable, and thus popularly misperceived as prone to criminality (L. Zhang 2001; Zhao Shukai 2000). As a corollary to these obstacles, marriages between rural women and urban men share certain general characteristics. Women tend to come from poorer households and are much younger than their spouses. Their husbands are older than most urban men are at the time of marriage, and are more likely to be disabled, unemployed, divorced, or without a complete set of parents, factors that decrease their value in the urban marriage market (Fan and Huang 1998; Tan and Short 2004). Nonetheless, several of my informants successfully married Beijing bachelors introduced through family, colleagues, or even employers.

Yaling worked as a domestic worker for a cadre household in Beijing in the late 1980s, a job that was arranged through her father's social network. Her older Beijing husband was introduced to her by her employer, at her parents' request, in 1991, when she was twenty-one. When I met them in 2000, he was unemployed, having been laid off from his state-sector job, and received only a monthly subsistence. The couple had a five-year-old son, and lived with the husband's elderly parents in a ramshackle house in a Beijing *hutong* ("warren") with the husband's younger brother, the brother's wife, and their four-year-old daughter. Their son attended the neighborhood kindergarten at an annual cost of several thousand *yuan,* paid for by the grandfather. Although old enough for primary school, the boy was prevented from matriculation due to the lack of Beijing *hukou* and prohibitive "introductory fees" (i.e., an illicit charge). Sharing a modest meal with her extended family one afternoon revealed some of the tensions around her entry into this urban family. The younger brother spoke disparagingly of how *waidiren* are competing for Beijing workers' jobs, and his wife later told me that her husband objected to his father's support of the grandson's exorbitant school fees. Yet Yaling's mother-in-law praised Yaling's skills in housework and disparaged so-called modern Beijing women whom she said "demanded too much" and were "not very traditional." When I asked Yaling later whether she felt accepted by her new family, she responded: "Now that I have a son, I have security." Bearing children is critical for rural women to gain acceptance into urban families that are otherwise suspicious of their intentions and mobility (Hoy 1999; Tan and Short 2004). A filial son—as part of the "uterine family" created by women—has also traditionally been a woman's best support for her future in the context of patrilineal kinship and patrilocal marriage customs (M. Wolf 1972).

In the summer of 2001, just shy of age twenty, Shuqin accepted the marriage proposal of an unemployed Beijing bachelor sixteen years her senior, who had been a manager at the hotel where she worked. She had initially discouraged his attentions because she was "fearful" of his intentions. Eventually he won her over with frequent invitations to the cinema, to Pizza Hut, and other places she had never been. The couple legally registered their marriage, and Shuqin moved into the small three-bedroom apartment where he lived with his widowed mother, divorced sister, and the sister's son. The apartment was quite old as it had been allocated to his parents by their work unit, and later purchased with subsidy. Despite her husband's seniority in the family as the only son, Shuqin was often at the mercy of her mean-spirited new relatives, who called their marriage a sham and accused Shuqin of marrying for money. Shuqin confided to me retrospectively that when she became pregnant two years later, she had considered abortion and even divorce, but stayed in the marriage because of her feelings for her husband. "He is good to me," she explained.

Shuqin's pride and concern for her natal family's reputation also stopped such thoughts. She and her husband held a small ceremony in her home village during the 2002 Spring Festival holiday, after holding their larger ceremony with his family in Beijing. To avoid the opprobrium of inquisitive friends and covillagers, Shuqin disguised her husband's older age and unemployed status. She and her parents also kept secret from kin and neighbors the truth that the groom's family did not offer any bride wealth. Bride wealth typically involves negotiations between two families of equal status and would not be appropriate to a hypergamous love match across the rural-urban class divide. "We didn't ask for it," her mother simply explained. Rather, Shuqin allowed villagers to believe that the groom's family, being from Beijing, was rich and therefore generous with the betrothal and marital gifts. Her pursuit of upward mobility through free-choice marriage to an urbanite meant that Shuqin circumvented traditional conventions like gift exchange, and this left her and her parents without resources to make future claims, including for her well-being and fair treatment, on her husband's family.

Despite Shuqin's mixed success at finding happiness, her sister nonetheless aspired to an urban match, on the condition that that her future spouse be "good looking and not *too* old." Then, in 2005, Shuchun was tricked into marrying an urban playboy, introduced to her by a distant relative. She discovered his infidelity soon after they set up an apartment together, but before hosting a wedding banquet in her natal village. Humiliated and devastated, Shuchun left her husband and sought refuge temporarily with her sister and brother-in-law in Beijing (and her new niece, born to Shuqin in 2004). Against her parents' wishes, Shuchun demanded a divorce, on the grounds that there was no love or fidelity between the couple. She blamed herself for being seduced by her ex-husband's good looks and relative prosperity, and not taking the time to really get to know his character. Her divorce was finalized in 2006. By then Shuchun was working as a chambermaid in another Beijing hotel where no one knew of her shameful status as a divorcée, and hence of her sexual impurity, and she did not speak of her past.

Over the next few years, Shuchun went on dates with numerous potential mates, most of whom were introduced to her by coworkers, including the middle-aged

Beijing "aunties" with whom she and her sister had worked at the four-star hotel years before. In 2008 she had several dates with a bachelor featured on a Beijing Television Channel 7 dating show, *Love Life* (生活秀). After seeing this man on the show and learning of his personal particulars, Shuchun submitted her contact details and brief biography by text message to the number flashed on the screen. She felt they would be compatible, despite his having a Beijing *hukou*, because of his relatively low level of education, modest job as a postal carrier, and basic accommodations—a house shared with his parents on the far outskirts of Beijing (in an "urban village"). Soon after, a representative of the television station contacted her, and passed along her information to the bachelor, who called and invited her to meet. They went out several times before parting ways. Finally, in 2009, just after turning thirty, Shuchun met and then married a divorced thirty-five-year-old Beijing man introduced to her by the husband of her friend and former coworker in hotel housekeeping, Yarui. The couple legally registered their marriage, but to save money they did not hold a wedding banquet. They settled into an apartment shared with his retired parents that had been allocated by, and later purchased from, his father's (former) work unit.

Yarui met her husband in 2005, when she was twenty-three and he was thirty-four. They dated for over two years before they registered their marriage, in 2007, after his divorce from his first wife was finalized. When I met up with Yarui later that year, she still referred to herself as only "engaged." Her parents did not approve of the match, and they would not consider the couple to be legitimately married until they had held a wedding banquet in her village, which they finally did in 2008. Although her husband had the Beijing *hukou*, he was not particularly wealthy. Having been laid off from a state-sector job, he worked as a shuttle and tour bus driver for the same hotel in which Yarui also worked booking guests' flights and tours.

Agency and Power in Courtship and Marriage

Working away from home and spending their youth in the city, migrant women have found the space, time, and means to postpone marriage and experiment with a burgeoning modern dating culture, including engaging in premarital sex, although the latter incurs certain risks. Migration further provides young rural women the chance to imagine different futures that could be achieved through making a better match than would be available in the countryside. However, few rural women succeed to marry above their social status, as numerous obstacles weigh against rural-urban marriages. On the whole, migrant women incrementally help transform dominant rural patterns of courtship and marriage, and in so doing gain greater autonomy and control over their immediate futures.

Clearly, the marketization, migration, and urbanization of the postreform period have rapidly accelerated the shift of power in rural China from the older to the younger generations, a process that has been underway since the early years of socialism (Y. Yan 2002). This shift has especially empowered young brides and wives to assert themselves and maneuver within the patriarchal marriage system to their greater advantage (Yan 2006). Legal reforms initiated by the CCP, most notably the 1951 Marriage Law, weakened parental authority in marriage by decreeing freedom of choice in spouse selection and outlawing such practices as arranged marriage, bride wealth payment, and child betrothal. Yet romantic courtship and free-choice marriage have only been realized in the postreform period with the emergence of a modern dating culture made possible by consumerism (Whyte 1990; Y. Yan 2003).

Likewise, while land collectivization undermined the system of ancestral property inheritance by stripping patriarchal elders of the basis of their authority over sons, patrilineal-organized families and even villages were incorporated into the collective and commune structures such that agnatic-related men continued to wield political authority (e.g., controlling job allocation) (see Judd 1994). In contrast, the market economy and the logic of the "spring rice bowl" favor young workers, whose superior earning power can be leveraged for greater autonomy and control over their futures (Zhang Zhen 2000). Under conditions of market socialism, young migrant women thus are enabled to make independent choices in love and marriage.

Shifting demographics may also favor young rural women's agency in marriage. China's sex ratio at birth has grown increasingly disproportionate since the mid-1980s, peaking at nearly 120 boys per 100 girls in 2010 (Poston, Conde, and DeSalvo 2011).[4] The imbalance negatively impacts poorer, rural men's marriage prospects (Attané 2012; Cheng, Xuehui, and Dagsvik 2011; Poston, Conde, and De-Salvo 2011). As a result, young women may be more selective about marital partners and have greater bargaining power in negotiating the terms of marriage (Attané 2012). However, such changes have not gone so far as to dismantle the patrilineal-patrilocal marriage system and the gender inequality it maintains. As emphasized in Chapter 1, rural women must marry to ensure livelihood and security for the future, and would be hard-pressed to remain independent. Moreover, as in the examples above, rural women who marry hypergamously to urban men are outsiders in both their new households and the city, and are particularly dependent on their husbands to facilitate their inclusion and instill a sense of belonging.

Finally, under revolutionary socialism, ancestor worship and filial piety were targeted in numerous campaigns as competing ideologies with socialism, which required individuals to be loyal to the party-state above the family. Yet the state continued to promote the intergenerational contract, the mutual responsibility of nurture between parents and children, which the Constitution stipulates is the duty of all citizens (Ikels 2004). As the next section makes clear, the impact of migration, marketization, and urbanization on postmarital family structure poses new challenges to filial piety and intergenerational relations. Below, I first describe the postmarital experiences of Ruolan and Changying, who married fellow migrants, and then present the experiences of Shuqin, Shuchun, and Yarui, who married into Beijing families.

My informants' experiences show how postmarital migration and work further enhance the position of daughters-in-law in the rural family, and in turn shift intergenerational authority from elders to youth. Yet, their stories also reveal that migrant wives and mothers continue to invest in traditional identities and filial piety as these provide meaning and support amid the uncertainties and instabilities posed by migration and work to their the conjugal family and household.

Postmarital Experiences

RUOLAN

After marrying in 1999, Ruolan and her husband continued their working lives in Beijing: she as a cashier in a grocery store, and he as a cook. Shortly thereafter, Ruolan became unexpectedly pregnant. She considered having an abortion, because she did not feel they were financially secure enough to have a child, and she wished to continue working; her husband convinced her otherwise. Nonetheless, Ruolan kept at the job well into her third trimester until she could no longer do the work, which in her words "involved heavy lifting." Like most migrant workers, she was not entitled to any maternity benefits and was terminated upon taking leave. Unable to afford a hospitalization in Beijing, Ruolan moved in temporarily with her in-laws (now her official place of *hukou* registration) for the birth. She suffered high blood pressure late in the pregnancy, and their son, Xiao Han, was born prematurely in the local hospital, by emergency C-section. During the traditional monthlong postpartum lay-in, Ruolan rested at her in-laws', but was cared for by her own mother and her unmarried younger sister. Uncomfortable around her in-laws, she then made the unusual decision to move back to her natal village, where she raised Xiao Han, with the assistance of her unmarried sister and her elder brother's wife, in her parents' home, until his second birthday. During these two years, except for a brief visit shortly after the birth of their son and an extended visit at the Lunar New Year holiday, Ruolan's husband continued living and working in Beijing.

In 2001, Ruolan, her husband, and their son were reunited in Beijing. Ruolan found work as a restaurant cashier and paid for her son to attend a local daycare. This arrangement was expensive and difficult due to Ruolan and her husband's long work hours. When I asked Ruolan why she had brought Xiao Han to Beijing at such a young age, she explained that she felt it was important for him to "bond with his mother." Her opinion reflected modern ideas of "scientific childbearing and childrearing," and a different understanding of motherhood than held by a previous generation of women (see Evans 2008; Gottschaung 2007; Greenhalgh and Winckler 2005; Zhu 2010). The latter were encouraged to entrust their infants to communal crèches, or to kin or hired help, in order to fulfill their patriotic duty to contribute their productive labor to socialist construction (Sidel 1972; Wolf 1985). In the postreform period, the state promotes a small family ideal that emphasizes the quality of offspring, and places primary responsibility on mothers to bear and raise a healthy and intelligent child, who will become a productive citizen (Greenhalgh and Winckler 2005).

Modern motherhood is increasingly a full-time occupation that involves following expert advice and utilizing a plethora of technologies and consumer products (Gottschaung 2007; Zhu 2010). Yet this bourgeois ideal is quite difficult for migrant mothers to achieve given their limited income and lack of access to requisite resources. In fact, Ruolan had counted on her mother-in-law's assistance in raising Xiao Han, a typical arrangement dictated by the intergenerational contract and essential to maintaining a flexible migrant labor force. Thus she was disappointed that her mother-in-law did not offer to provide help. However, she understood that the older woman was under pressure to provide care exclusively to the children of her eldest son, who lived in a new house in the village with his wife and two daughters. Toward the end of 2002, Ruolan's mother-in-law relented and Xiao Han spent the next two years living with his grandparents in the countryside, while his parents remained in Beijing to work. Ruolan provided indirect payment to her mother-in-law in compensation for Xiao Han's care, including cash at the Chinese New Year and gifts of household goods and clothes. But as her husband's brother and sister-in-law continued to complain of the grandparent's alleged favoritism toward their only grandson, and neglect of their granddaughters, Ruolan eventually decided to make alternative childcare arrangements.

In 2005, Ruolan and her conjugal family relocated to the small-but-growing prefectural city near the (father-in-law's) village, where they rented a two-bedroom apartment shared with another young family. For about a year, they struggled financially as they spent their savings to build a new life together in this developing small city. In addition to rent, the couple's expenditures included purchasing a motorcycle for long-distance transport between the city and the village, to which they later added a battery-powered scooter. Ruolan's husband invested in a driver's education course and earned a license, then found work as a chauffeur for the CEO of a private company. The couples' biggest expense was the annual tuition and room and board fees at Xiao Han's elementary school. The "tuition" was actually an arbitrary and illicit fee demanded by the school for admitting students like Xiao Han, who had rural, nonlocal *hukou*.

Ruolan trained as an apprentice for six months, during which time she did not receive wages, to learn to stitch gloves and leather accessories for a small export apparel factory. While her husband drove his boss around the provincial city and out to rural factories, often not getting home to rest until the wee hours of the morning, Ruolan worked long and irregular hours six days a week. She was paid by piece-rate. Although she earned less than what she had earned, or could earn, in Beijing as a cashier, Ruolan spent less due to the lower cost of living in the smaller city. When the factory sat idle because it had no orders, Ruolan sewed clothes or did alterations for private clients on a secondhand, pedal-operated sewing machine that cost her nearly a month's salary. The couple also spent some money renovating their rural property, three mud-and-brick rooms on one side of a traditional courtyard house shared with Ruolan's in-laws, who lived in a set of rooms opposite. As customary, Ruolan's father-in-law had bestowed this family property on his younger son and Ruolan at their marriage; his elder son was given cash to build a new house at his marriage.[5] When possible, Ruolan and her family returned to the village, about one hour's drive by electric scooter or motorbike from the city, to spend time with her in-laws and other relatives.

After the New Year celebration of 2007, Ruolan's husband returned to Beijing on the motorcycle to take up a better paying job as a cook, having learned of the job opportunity through his former coworkers. Once again, the household was restructured. Ruolan moved with her son into a rented room (with access to a communal toilet) near his school. Xiao Han no longer needed to board overnight because he was now old enough to walk home after school on his own. He obediently completed his homework while waiting for his mother to return after her shift at the factory and cook his dinner. On Friday evenings, mother and son rode the scooter out to the village to join Xiao Han's grandparents for a meal and some conversation. Mother and son slept in their newly renovated set of rooms, now equipped with steam heaters (but no indoor plumbing). Despite their advanced age, Ruolan's in-laws still farmed a plot of land, and grew enough to feed themselves and earn a decent living by selling the surplus. On Saturday morning, in a gesture of filial respect, Ruolan usually went into their fields to help a bit and to gather some vegetables for the noontime meal, which she cooked for everyone. After lunch, Xiao Han and his mother returned to the city. Saturday afternoons, Xiao Han attended English-language or swimming classes; these were extra lessons that Ruolan insisted he have and for which she paid out of her earnings.

In 2010, her husband still working in Beijing, Ruolan secured a 115,000CNY, twenty-year bank mortgage and paid a down payment of equal amount, using up her family's savings and money borrowed from her own sister and brother, to purchase an apartment, still under construction, in a large new complex on the city outskirts. Taking me on a tour of the family's future residence, Ruolan pointed out the three bedrooms, living room, heat and hot water, air-conditioning and bathroom with shower, a vast improvement over their rustic village accommodations. She had already invited her in-laws to move into the apartment when they were ready to "retire" from farming. The elderly couple preferred to stay in the village where they had an extensive network of kin, but eventually they would need hands-on care, and they had not been invited to live with their (less filial) elder son. Moreover, a rumor was circulating that the provincial government was planning to re-possess the village land for an environmental improvement project. Property owners would be compensated with a new home elsewhere. Anticipating such compensation, Ruolan and her husband planned to keep the family's household registration in the village a bit longer, although as new property owners in the city they were eligible for a transfer and eager to have local, urban *hukou* to facilitate Xiao Han's continuing education.

CHANGYING

Changying married her boyfriend in 2001, at age twenty-five, and gave birth to a son within a year, as is typical. As with Ruolan, Changying chose to give birth in her place of *hukou* registration and avoid the exorbitant fees charged by city hospitals. However, unlike Ruolan, Changying's birth was a positive experience. For the duration of her pregnancy, Changying moved in with her mother-in-law and her husband's brothers' wives, back in the countryside. (At the time, three brothers were working in Beijing together.) Ten hours after her water burst, with birth imminent, she went to the nearest hospital, accompanied by her husband, and he remained present at the birth of their son.

Telling me about her birth story retrospectively in 2006, Changying explained that conventionally only (female) midwives were present at births, and still today husbands are not permitted or expected to witness the procedure. (However, in large cities like Shanghai husbands may witness their wives give birth, for a fee.) At Changying's insistence, the couple had utilized the family's *guanxi* ("social connections"; see Chapter 3) at this hospital to gain such a privilege. Her labor was smooth and quick, but undertaken without pain medication. Afterward, she was gratified when her husband told her, "You women have it really tough."

The couple innovatively named their son by combining both of their surnames, which is highly unusual, as conventionally children receive their father's surname. Changying was also expressly antitraditional about other aspects of maternity. For example, she ignored her mother-in-law's entreaties, also a widely followed prescription, to refrain from bathing during the postpartum lay-in. As Changying's own mother passed away in her youth, she relied on her older sister, who came to stay with her immediately after the birth, along with her three sisters-in-law.

As the first of four daughters-in-law to bear a son, the birth elevated Changying's position in her mother-in-law's eyes. Such a boost was badly needed, as the rather conservative elder woman was prone to making derogatory comments about Changying, attributed to her daughter-in-law being an "outsider"—that is, hailing from another province. Her petty and mean attitude possibly stemmed from insecurity about her own future due to her son's independent choice of his wife, as well as her suspicions about Changying's long-term reliability as a daughter-in-law.

However, Changying was highly respected by her sisters-in-law, who perceived her as educated and worldly, and because she was quite generous with her savings (remittances). For example, she and her husband gave the most generous wedding gift (5,000CNY) to his younger brother at his wedding. Through frequent gifts of clothes and household goods bought with her savings, Changying eventually won the favor not just of her brothers- and sisters-in-law, but even her critical mother-in-law. Further, each year Changying gave 1,000CNY to her widowed elderly father, who still lived in her natal village and was cared for by her coresident younger brother and his wife. Although she knew her husband objected to this practice, Changying explained that he never voiced complaint because, "after all, it is my money to spend as I please."

Changying remained in the countryside for just over a year after giving birth, before returning to Beijing with her son, to reunite with her husband. For the next few years, the nuclear family rented a one-room shack in a migrant enclave on Beijing's outer limits. The conditions were rudimentary—there was no heat/air-conditioning or refrigerator, and water had to be fetched from a pump shared with ten other families, located at the end of an alleyway. But when I paid them a visit in 2006, Changying quipped, "at least the roof doesn't leak"!

Changying relied on her social network of former colleagues to find new work as a teacher at another school for children of migrant workers, operated by a charitable organization, and enrolled her son in its preschool program. The job paid well, about 1,300CNY per month, on the condition that Changying make progress toward earning a *dazhuan* through self-study. To do so, Changying had first returned to her hometown—her place of *hukou* registration—to take the national qualifying exam, which she successfully passed in 2005 on her second attempt. When I met with her in 2006, she had already completed a year's worth of independent-study courses. Each day, mother and son rode on a bicycle to school. After school, Changying cooked their dinner on a small coal-burning stove outside while her son played with neighborhood kids. Later he practiced characters or did sums by the light of one lamp while she attended to her studies. Mother and son slept together on the one-pallet mattress. Changying's husband stayed overnight at whatever construction site he worked at elsewhere in the city, returning just once each month. Such an arrangement led some of her female neighbors, also migrants, to tease Changying: "Are you divorced?!"

In 2008, Changying changed jobs, joining the faculty of a private elementary school on the city outskirts, which catered to children of better-off migrant workers, and again enrolled her son at the school. The new job paid well and, more importantly, it provided accommodations. By saving on rent and working extra as a tutor on nights and weekends, Changying could earn as much as 2,000CNY per month, matching her husband's earnings in construction.

Like Ruolan, Changying remained close to her natal family in addition to providing financial support. Traditionally, a wife should spend the Chinese New Year with her own family (that is, her husband's parents), and only visit her natal home after the holiday. However, Changying bucked convention and regularly spent the entire holiday in her natal village. When, in 2006, her sixty-year-old father decided he could no longer get along with his son's wife back in the village, Changying intervened to smooth over relations. She arranged for her father to join her own husband in construction in Beijing, and the two men shared rental accommodations near the construction site.

In late 2008, the construction frenzy of the lead-up to the Beijing Olympics dissipated, and construction jobs grew scarce. Changying's husband and his brothers eventually migrated to remote Gansu Province for work, and Changying then returned to the village and her mother-in-law. Drawing upon her savings and her extensive education experience, Changying established a community kindergarten. By 2010 the school was quite lucrative, and she was earning about 800CNY monthly. She sent her son to board at an elementary school in a nearby township, where he would have the chance to attend a decent middle school and perhaps even high school in the county-town. Despite living and working in the village, Changying and her husband still had not renovated their village dwelling, as migrants typically do, intending to settle in the village upon retirement. Rather, like Ruolan, Changying planned to buy property in the nearest county-town, where she hoped their son would eventually attend a key middle school and later enter into high school. Property ownership would enable Changying's family to transfer their *hukous*, and enroll her son in the public school system without being charged nonlocal *hukou* tuition and fees.

Meanwhile, the couple loaned a large sum of money to Changying's brothers-in-law, to enable them to renovate their homes, and Changying also loaned some money to her own brother for the same purpose. The home renovations would further enable and obligate the brothers to fulfill their filial responsibilities to care for Changying's aging mother-in-law and her father. As symbols of Changying's filial devotion (*ganqing*), the loans allowed her to live independently without being perceived as unfilial, and also raised her status among her natal and marital kin.

YARUI

Yarui's story is especially poignant. After marrying her fiancé, she suffered a miscarriage during her second pregnancy late in 2007, which she believed was triggered by anxiety she felt about a precarious living situation. At the time, the couple was renting an apartment on the outskirts of Beijing. Yarui's husband co-owned a flat with his ex-wife, who refused to relinquish her share of the property. She both refused to vacate "her" rooms in the apartment and to co-reside with her ex-husband and his new wife. Yarui's retired in-laws also owned a large apartment in Beijing, which they had purchased from their work unit and now shared with their eldest son and his wife, a childless couple. When I met with Yarui in Beijing in June 2008, she expressed frustration both at the housing situation and her weak reproductive system. She ominously intoned that, "without a child, this marriage will not survive." Yarui no doubt felt pressure to bear a child in a timely manner in order to gain her in-laws' trust and acceptance, all the more difficult as a rural bride and as their son's second wife. Her husband also desired a child. Yet, Yarui also said she was lucky to have an unusually generous husband, who was willing to help out his wife's siblings from the countryside. In 2008, Yarui's younger brother decided to come to Beijing for work, accompanied by his young wife and child. Yarui's husband arranged for them to stay in the contested flat, without revealing to his ex-wife their true identity as his new wife's kin! During my visit in 2008, I also met Yarui's younger sister, who was staying with Yarui while completing a summer internship as a preschool teacher. I learned that Yarui was paying her younger sister's tuition and board at a residential high school in the provincial capital, where she would graduate with a *zhongzhuan* degree in early childhood education. Yarui's younger sister told me, "My sister is so good to me; she never says 'no' and gives me a lot."

In 2009, Yarui successfully carried to term a healthy baby boy. Unlike Ruolan and Changying, she gave birth in a Beijing hospital, paying out of pocket as her husband's insurance did not cover her maternal care, due to her nonlocal *hukou*. (However, the insurance did provide care for the newborn.) Yarui's father-in-law was especially thrilled to have a grandchild finally. According to Yarui, her sister-in-law was a "modern woman" because she chose to remain childless, not wanting to be burdened by the demands of motherhood. When I visited Yarui and her baby in 2010, the housing situation had improved slightly. Her husband's ex-wife had accepted their offer of some compensation and vacated the apartment, and it was being renovated in preparation for Yarui, her husband, and their son to move in. Yarui's younger sister had come back to Beijing to help care for the new baby, and had stayed on after finding a job as a kindergarten teacher, sharing the apartment with her sister, brother-in-law, and new nephew.

Having quit work soon after getting pregnant, Yarui now spent her days caring for her infant, helped by her sister in the evenings. She spent the daytime in the in-laws' more spacious apartment, and took her lunch with her retired father-in-law, who was affectionate with his grandson; sometimes he took the baby for a stroll in the carriage while Yarui did laundry or napped. At the end of the day, Yarui returned to the rental flat, and cooked dinner for her sister and herself, leaving leftovers for her husband who worked long and irregular hours. Unfortunately, Yarui's mother-in-law continued to be aloof and even rude to her daughter-in-law from the countryside, derogatorily calling Yarui *tu* ("rustic"), and spending her days playing mahjong with her friends rather than helping out with childcare or cooking. Through her unkind words and refusal to enter into a reciprocal relationship with Yarui, the mother-in-law symbolically rejected Yarui as a legitimate daughter-in-law, to Yarui's great distress.

Shuqin

In Shuqin's household, intimacy was frequently compromised because she, her husband, and their daughter shared a small, cramped three-bedroom, one-bath apartment with his elderly mother, his sister-in-law, and her son. Shuqin's husband was in the unenviable position of moderating tensions among his aging mother and his sprightly wife as well as his cantankerous older sister, herself divorced with child. In such situations, he would avoid taking sides, and disappear until tensions abated. When pressed, he readily conceded to his wife's wishes against his sister's demands, but rarely to his mother's wishes against his wife's demands. Fortunately, there was little tension between his wife and mother. Nonetheless, the couple was dissatisfied with their living arrangements. Shuqin once expressed her opinion that her husband, as the only son, had more right to his parents' property than his sister, invoking patriarchal tradition to serve her own interest and ignoring the law on equal inheritance. Shuqin and her husband both contributed their earnings to the joint family household, but their combined income was insufficient to afford their own apartment. However, during Shuqin's pregnancy until just after the birth of their daughter in 2004, the couple lived in a rental home, joined by Shuqin's mother and her sister Shuchun, who assisted with postnatal care. In retrospect, Shuqin spoke fondly of her confinement as a period of independent living and freedom from serving others.

After her 2001 wedding, Shuqin had continued to work in hotel housekeeping up until her pregnancy. During this time, she was the major breadwinner for her household, while her unemployed husband upgraded his knowledge by enrolling in technical training courses, earning a certificate in tourism. When Shuqin was forced to leave her job due to pregnancy, her husband found temporary work. In 2004, Shuqin reentered the workforce, and by 2006 she was in a management position at a state-owned hotel. The regular 8 a.m. to 5 p.m., Monday to Saturday schedule allowed her to be home each night with her family. Shuqin enrolled her toddler in a subsidized daycare affiliated with her (retired) mother-in-law's work unit, which also employed Shuqin's sister-in-law.[6]

During summer months and holidays when that daycare facility closed, Shuqin arranged for ad-hoc childcare by involving her mother-in-law, sister-in-law, husband, and even her sister Shuchun. But, during the 2007 Lunar New Year holiday, no one was available to provide childcare, so Shuqin was forced to quit her job and stay home. Fortunately, by this time her husband had steady work as a construction site supervisor. Shuqin envied wealthy women who could afford to be "full-time mothers," and worried that her daughter did not receive adequate nutrition in the daycare facility. But she also felt it was boring to be a full-time caregiver. Moreover, she aimed to earn more money so that her family could live better. Thus, within a month, when the daycare facility reopened, she had already found employment at another hotel, also as a housekeeping manager. Half of her salary (1,600CNY) went to the daycare facility, the other half to household living expenses. Still, it was enough to allow her to support her husband again while he invested in the courses of study necessary to earn a driver's license and become certified as a taxi driver.

When I visited Shuqin in 2010, her situation had improved greatly. Although her job kept her extremely busy and made her exhausted, Shuqin enjoyed the salary and perks of being in management. I watched a video taken by her sister of a banquet Shuqin arranged (on discount) earlier that year at the hotel restaurant to celebrate her husband's sister's remarriage, attended by Shuqin's affinal relatives (and her sister). Shuqin's relationship with her sister-in-law, who had gained a new apartment (and a second teenage child) with remarriage, seemed quite amicable. Though Shuqin herself still lacked a local, Beijing *hukou* (which she said required ten years of Beijing residency after marriage) and related benefits like health insurance, she was hopeful of having these within a few more years. Her husband received health benefits, which extended to their daughter, through his former work unit. Their daughter attended a public kindergarten, so Shuqin no longer needed to pay for daycare. Furthermore, her husband had some flexibility as a taxi driver, and was available to drop off and pick up their daughter from school each day, allowing Shuqin flexibility to attend to her very demanding job in hotel-restaurant management.

SHUCHUN

With her (re)marriage in 2009, Shuqin's elder sister Shuchun likewise seemed more content. She no longer needed to sleep in a stuffy and crowded dormitory shared with other housekeeping staff. She had reached the supervisory level at her job, and earned 1,200CNY per month plus overtime. As a loyal long-term employee of the hotel, she received perks that pleased her, including an annual New Year's gala, a weekend outing to a wilderness spot, and a three-day trip to Shanghai during the 2010 World Expo to help at another branch of the hotel. However, her workday was now quite long. Each day she arose at 5 a.m. and commuted 1.5 hours from the apartment shared with her in-laws on the far outskirts of Beijing to the tourist hotel in the city's center where she worked. From Monday through Saturday, Shuchun usually ate both lunch and dinner at the hotel staff canteen. Her husband, who had been unemployed for about two years before their marriage, had finally found steady factory work. Her in-laws warmly welcomed her into their household. Shuchun proudly explained that her mother in-law did all of the food shopping and cooking, a reversal of traditional role expectations that conveyed the older woman's appreciation for Shuqin's financial contributions to the household and respectful acceptance of her son's bride.

However, the future will hold definite challenges. Like Yarui's husband, Shuchun's husband also has a brother who has equal claim to their parent's property. Their family was originally from the countryside, but when the military transferred the father to Beijing to take up a new post, only the younger brother was eligible for the city *hukou*. The older brother remained in the countryside with his family, farming the family's plot of land. Shuchun's father in-law suffers from Alzheimer's, and will need extensive care in the coming years. Two years after her marriage, Shuchun became pregnant. She quit her job and relocated to her natal home in north China, where her local *hukou* registration entitles her to affordable medical care and hospitalization.

Shuqin and Shuchun had always been close to their parents and their younger brothers, and remained so even after their marriages. The sisters' financial support was critical to their siblings' economic success and social mobility. On his sisters' recommendation back in 2000, their eldest brother had been hired onto the janitorial night shift at the four-star hotel in Beijing. Eventually he went to Shenzhen, where he worked several years as a supervisor at a facilities and security firm contracted to a large state-owned company, earning up to 3,000CNY per month. The sisters also supported their younger brother to study auto mechanics and earn a driver's license in their home county. In 2004, the brothers and their parents pooled their savings to purchase a two-story apartment house in the county-town (a former township that had been newly designated a "small city") nearest to their natal village. Shuchun contributed a 10,000CNY loan toward the 180,000CNY purchase. Their parents moved into the apartment along with their youngest son. Their purchase of property and relocation enabled the sisters to transfer their *hukou* to the prefectural city and change its type to "urban" (i.e., nonagricultural), which they heard would help their application for a transfer of *hukou* to Beijing. Also in 2004, their father purchased a van and, helped by his youngest son, began a small-scale transport business, shuttling goods and people between the prefectural city and townships and hotel accommodations.

Postmarital Aspirations and Realities

Having experienced modern courtship and freely chosen their marital partners, all five of my key informants expected conjugal intimacy and autonomy after marriage. Yet, nuclear households, which would be most conducive to these rather personal goals, were difficult to establish and maintain due to economic deprivation, lack of affordable health care and housing, the volatility of the informal labor market, and obstacles to obtaining reliable childcare and public education for their children. Against such challenges, flexible household structures and divisions of labor were strategies they adopted to incrementally boost their families' economic and social standing. These innovative arrangements enabled my informants to continue working after marriage and childbirth, and thereby fulfill their new aspirations. They were also empowered to renegotiate intrafamilial relationships to their advantage. However, these negotiations also gave rise to much emotional and physical stress.

Initially after marriage, all five women continued working in Beijing. But as none had (nor ever obtained) health insurance or maternity benefits through their employers, each was forced to quit work to give birth. They similarly faced the difficult decision of where to give birth: in Beijing or in their place of household registration. Due to financial and hospital access constraints, Ruolan and Changying both opted to receive maternity and postnatal care in the countryside, and so endured extended separations from their migrant-worker husbands, until their newborns were sufficiently weaned and grown. Yarui and Shuqin both chose to give birth in Beijing, to be near their husbands, but they paid a high cost, not only for out-of-pocket hospital care but also to provide accommodation for their attending female kin. Shuchun, who bore a child 2011, ought to have benefited from a 2009 directive aimed at providing reproductive and maternity care to rural women working away from their place of *hukou* registration. However, like related schemes initiated under the government's agenda to provide universal health care by 2020, the plan has not effectively reached migrants, because medical reimbursements to providers and consumers continue to be linked to the household registration system (Qiu et al. 2011; Selden and Wu 2011). So Shuchun too returned to her place of household registration to spend her maternity period under the care of her mother.

In general, the households formed after marriage by Ruolan and Changying were especially unstable. For years, the women and their young children made do with cramped rented flats in migrant enclaves among the working poor, while their husbands roomed in dormitories at their work sites. When they left Beijing to settle back in the villages or towns and small cities in their home provinces while husbands remained in Beijing or migrated further afield (e.g., to Gansu), their families endured even longer durations and distances of separation. Such divided households caused emotional strain to couples and children. Both women implicitly trusted their husbands' fidelity, but worried for their husbands' well-being. Ruolan admitted feeling concerned about her husband's indulgence in drink and card games (i.e., gambling) on his weekly day off, but reassured herself that he needed an outlet to relieve stress and homesickness, living apart from his wife and child. The mothers also strove to prevent estrangement between absent fathers and children. Nonetheless, Ruolan's husband complained to me in 2010 that his son no longer recognized him when he returned home for an annual New Year's visit. These situations also placed a heavy burden on working mothers to balance wage work and childcare without support of their husbands or access to social services. Their sole responsibility for childcare on top of their long hours of paid labor sometimes made them dependent on the labor of others, particularly female kin. Among other reasons, the need for childcare assistance motivated their relocation from Beijing to places nearer to such caregivers, forfeiting lucrative employment and compromising their autonomy.

My informants who married into urban families did not automatically gain a solid foothold in the city, as might be expected. Previously married and un(der)-

employed husbands especially were in no position to provide their new wives with a neolocal residence separate from in-laws, as is increasingly common among young newlyweds in rural villages, who likewise desire conjugal autonomy (Y. Yan 2003). Sisters Shuqin and Shuchun made do with nicely renovated bridal suites as part of stem households. (In the latter's case, the renovation had been undertaken for the first wife.) Living in a rental property near her in-laws' home, Yarui's situation was precarious for several years, but had turned promising, as she anticipated living as a nuclear household. Because of their inferior social status, rural women who married into urban families were susceptible to a range of prejudices and even mistreatment by their new kin. They preempted or countered negativism by proving themselves to be industrious, frugal, and deferent daughters-in-law as well as virtuous wives and good mothers. Bearing a child, especially a son, soon after marriage was another means both to win their in-laws' hearts and set their minds at ease, dispelling (prejudicial) fears of runaway brides from "outside."

Flexible household and domestic labor arrangements enabled these women to continue with migrant work after marriage and childbirth, which in turn afforded them greater leverage and status within their households and wider kin groups. With the exception of Yarui, who was estranged from her in-laws until the birth of her son, most of these women contributed financially to their in-laws' households, whether they were coresident with them or not. Shuqin and eventually Shuchun contributed half their wages directly to their extended families' household budgets. Further, they took care not to overly burden their mothers-in-law financially or physically by electing to eat most of their meals at their places of employment. Ruolan and Changying both gave gifts of cash and goods directly to their in-laws and also helped with housework or farm work during their visits. All four women provided emotional care and physical labor to their in-laws, which indirectly produced economic value. Finally, by offering wages as loans, Changying, together with her husband, has helped his siblings and their households to grow and prosper.

Importantly, these forms of economic capital gave these migrant women a fair amount of power in their relationships with in-laws, without compromising their image as good daughters-in-law. In return for their generosity, they have gained respect, admiration, and, above all, reciprocity from affinal kin, especially important as they relied upon female kin for childcare provision. Thus Shuqin views her large financial contribution to her joint family household to be mutually beneficial, because her mother-in-law provides meals and childcare for her granddaughter, and sometimes Shuqin's sister-in-law lends a hand. Further, Shuqin is exempt from providing personal care to her mother-in-law, who prefers to rely on her own daughter (who was coresident until 2010).

In addition, all of these women have continued to provide financial support as needed to their birth parents and siblings, even after their exit from these households at marriage, against convention and despite the objections of their spouses. Doing so has enhanced their social standing among their natal families, while improving the latter's socioeconomic standing. In addition, and probably more importantly, these women have aided their natal families and communities by helping to extend social networks from the village to the city. Patrilocal marriage and hypergamy have long been conduits for expanding social networks in rural China; today these networks may extend further afield. Informants married to Beijing men have been especially well positioned to provide temporary accommodations and job introductions to their siblings and covillagers. Migrant women of course benefit from maintaining close connections with their natal households, both emotionally and materially, such as during and after childbirth.

Flexible households and creative divisions of labor within the household have helped these migrant women to work toward a central goal of improving their conjugal family's socioeconomic status and securing their children's brighter future. Given their own limited economic pathways and their unquestioned identities as primary caregivers, these women were pragmatic in investing in their husbands' careers on the one hand and their children's educations on the other. At various times, all but Yarui have taken turns being the primary breadwinner in their household, to enable husbands to return to school and learn new skills, or search for new jobs after unemployment, or start new business ventures. Some have also endured the hardships of prolonged separation from their spouse and the burden of sole caregiver to meet this goal.

Over the years, the women have variously adjusted their employment and even their place of residence to accommodate their children's educational needs amid the biased educational environment created by state policy. Without local urban *hukou,* migrant children still have limited options for education in Beijing. As a result, most migrant parents leave their school-age children in the countryside, in the care of grandparents or other kin. Yet this solution does not appeal to young mothers influenced by modern ideas of childbearing and childrearing, which reinforce the state's modernization agenda and objectives of improving population quality. They worried that grandparents will only spoil their grandchildren and cannot adequately supervise their academic studies. Rather, they aim for their children to attend relatively better quality schools in urban areas, which receive the lion's share of state educational investments. By strategically concentrating their resources on their children's educations, these mothers expect their children will go further academically and thus reap greater economic opportunities in the future. Indeed, Ruolan and Changying both intend to send their sons to university. Through selfless provision of resources to ensure their children's future success, these women and their husbands also secure their own futures, as they can one day expect to receive their filial children's reciprocal support (Fong 2004). Such strategic planning simultaneously reflects and fosters the state's neoliberal approach to social welfare that emphasizes family responsibility.

Summary

Migration greatly impacted the views and behaviors of my rural migrant women informants in regard to courtship, marriage, and family. Migration allowed them to assert more control over the timing of their marriage and choice of marriage partner, to experiment with an emergent dating culture, and to pursue a better match than otherwise possible. Raised expectations of the future and demands for a partner with good conditions reflected their increasing sense of self-worth and achievement. It also manifested their ambitions to make something of themselves by taking advantage of the opportunities for social mobility through marriage provided by living away from home and in the more commercialized urban environment. Their emphasis on mutual affection as a basis of marriage in turn provided a moral framework within which to justify both their desires for material betterment, and the behaviors, such as premarital sex, necessary to attain that goal (Farrer 2002). They were also able to counter urban stereotypes of rural brides as mercenary and conniving. These changes in viewpoints and behaviors challenged patriarchal authority vested in parents and rural elders, and demonstrated migrant women's agency in matters of sexuality, dating, and marriage.

However, pursuing romance away from the village was rather risky, and marriage to urban men was a rarity. Ultimately, most migrant women return to the village to settle down, as did Qiaolian and Xiaofang. Exceptional women like my key informants who married fellow migrants or urbanites could continue with migrant work after marriage. But maintaining employment during pregnancy and while raising a child proved especially difficult, due to the many economic and social disadvantages that stemmed from their status as migrants. Migrant working wives and mothers met such challenges by adopting flexible household and division-of-labor arrangements, which in turn propelled them into new and often unconventional gender roles and identities, including as scientific mothers and household managers, as moneylenders and entrepreneurs, and even as primary breadwinners. These roles in turn enabled them to renegotiate traditional expectations of daughters and daughters-in-law and the distribution of power in the family to their own advantage. Despite living in extended-family households or temporarily divided households, they have successfully maintained their relatively autonomous conjugal families and egalitarian companionate marriages.

My informants may seem to epitomize the traditional feminine virtue of self-sacrifice, putting the needs of their nuclear family before their own, but closer inspection complicates this picture and indicates their agency and individualism. Terminating a pregnancy due to financial insecurity, becoming the family breadwinner temporarily to support a husband's career change, and raising a son apart from his father were carefully plotted strategies they devised to maximize their household's income and ensure a secure future amid social and economic instability and inequality. At present, these informants aspire for their families to join the new "middle class," indicated by urban residence and home ownership, steady and lucrative employment, social insurance, and a well-educated child (L. Zhang 2010). Achieving such markers of status and identity will require the state to fully dismantle remaining barriers to migrants' settlement in cities and assimilation into urban society, and address the needs of the migrant working class.

Conclusion
The Changing Lives of Rural Women

During a Chinese New Year visit to Qiaolian's natal village back in 1999, Qiaolian's mother gave me a precious gift of handwoven and dyed batik cloth, which she had kept stored in a trunk. Qiaolian and I admired the intricate handiwork of the faded material as we listened to her mother's moving account of how, as a young woman, she labored into the night weaving and dying this material. On her wedding day, she used the material to bundle together her meager dowry, just a spare outfit and a few jewels, which she carried over her shoulder as she walked to her husband's village, where she would live with his parents as their new daughter-in-law. Hearing of my interest in handwoven cloth, Qiaolian's aunts gave me samples of their textiles. Produced in an era of relative scarcity and thrift, when hand-sewn clothes were the norm, such textiles were no longer valued in the market economy, with its convenient ready-made fashion. They were meaningful only as nostalgic representations of women's youth and former skills.

The story evoked by the gift of cloth emphasized to me the different trajectories of two generations of rural Chinese women, whose lives were conditioned by the distinct historical contexts, and related gender configurations, in which each came of age. Raised under revolutionary socialism, Qiaolian's mother left her natal village only at marriage, and did not venture very far. Her wedding ceremony reflected the socialist ethic of frugality during leaner times. Her modest dowry showcased her handicraft skills and industriousness, qualities certain to recommend her as both a housewife and worker in her husband's agricultural collective. Her daughter, raised under market socialism, left the village initially to work in distant Beijing, in the service sector, and to continue with her studies toward a college degree. She explored different jobs and even helped start a business; she adopted a more feminine and up-to-date appearance and she continued to learn. In her mid-twenties, through her social network, she was introduced to an educated man, a schoolteacher from a town near her home. After marriage, she collaborated with her husband to establish an elementary school that could serve the villages outside the town.

Revolutionary socialism incited rural women to become productive workers and loyal citizens of the party-state. The new society improved women's lives in myriad ways, including promoting literacy and combating forced marriages, opening occupations and political roles to them that were formerly reserved for men, and extolling gender equality even in matters of appearance and dress. Despite such achievements, gender equality remained a distant ideal. In particular, women were still held responsible for the domestic sphere as "virtuous wives and good mothers" and thus not treated as equals to men in the workplace (whether farm or factory). A patrilineal-patrilocal marriage and family system continued to disadvantage women in regard to resource distribution in the family and household as well as in the male-dominated public institutions of work units and collectives.

China's shift to a market economy and opening to global capitalism presented rural women with alternative and plentiful possibilities for their futures. Their generation could imagine and, to varying degrees, also experience, living independently away from home and family, working for a wage and for a boss, and building a social network and accruing social capital and status. They could also develop their talents through technical training or higher education, experiment with cultures of consumption and dating, choose a spouse independently of go-betweens, marry far from the village, and advance toward a middle-class lifestyle. Once again, many of these options were previously available only to men. For example, Shuqin once shared with me her happy childhood memory of running down the mountainside from her village to greet her father and uncles returning from weeks of toiling in the coal mines of north central China, and reaching inside their pockets for gifts of sweets. Then she proudly intoned, "Now, I'm the returning villager whom the kids run to for presents!" Indeed, each year since 2004 she and her sister have returned to their natal home together—by airplane! However, the shift to market socialism also presents new obstacles to improving rural women's lives. As a consequence of so many choices, as well as challenges, what it means to be a rural woman and how a rural woman should behave, and the progress of gender equality, are in rapid flux.

In this book I have described the experiences of young women like Qiaolian who migrated to Beijing from rural villages during the 1990s and early 2000s to help spearhead China's economic development and growth in the era of reform and opening. Gender is integral to their experiences of migration and modernity, which in turn have profoundly impacted gender roles, identities, and relations. These young women forged new paths out of the village and made their own way in the city. At every step, they encountered discrimination as migrants who traversed the rigid ideological and administrative rural-urban boundary, as menial laborers in an emergent capitalist system of class inequality, and also as women subjected to patriarchal gender ideologies and structural gender inequality. In particular, the restrictive policies and regulations tied to the household registration system and the rural-urban class divide it helps maintain served as a barrier. The constraints of the patrilineal-patrilocal marriage and family system and a gender-biased labor market also limited their livelihood options, their settlement possibilities, their marital prospects, and hence their futures. These first-generation migrants also bore the burden of relative educational and economic deprivation. Thus they contributed most of their hard-earned wages to their natal households, where they were applied to siblings' school fees, to medical expenses, or to pay down farm debts. In time, each also faced the inevitability of marriage that results from social pressure to form a family as well as pragmatic concerns for their future economic security. As wives and mothers they encountered the additional difficulty of balancing wage work with domestic obligations, and balancing family unity with the flexible household configurations required to achieve socioeconomic mobility through continuing to migrate for work.

The uniquely migrant-centered and longitudinal approach of this multisited study highlights the intersection of structure and agency as revealed in the minutiae of everyday social relations and interactions, in multiple social contexts, including the workplace and the domestic sphere, and at various times in an individual's life. My research indicates these women were not powerless victims but participants who determinedly seized upon new economic and social opportunities presented by market socialism and made them personally meaningful and beneficial. As agents, they creatively drew upon available resources to understand and navigate the complex situations and environments they encountered through migration. They used their individual backgrounds and personalities; their various and shifting social relationships, roles, and identities; as well as ideologies of difference (i.e., gender, rural-urban, and cultural quality) to negotiate authority vested in rural elders, employers, urbanites, and state representatives. In this way they gained personal advantages and furthered their own evolving aims. Particular strategies they deployed included augmenting their natal families' wealth and status, by which they garnered security and prestige, and cultivating social networks that connected them to more desirable jobs and marriage prospects. They also carefully selected future spouses who shared their vision of social mobility and made smart economic and emotional investments in their spouses, children, and affine kin, in return for practical support and respect for autonomy.

Overall, I conclude that migration promotes agency and advances gender equality by creating more opportunities for young rural women to make money, learn new skills or further their education, earn recognition and respect for their contributions to their rural households and communities, and exercise greater control in matters of marriage and family. However, I also find that individual migrant women's empowerment is not necessarily or always aligned with the goals of gender or sociospatial equality, nor sufficient to dismantle durable structures and enduring discourses of inequality. Further, I observe that the capacity for these women to develop agency by grasping and utilizing novel possibilities offered through migration increased with experience over time. Yet as the opportunities available at particular moments of the life course vary, so too agency does not simply increase or decrease with age. Rather, individuals draw upon their experience to capably respond to the given circumstances. For example, in their teens and early twenties, my informants were naïve and vulnerable, and subordinate to authority figures such as parents and employers. Yet their youthful energy and beauty were assets in the labor market and consumer culture, and they deployed them for personal gain and empowerment. Into their thirties, they had the advantages of knowledge, skills, and resources accumulated through extensive experience of migration and work to help them to discern among options and make informed decisions, as well as generational authority over their children and others. But their youthful advantages declined, and their responsibilities as working wives and mothers were complicated, requiring more complex negotiations and compromises to meet expectations, fulfill desires, and maintain some autonomy.

I explored in Chapters 1 and 2 how rural women are rendered structurally and symbolically marginal in development and modernization discourse and policy, in the labor market and urban society, as well as in their households and families, as a result of social constructions of gender and occupational hierarchies, patrilineal-patrilocal kinship practices, and the sociospatial class divide maintained by the *hukou* system. Paradoxically, these disadvantages produce new desires and the impetus for change, as young rural women aspire to become more modern and improve their cultural quality by leaving the village for the city, and by rejecting agriculture to take up the menial jobs offered to them. Through migration they join social networks and become migration brokers, service workers and wage earners, savvy consumers and cosmopolitans, or even college students and service managers, as described in Chapters 3, 4, and 5 respectively. These new roles and identities instill young rural women with self-confidence and assert their significance to economic development and modernization while challenging their exclusion from urban society. Further, their remittances of wages and consumer goods as well as information enhance their social standing in the family and household and among their rural community.

Chapters 3, 4, and 5 also demonstrated the micro-strategies by which migrant women manipulate the patriarchal power of parents and rural elders, employers, and representatives of urban society and the state in order to ensure desired outcomes of their migration decisions: a safe journey and successful search for work, decent wages and a tolerable work environment, and eventual integration into the middle class. Their efforts are often contradictory; in their struggle to advance their own interests, young migrant women sometimes subvert and at other times reinforce normative constructions of gender and rural-urban difference that rationalize and perpetuate structural gender and sociospatial inequality. For example, young migrant women's involvement in social networks and *guanxi* relationship building subjected them to indirect patriarchal control over their behavior while away from home through enforcement of standards of female respectability, even as such activities increased their public visibility and value to their households and the rural community. Similarly, young migrant women took pleasure and power in emulating modern fashions and urban lifestyles, as it enabled them to better blend into urban society and even move out of menial jobs, yet such practices promoted stereotypes of femininity and rusticity that reinforced gender and rural-urban hierarchies. Further, their tactics and successes were individual and inadequate to dismantle durable structures of inequality, such as the *hukou* system and gender-discriminatory labor market. Thus their impact could only be ephemeral; ultimately young migrant women sought out marriage in order to secure their future.

Nonetheless, rural women's changing visions of themselves and their futures, gleaned through labor migration, reflected awareness of other possibilities for being-in-the-world that formed a basis for social change, starting with their own lives. Migration is a process that unfolds across the individual life course, and indeed all of my informants documented personal growth and self-transformation over time. As Chapter 6 especially makes clear, migration significantly impacted rural migrant women's perspectives and behaviors in regard to courtship, marriage, and family formation, as well as postmarital gender identities, roles, and relations. My findings show that, over the long-term, migration especially empowers some rural women and advances gender equality by enabling greater autonomy in courtship and marriage. Migration also supports more egalitarian, companionate marriages, strengthens the position of the daughter-in-law in the patrilineal family, and encourages nonnormative gender divisions of labor in the household, such as the wife as breadwinner. However, migration also introduces rural women to middle-class expectations of scientific mothering that reinscribe women in the domestic sphere as managers of their children's development. Further, the instability of the migrant labor market and the high cost of housing, medical care, and children's education for "outsiders" in the city forced migrant women to endure long separations from their husbands, which increased their domestic burden and no doubt put stress on their marital relationship, or forced them to sacrifice conjugal independence to reside with in-laws in a more traditional household arrangement.

Situating women's experiences of labor migration and its impact on identity and agency within the wider social relations of family and kinship as well as the individual's life course is a unique contribution of this book to a growing literature on migrant women workers in contemporary China. Significant works have focused on industrial relations and labor politics through investigations of women factory workers in China's export manufacturing industries (e.g., C. K. Lee 1998; Pun 2005; Feng Xu 2000), or of migrant women workers in domestic service (e.g., Sun 2009; H. Yan 2008), hotel hospitality (Otis 2011), and home-based enterprises (L. Zhang 2000). Others look outside the workplace to encompass migrant women's use of urban space and technology (e.g., Wallis 2013) and to compare the experiences and identities of two cohorts (i.e., single and married) of migrant women in the city (Jacka 2006). Broadening the scope to encompass household and family, kinship and social networks, and urban space and consumer culture in addition to informal-sector service work, and by adopting a longitudinal perspective, this study illuminates migration as a process that impacts rural women's identity and agency in multiple contexts and over time. Such an approach furthers our understanding of migrant women's complex and context-dependent agency and empowerment.

Migration creates a position of ambivalence that can lead to critical insight as rural women compare and contrast their community of origin with their destination society. They also may evaluate their past experiences and selves against their lives in the present as well as the different gender configurations of the places and times in which they have lived. For example, in a conversation with Yarui in 2002, she spoke of hurt feelings after being bullied by her Beijing coworkers, who called her an "outsider" behind her back. She surmised: "In an ideal society, everyone would be equal, like they were under socialism." Yet in the next breath, she reconsidered: "Society must be socially stratified, like feudal society [was], and not stay as under communism, or life would be boring and pointless." She elaborated that society required internal friction to stimulate "differences of opinion" that would create a more interesting society. Then she gave the example of her family as a "typically feudal" one that, I presumed, met the requirements of so-called internal friction: "At home, no one can be seated at the dinner table until my grandfather has sat down, and no one dares to pick up their chopsticks until he has raised his rice bowl to his lips."

It could be that Yarui was reflecting on the social changes wrought by market socialism and their impact on the lives of rural women in particular. Market socialism offered Yarui a new direction in life and a different fate than previously available. By choosing to migrate, then pursuing romances in the workplace, and finally marrying and settling down in Beijing, Yarui challenged the gender and generational inequality characteristic of her rural household and family, which she envisioned as a holdover from the (mythic) feudal past. But as a rural migrant and menial worker in the city, she was disadvantaged relative to urban coworkers and employers, who treated her as an outsider and an inferior. No wonder she voiced ambivalence about her plight and that of contemporary society generally.

For much of China's history, patriarchal kinship and family determined women's identity and destiny. Socialist revolution provided possibilities for rural women beyond the domestic sphere as determined by a patriarchal state. In contemporary China, neoliberal capitalism opens up seemingly endless opportunities for self-making and greater space for autonomy and individualism (Y. Yan 2010), yet it creates new vulnerabilities due to market competition. This system also creates new inequalities rooted in development policies and institutional practices, including the household registration system and the discriminatory labor market, and ideological constructions of gender and sociospatial difference. The ethnographic evidence presented in this book, particularly the stories of my key informants, provides hope for China's future. Through small accomplishments in their own lives, rural migrant women are gaining traction and moving ahead.

NOTES

Introduction

1. The Chinese term literally means "protector mother" or "swaddling mother," and is perhaps best translated as "dry-nurse," one of two forms of "menial mothers" of the late imperial-republican periods that also included the "wet-nurse" (*ruma, naima*) (Lieberman 1998: 158–159). In the late Qing, dry nurses were usually mature women who had borne children and who were hired to care for the children of elites and might also perform routine domestic work. In southern China, they were called *amah* (Mandarin *aiyi*), a term still in use today. In contemporary parlance, *baomu* generally refers to the young rural women employed in urban households as full-time, live-in maids or nannies. I translate *baomu* as "domestic worker" rather than the more pejorative "maid," unless the text is meant to convey such a connotation. Feminists use the term "domestic worker" to promote recognition of maids and nannies as rightful workers, not servants or slaves.

2. As I explain below, institutional barriers to permanent settlement, especially in the largest cities, force millions of people in China to "float" between rural and urban spaces, hence the term "floating population." Note that the term incorrectly suggests that people migrate "blindly," as aimless drifters or vagrants. Dutton (1998: 63–65) traces the etymology of the term to negative associations with social disorder or chaos, as in "hooligan" (*liumang*). The rural women who are the subjects of this book are considered temporary residents no matter their length of stay in the city because their household registration remains in the place of origin. By contrast, those whose migration entails a change of official registration are indicated by the term *qianyi renkou,* more akin to the English term "immigrant." Approximately 262 million people living and working in urban China in 2012 lacked the local household registration ("Migrant Workers" 2013). Legal and illegal statuses further distinguish among "migrants" as I use the term. The latter include those lacking documentation, stable shelter, and stable employment (i.e., the "three-withouts" [*sanwu*]).

3. Overall migration patterns since the 1980s have followed economic indicators, as labor flows from poorer, inland regions (primarily in China's central and western regions) to the wealthier, eastern and southern seaboards, and, within the eastern region, concentrating in urban areas and Special Economic Zones (Chan 2012; Fan 2007; Mallee 1996). Long-distance, interprovincial migration, responsible for about one-third of all migration, has continuously increased since the 1990s, and is mostly from village to city (Chan 2012). Age and marital status are important determinants of women's migration in China as elsewhere (Riley and Gardner 1993). The migrant worker population has consistently been youthful (Rozelle et al. 1999): about 40 percent of migrant workers from 2008 to 2012 were under age thirty, reflecting a preference for youthful workers in manufacturing especially (Chan 2012; "Migrant Workers"

2013). Within the migrant population, women tend to be younger, and therefore a greater percent are unmarried, when compared to men (Goldstein et al. 2000; Zai and Chan 2004). This is not to say that married women and mothers do not migrate (Roberts et al. 2004). Indeed, demand for more mature workers, which includes married women and mothers, has increased over the past decade, due to factors such as a declining birthrate and an expanding service sector (Chan 2012; Connelly et al. 2012; "Migrant Workers" 2013).

4. For overviews of this interdisciplinary field of scholarship, see Hondagneu-Sotelo (2005); Mahler and Pessar (2001, 2006); Pedraza (1991); Pessar and Mahler (2003); Silvey (2004); Willis and Yeoh (2000).

5. For much of modern Chinese history, debates about modernity and national identity have taken place on the symbolic terrain of gender difference and constructions of womanhood (Barlow 1994). See my discussion of "the woman question" in Chapter 1.

6. The terms *tongxiang* or *laoxiang* refer to people from the same place, be it a village, county, or province, and imply a reciprocal social relationship as among kinswomen and close friends.

7. Such illicit schools sprung up in Beijing in the 1990s to meet the needs of the children of rural migrant workers, whose access to free public schooling is restricted without the local *hukou*. See Chapter 4 (note 1).

8. Thus, agency has ideational, experiential, and material components. Anthropologists influenced by existentialism and phenomenology describe agency as the capacity to make sense of our lives and social worlds, and in our natural or cultural need to live meaningfully, to construct a worthwhile life (Jackson 2005, 2008; Scheper-Hughes 2008). Feminist scholars have emphasized that agency may be "action taken in specific contexts, but not entirely autonomously or without constraint" (Joan Scott, quoted in Wolf 1992: 23). Further, "agency can involve passivity, accommodation, and withdrawal as much as defiance and resistance" (Wolf 1992: 24).

Chapter 1. Rural Women and Migration under Market Socialism

1. The national women's organization, the All-China Women's Federation, was created in 1949 as a "mass organization" under the Chinese Communist Party (CCP) to represent and safeguard the rights and interests of Chinese women and tasked with promulgating laws and policies. In 1995 it was reinvented as one of the largest nongovernmental organizations (NGOs), also known as a GONGO: government-organized NGO. See Wesoky (2001) and Judd (2002) for contemporary studies of the Women's Federation, and Wang (1999) for a historical view.

2. The few men who have passed through companies like the March 8th were newsworthy. An article in the *Beijing Evening News* (22 May 1998) announced the arrival of the "first male maid" at Beijing's Chongwen District Trade Union Household Service Reemployment Center, a forty-six-year-old laid-off steelworker who received free retraining in household service at a reemployment center. He is quoted as saying to the reporter: "What, don't you believe this? Should I feel ashamed? Once you are no longer ashamed, you can do this." Such reports helped construct domestic work as properly women's work that is demeaning or ludicrous when undertaken by men.

3. In the 1990s, however, numerous for-profit domestic service placement agencies emerged in Beijing.

4. A widely accepted view in China of gender relations is that women, especially rural women, have a lower status than men. As Peng Peiyun, former chairwoman of the All-China Women's Federation, stated: "Due to the obstacles of traditional customs and the level of social develop-

ment in China, women's status is still lower than men's, rural women's status is lower than that of urban women, [and] in order to realize real equality between men and women and bring the initiative of women into full play, it goes without question than we still have a long way to go" (1995: 6).

5. According to revolutionary socialism, women's liberation and gender equality were narrowly conceived to be the movement of women into socially productive labor—work located outside the home and oriented beyond the household, which was to be facilitated by the socialization of domestic responsibilities (Honig 1985: 330). In retrospect, revolutionary socialism fell short of its lofty goals for women's liberation and gender equality. Deeply rooted notions of gender difference and male superiority, inattention to gender inequality in the family and household, resistance from the male peasantry, and pursuing expediency over ideals together impeded women's ability to fully participate in production and the public sphere as men's equals (see n. 10 below). In rural China, for example, the continuance of the patrilineal-patrilocal marriage and family system perpetuated gender inequality. Upon marriage, women might depart one agricultural work team and enter another, causing the former work team or brigade to lose their labor power. This reinforced the perception of women as temporary workers, and negatively impacted their overall opportunities for training and promotion (Lai 1995).

6. Hanchao Lu (2002) and others note that Shanghai became synonymous with a modernity equated with Westernization that was at first alien to the nation; Faure and Liu (2002) stress that Beijing, Nanjing, and Guangzhou were more attractive to intellectuals and socially mobile elites not because they were, like Shanghai, Western treaty ports, but for their prior cultural importance as centers of learning. On the discourse of (Western) modernity in China, see also Shih (2001).

7. In early twentieth-century literature, the peasantry was portrayed as a culturally distinct and alien "other," passive, helpless, and unenlightened, in the grip of ugly and fundamentally useless customs, desperately in need of education and cultural reform, and for such improvement in their circumstances totally dependent on the leadership and efforts of rational and informed outsiders (Cohen 1993: 154–155).

8. In speeches, Mao often invoked the metaphor of women in binds or shackles due to "feudal patriarchy" (a gender and class system of oppression) and the fetters of traditional, "superstitious" (*mixing*) beliefs and practices. See, for example, his "Report on the Investigation of the Peasant Movement in Hunan" (Mao 1965 [1927]).

9. Dorothy Ko explains: "To claim credit for the 'liberation' of women, the CCP and its sympathizers perpetuated the stark view of China's past as the perennial dark age for women" (1994: 2). From the work of social historians like Ko and others (e.g., Bray 1997; Hershatter 1997; Mann 1997), a more nuanced image of women in "traditional," or imperial and republican-era China has emerged that emphasizes the regional, ethnic, and class differences among women and is attentive to historical change.

10. Feminist studies of the CCP and "the woman question" have criticized the failures of political praxis and policy to address the roots of gender inequality, namely entrenched gender ideologies and the patrilineal-patrilocal marriage and family system. However, many also acknowledge improvements to women's lives under revolutionary socialism, such as gains in literacy and education, life expectancy and maternal health, and work opportunities, as well as the abolition of forced marriage, child-brides, and other practices harmful to women. For an overview, see Honig (1985). On the CCP's gender politics, see Gilmartin (1995), Johnson (1983),

Stacey (1984), and Wang Zheng (1999). Women's lives under revolutionary socialism are chronicled in Croll (1978), Davin (1976), Hershatter (2000), Honig (2000), and Wolf (1985).

11. Ironically, the implementation of the *hukou* system undermined Mao's promise that the socialist revolution would abolish the antagonistic, exploitative relationship between the city and the countryside (Kipnis 1997: 165–168).

12. For more details on the *hukou* system's development during the 1950s, its temporary suspension during the Great Leap Forward (1958–1961), and its reimplementation in the wake of mass famines and upheaval that resulted from that failed experiment in rapid industrialization, see Cheng and Selden (1994). On its use in political control, see Fei-Ling Wang (2004 and 2011). On *hukou* and managed urbanization, see Chan (1994).

13. For several years after the policy change, migrant children born to Beijing fathers and rural mothers (including those of my informants, see Chapter 6) were still being denied local *hukou* in practice, making it virtually impossible for their offspring to gain equal access to urban education and medical services.

14. See Chapter 6 for a discussion of the persistence of bias against rural-urban intermarriage.

15. Economic reforms were introduced in two stages (Naughton 2006). The early phase of reforms concentrated on agricultural productivity and the transition to a market economy. Between 1978 and 1984, rural reforms were introduced that involved redistribution of collective land to households, who in effect contracted land from the state in perpetuity. Households were permitted to make their own decisions about farming and to sell their produce on the market after contributing a grain quota or tax to the government. This "household responsibility system" reversed the "scissors effect" of agriculture subsidizing industry via state extraction of rural profits that characterized prior decades. In the industrial sector, state-owned enterprises (SOEs) were likewise given leeway to sell above-quota products for profit. Urban reforms, with gradual privatization of industry and land at their core, were the focus of economic policies after 1985. The years 1996–1997 saw a major push toward privatization of the SOEs; privatization of real estate was stepped up after 2000.

16. In 1981, China began to manage population growth through restrictions on numbers and timing of births, using a quota system. For a thorough study of the background and history of population planning, see Greenhalgh and Winckler (2005).

17. China is linguistically diverse, having numerous regional and local dialects, including Cantonese and Mandarin (Putonghua), which is also the official language of the nation. Inability to speak proper Putonghua may be indicative of a lack of formal education and perceived by urbanites as a sign of low *suzhi*. See Pun (1999) for a description of how dialect is used as a tool by native supervisors and bosses to discipline and control rural outsiders and migrant women workers in the export-processing industries of southern China.

18. In the late 1990s, some of the lowest-paid female migrants were domestic workers like Qiaolian, who earned about 400CNY per month. Hotel housekeepers earned similarly low wages. By contrast, the average monthly wage of a (male) migrant construction worker was about 900CNY (Xin 2000). Gender rather than education or age appeared to account for such a discrepancy in wages, at least among rural-to-urban migrants. For example, Wang and Zuo (1997) found that when other factors (education, experience, age) were controlled, a female migrant still earned 22 percent less than male migrants. Magnani and Zhu (2012) calculated that male migrants earned an average of 30 percent more than women migrants, and that relative gender wage discrimination was greatest at the lowest income levels. An experiment conducted by Guang

and Kong (2010) similarly found that when all other factors were controlled, being a rural and female migrant sharply diminished the likelihood of a job applicant being hired by companies in Beijing.

19. In elite households of late imperial China, women and men were accorded separate living quarters, with women secluded in the interior behind walls. Work performed in the inner quarters was equated with feminine virtue and elite status, while activities that took women outside this realm were comparatively less virtuous or "womanly" and indicated lower social status. For more details, see Bray (1997), Ko (1994), and Mann (1997). Chapters 2 and 3 also discuss migration and service work in regard to gender transgression.

20. The (re)migration decisions of married women are closely tied to the age and sex of their children; the availability of childcare provided by in-laws, parents, or other close kin; and their educational needs (Connelly et al. 2012; Fan, Sun, and Zheng 2011).

21. Thus, the Goals for the State Council's Program for the Development of Chinese Women (1995–2000) were "to increase the employment of women and expand their areas of employment in the course of establishing a socialist market economy, readjusting the urban and rural industrial structure, and developing the tertiary industry."

Chapter 2. Dutiful Daughters and Migration Desires

1. I discuss *guanxi* in more detail in Chapter 3.

2. The conviction that investment in education will enhance social mobility is pervasive despite the reality that institutional and social barriers thwart the advancement of rural youth. See Hannum and Park (2007) and the collection of essays in Postiglione (2006a) for further information.

3. Socialist model workers in agriculture and industry, such as the Iron Girls, exemplified the gender-neutral or androgynous look. In 1950s and 1960s propaganda posters, they were posed with heavy equipment and tools, wearing overalls, and sporting short hair. But close readings of such visual images indicate subtle gender differences, according to Evans and Donald (1999). Indeed, socialism did not entirely erase gender difference or inequality.

4. Urban working mothers at least had some social support as recipients of state benefits distributed through the work units; rural women, working in self-sufficient agricultural collectives, did not, despite their more onerous double burden (see Sidel 1972: 84–85; M. Wolf 1985: 121–122).

5. The state has taken steps toward a goal of universal coverage (by 2020) by improving the availability and quality of rural health care, such as by building more hospitals and training more medical personnel and establishing a cooperative insurance system in rural areas equal to that provided to urban citizens since 1998 (Yip 2010).

6. Land reform and collectivization interfered with the traditional patrilineal inheritance process and weakened the father-son bond. In the postreform era, the greater cash-earning power of adult sons has increased their bargaining power over their elders. Indeed, "inheritance" is often passed to sons at marriage, before the parents' death (Y. Yan 2003).

7. A daughter's temporary membership in her natal household should not, however, be exaggerated. Anthropologists and social historians have shown the ongoing links of married women with their natal households (e.g., Judd 1989) and the importance of affinal ties that are forged through marriage to rural social life and economy (Croll 1984).

8. In very poor households having few laborers, young women's help in family farming is certainly critical to the household economy, but those who can migrate are already somewhat

peripheral to that economy. Hence their remittances tend to supplement the household budget, allowing for enhanced consumption power (see Fan 2004 and C. K. Lee 1998).

9. I interviewed Shanshan, who I met through Qiaolian and Changying, in 2000, when they were neighbors in a migrant enclave in Beijing. Shanshan was unemployed at the time and busy caring for her husband, also a migrant, and raising their newborn.

10. Fortunately, this gender gap in compulsory education appears to be narrowing since the implementation of new government initiatives in 2005 (Ibid.).

11. Interestingly, as I will explain in Chapter 5, one positive, unintended consequence of migration and work is that it allows young women to reflect upon and question the fairness of gender-selective practices with regard to schooling decisions made in their own households. Equally encouraging, some scholars have found that demand for young women's labor in south China's export industries, together with the smaller families created by the family planning policy, are favorably influencing parental attitudes toward investing in daughters' educations (H. Zhang 2007).

12. Not only is there pressure for young couples to procreate, but there is also pressure on rural women to bear sons. Pressure on rural households for male farm labor under the household responsibility system contributed to undermining the initial "one-child" family planning policy (Greenhalgh and Li 1995). The overall sex ratio has become imbalanced; technology enabling fetus sex identification and sex-selective abortion accounts for the "missing girls" (Greenhalgh and Winckler 2005). On the other hand, recent scholarship points to lessening of son preference in areas where women's employment opportunities, including via migration, are established and in concert with the promotion of smaller families through family planning (Short 2003). See also Chapter 6.

13. Poverty itself was shameful but so too was the grandmother's transgression of traditional gender prescriptions of virtue by migrating from the inner quarters to the public streets (see Mann 1997: 30–44).

Chapter 3. Gendered Social Networks and Migration Pathways

1. For example, while gender identity may have become less relevant after 1949 for women who positively embraced the class label of "worker" (Rofel 1999: 80), this may not have been possible for the rural female *domestic* "worker" of the post-1949 period. In her analysis of women who had migrated out of China's villages and found work in urban domestic service in the 1970s, Hairong Yan (2003a: 582) points not only to their violation of the norms of rural patriarchy, but also to their failure to become the liberated subjects of state socialism:

> In both the city and the countryside, these rural migrant women were transgressors: In the countryside they had transgressed the sphere of local patriarchy and thus raised anxiety about their gendered personhood; in the city they were transgressors of the proper subject position of rural woman as defined by ideologically espoused heroic agricultural labor, and they reinvoked the specter of the past through domestic service. This notion of transgression and contamination thus constitutes a vague source of shame for these women—vague because it is caught uneasily between the state ideology of women's liberation and the continued presence of patriarchal power that defines what a proper woman is through the spatial circumscription of her labor.

2. Trafficking in women is an officially acknowledged and widely reported crime that has been on the increase, or simply made more visible (Whyte 2000), in the postreform period. The rise of trafficking may be connected to the demographic sex imbalance.

3. Security deposits served as collateral to discourage migrant workers from spontaneously quitting employers.

4. See Hu (1944) and Yang (1965: 167–172) for anthropological discussions of this Chinese concept.

Chapter 4. Menial Women and Model Workers

1. Children of migrant workers have long been denied access to public schooling in large cities (Kwong 2004). Until educational policy reforms adopted in the late 2000s, enrollment in public schools was limited to local *hukou* holders (Hannum, Wang, and Adams 2010). Many public schools charge illicit arbitrary fees to enroll migrant children. Most migrant workers therefore send their children back to the village when they reach school age, to be looked after by kin, or enroll them in cheaper, makeshift schools operated mainly by migrant entrepreneurs. Such schools tend to be of substandard quality and insecure, as they might be demolished or closed down on short notice by authorities (see Jacobs 2011). Students who receive early education in Beijing must return to their place of *hukou* registration to sit for post-secondary school entry exams, which may be based on an altogether different curriculum. This link between education and *hukou* is a main impediment to the permanent settlement of migrant families in Beijing ("Migrant Workers" 2013).

2. In 1994, domestic service was officially recognized as a technical occupation, and deemed the science of "home economics" (*jiazheng*) (Wang Zheng 2000). Through its affiliated domestic service employment agencies, the Women's Federation instituted training centers and awarded certificates in the new science. The changes were aimed at the reemployment of urban women workers laid off from restructured state-owned enterprises, who were reluctant to enter an occupation they found shameful due to its association with servitude as well as rural migrant women.

3. Maids, nannies, and even wet nurses were available for hire after 1949, but they grew increasingly rare (Tang and Feng 1996). Without local *hukou*, it was extremely difficult for rural women to procure basic necessities of food and housing in the city. Moreover, it was a violation of regulations to reside away from one's place of *hukou* registration.

4. A Beijing cadre who was retired from the Foreign Service explained to me that the state provided subsidies to households like his during the 1950s and 1960s, in variable amounts and forms depending on the cadre's rank in the government agency, expressly for securing domestic help, usually middle-aged women from the countryside. His household received a stipend for their domestic workers' salaries and extra ration coupons for rice and other staples. His work unit also arranged for the transfer of their domestic workers' household registration to Beijing, where it was entered into his family's register. However, many more rural women who became nannies in the 1960s and 1970s did not secure urban *hukou* (H. Yan 2003a: 582).

5. Given that the socialist revolution had purportedly eradicated class inequality and exploitation by eliminating capitalist labor relations as well as feudal servitude, their reappearance in the form of a market in private caregivers in the 1980s was jarring (Chen and Sun 1984–1985). Much effort was made to reassure the emerging urban middle class that hiring caregivers was in keeping with socialist aims of development, and would be tolerated and even encouraged ("Baomu" 1986; Croll 1986).

6. In this chapter I rely on an extensive literature on the unique work conditions of domestic service, including Anderson (2000), Rollins (1985), and Romero (1992), to name but a few.

7. Some nurse's assistants (*hugong; huli*) are paid by the hospital as temporary staff; others are domestic workers hired by the patients or their families.

8. Wenling, from a poor area of north China, had worked nearly ten years in domestic service (in Xi'an and Beijing), and at the time of our meeting was already thirty-two years old, yet still unmarried. See Chapter 6 for a discussion of migrant women workers and the problem of later marriage.

9. Again, the existing literature on domestic service in other contexts, such as among immigrant and minority women in the United States, suggests similar hierarchies of "professionalism" by work arrangements and content. For example, live-in domestic workers rank below part-timers, and those working directly for a household rank lower than those working for a contractor (Salzinger 1991).

10. As explained in Chapter 1, most fees were eliminated with legislation introduced in 2003.

11. After switching from the four-star hotel to a (three-star) state-run guesthouse in 2001, Shuqin still kept details of her menial work to herself. However, when visiting her natal home, she boasted of meeting high-profile government officials (who had stayed at the guesthouse) and distributed gifts of souvenir pens inscribed with the titles of ministries that she received as perquisites of her job!

Chapter 5. From Country Bumpkins to Urban Sophisticates

1. China has over one hundred spoken languages, about 85 percent of which belong to any of seven dialect families.

2. Like many migrant workers, Shuchun rented a room in a house located on the far outskirts of Beijing, in a so-called migrant enclave. Her landlords were former farmers who received Beijing *hukou*s after their village was incorporated into the city administrative zone in the 1980s. Many migrants renting in such "urban villages" worked the fields belonging to their landlords, who in turn derived income from the rental property (see Jacka 2006).

3. The dismantling of rural collectives and restructuring of the state-run economic sector in the postreform period has undermined China's health-care system, which today is characterized by differential access and quality of care as well as skyrocketing prices. Key steps toward a goal of universal coverage (by 2020) have been improving the availability and quality of rural health care and establishing a cooperative insurance system equal to that provided to urban citizens since 1998 (Yip 2010). Rural migrant workers have been virtually excluded from the urban welfare regime; however, in 2003, municipalities began offering special social insurance schemes to migrant workers. Yet, by 2009, only a small percentage of migrant workers were covered by the major types of social insurance: pension, health care, unemployment, injury, and maternity. Further, as eligibility for each level of coverage is determined by household registration, migrant workers on the whole receive lower benefits. Moreover, insurance schemes are not portable, and thus most migrant workers who pay into the fund do not benefit over the lifetime (Selden and Wu 2011). For these reasons, migrants usually seek medical care back in the countryside.

4. The trial period evokes the apprentice system of the presocialist era, but in the postreform period serves to build employer's trust in the authenticity of the employee's résumé, in a context where phony college degrees are easily available for purchase.

5. The landlord and his family occupied the renovated rooms, which had linoleum floors and new furniture. They charged Yarui 150CNY plus utilities to rent the dilapidated room in

the rear of the house. She also paid a migrant management fee and public hygiene fee to the local village committee.

Chapter 6. Migrant Working Wives and Mothers

1. Several ethnographers of rural China have noted an increase in uxorilocal marriages, whereby the wife resides in or near her parents after marriage (H. Zhang 2004). Historically, such "minor" forms of marriage were undesirable but not uncommon, particularly in families without sons to inherit and tend to the property (Baker 1979). The implementation of family planning in the postreform period has led to smaller family size. Households with only one daughter may seek a uxorilocal marriage and be attractive, especially to poorer, landless bachelors (H. Zhang 2007).

2. The general rule of thumb for rural marriages historically was that a girl should remain within ten *li*, about three kilometers, of her natal village. Under collectivization, intravillage, intrabrigade marriages became a common phenomenon (Selden 1993).

3. In 2000, for example, Yaling's five-year-old son still did not have the Beijing *hukou*.

4. The sex-ratio imbalance is attributed to the restrictions on family size under the planned birth policies implemented since 1980, son preference, and the introduction of ultrasound technology that facilitates fetal sex detection (Poston, Conde, and DeSalvo 2011). In 2003 the state banned the use of such technology for elective sex-selective abortion procedures.

5. China has a long tradition of equal division of family property among sons, different from European primogeniture. Inheritance helped perpetuate the intergenerational contract: filial sons provided care and support to aging parents, and inherited the family property upon their death (see Baker 1979). In the postreform period, parents turn over property (and/or sums of cash) to their sons at marriage, and thus have less leverage to ensure their gifts are reciprocated with children's filial obligations (see Ikels 2004; Y. Yan 2003).

6. Under a practice called *dingti* in the socialist work-unit system, a high-school-educated daughter or son would be hired to take over his or her parent's job upon the latter's retirement.

Works Cited

Abu-Lughod, Janet. 1975. "Comments: The End of the Age of Innocence in Migration Theory." In *Migration and Urbanization*, ed. Helen I. Safa and Brian M. DuToit, 201–206. The Hague: Mouton.

Abu-Lughod, Lila. 1990. "The Romance of Resistance: Tracing Transformations of Power Through Bedouin Women." *American Ethnologist* 17 (1): 41–55.

————. 1991. "Writing Against Culture." In *Recapturing Anthropology: Working in the Present*, ed. Richard G. Fox, 137–154. Santa Fe, NM: School of American Research Press.

Anagnost, Ann. 1997. *National Past-Times: Narrative, Representation, and Power in Modern China*. Durham, NC: Duke University Press.

Anderson, Bridget Jane. 2000. *Doing the Dirty Work? The Global Politics of Domestic Labour*. London: ZED Books.

Attané, Isabelle. 2012. "Being a Woman in China Today: A Demography of Gender." *China Perspectives* 4:5–15.

Baker, Hugh D. R. 1979. *The Chinese Family and Kinship*. New York: Columbia University Press.

Ballew, Ted. 2001. "Xiaxiang for the '90s: The Shanghai TV Rural Channel and Post-Mao Urbanity amid Global Swirl." In *China Urban: Ethnographies of Contemporary Culture*, ed. Nancy N. Chen, Constance D. Clark, Suzanne Z. Gottschang, and Lyn Jeffery, 242–273. Durham, NC: Duke University Press.

"Baomu de sanda bianhua" [Three great changes in maids]. 1986. *Zhongguo Funü Bao* [China Women's News]. 9 June, 4.

Barbalet, J. M. 1998. *Emotion, Social Theory, and Social Structure: A Macrosociological Approach*. Cambridge: Cambridge University Press.

Barlow, Tani. 1994. "Theorizing Woman: Funü, Guojia, Jiating." In *Body, Subject, Power in China*, ed. Angela Zito and Tani E. Barlow, 253–289. Chicago: University of Chicago Press.

Bauman, Zygmunt. 2001. "Identity in the Globalizing World." *Social Anthropology* 9 (2): 121–129.

Beaver, Patricia D., Hou Lihui, and Wang Xue. 1995. "Rural Chinese Women: Two Faces of Reform." *Modern China* 21 (2): 205–232.

Beijing Laodongju [Beijing Labor Bureau]. 1995. *Waidi Laijing Renyuan Bidu* [Mandatory reading for migrant service workers in the capital]. Beijing: Industrial and Commercial Press.

———. 1999. *Waidi Laijing Renyuan Bidu* [Mandatory reading for migrant service workers in the capital]. Beijing: Industrial and Commercial Press.

Berman, Marshall. 1982. *All That Is Solid Melts into Air: The Experience of Modernity.* New York: Simon and Schuster.

Beynon, Louise. 2004. "Dilemmas of the Heart: Rural Working Women and Their Hopes for the Future." In *On the Move: Rural-to-Urban Migration in Contemporary China,* ed. Arianne M. Gaetano and Tamara Jacka, 131–150. New York: Columbia University Press.

Bossen, Laurel. 2002. *Chinese Women and Rural Development: Sixty Years of Change in Lu Village, Yunnan.* Lanham, MD: Rowman & Littlefield.

Bourdieu, Pierre. 1977. *Outline of a Theory of Practice.* Cambridge: Cambridge University Press.

Bray, Francesca. 1997. *Technology and Gender: Fabrics of Power in Late Imperial China.* Berkeley: University of California Press.

Brettell, Caroline B. 2000. "Theorizing Migration in Anthropology: The Social Construction of Networks, Identities, Communities, and Globalscapes." In *Migration Theory: Talking Across Disciplines,* ed. James F. Hollifield and Caroline Brettell, 97–135. New York: Routledge.

Brettell, Caroline B., and Carolyn F. Sargent. 2006. "Migration, Identity, and Citizenship: Anthropological Perspectives." *American Behavioral Scientist* 50 (1): 3–8.

"Building the Dream: Special Report." 2014. *The Economist* (online). April 19. http://www.economist.com/news/special-report/21600797-2030-chinese-cities-will-be-home-about-1-billion-people-getting-urban-china-work.

Cai Fang. 2003. "How the Market Economy Promotes the Reform of the Household Responsibility System." *Social Sciences in China* (Winter):118–125.

Cartier, Carolyn. 2001. *Globalizing South China.* Oxford: Blackwell Press.

Chan, Anita, Richard Madsen, and Jonathan Unger. 1992. *Chen Village under Mao and Deng: The Recent History of a Peasant Community in Mao's China.* Berkeley: University of California Press.

Chan, Kam Wing. 1994. *Cities with Invisible Walls: Reinterpreting Urbanization in Post-1949 China.* Oxford: Oxford University Press.

———. 2010. "The Household Registration System and Migrant Labor in China: Notes on a Debate." *Population and Development Review* 36 (2): 357–364.

———. 2012. "Migration and Development in China: Trends, Geography, and Current Issues." *Migration and Development* 1 (2): 187–205.

———. 2013. "Turning China's Cities with Invisible Walls into Cities of Dreams." *East Asia Forum.* 4 February. http://www.eastasiaforum.org/2013/02/04/turning-chinas-cities-with-invisible-walls-into-cities-of-dreams/. Accessed August 31, 2013.

Chan, Kam Wing, and Will Buckingham. 2008. "Is China Abolishing the *Hukou* System?" *The China Quarterly* 195:582–606.

Chan, Kam Wing, and Li Zhang. 1999. "The *Hukou* System and Rural-Urban Migration in China: Processes and Changes." *China Quarterly* 160:818–855.

Chang, Leslie T. 2008. *Factory Girls: From Village to City in a Changing China.* New York: Spiegel & Grau.

"Chaoyang jiawu fuwu gongsi chengli" [Chaoyang household services company founded]. 1983. *Beijing Evening News.* 21 December, 1.

Chen Baoming and Sun Zijun. 1984–1985. "The Social Function of Housekeepers: An Investigation of Several Middle- and Upper-level Intellectuals' Households in Shanghai." *Chinese Society and Anthropology* 17 (Winter): 96–106.

Chen, Nancy N. 2001. "Health, Wealth and the Good Life." In *China Urban: Ethnographies of Contemporary Culture,* ed. Nancy N. Chen, Constance D. Clark, Suzanne Z. Gottschang, and Lyn Jeffery, 165–182. Durham, NC: Duke University Press.

Cheng, Tiejun, and Mark Selden. 1994. "The Origins and Social Consequences of China's *Hukou* System." *China Quarterly* 139:644–668.

Cheng Yuan, Han Xuehui, and John K. Dagsvik. 2011. "Marriage Pattern in the City of Shanghai." *Chinese Sociology and Anthropology* 4:74–95.

Cheng, Zhiming, Fei Guo, Graeme Hugo, and Xin Yuan. 2013. "Employment and Wage Discrimination in the Chinese Cities: A Comparative Study of Migrants and Locals." *Habitat International* 39:246–255.

Chu, Julia Y. 2010. *Cosmologies of Credit: Transnational Mobility and the Politics of Destination in China.* Durham, NC: Duke University Press.

Cohen, Myron. 1993. "Cultural and Political Inventions in Modern China: The Case of the Chinese 'Peasant.'" In *China in Transformation,* ed. Tu Wei-ming, 151–170. Cambridge, MA: Harvard University Press.

Connelly, Rachel, Kenneth Roberts, and Zhenzhen Zheng. 2012. "The Role of Children in the Migration Decisions of Rural Chinese Women." *Journal of Contemporary China* 21 (73): 93–111.

Constable, Nicole. 1997. *Maid to Order in Hong Kong: Stories of Filipina Workers.* Ithaca, NY, and London: Cornell University Press.

Croll, Elisabeth J. 1974. *The Women's Movement in China: A Selection of Readings.* London: Anglo-Chinese Educational Institute.

———. 1978. *Feminism and Socialism in China.* New York: Routledge.

———. 1981. *The Politics of Marriage in Contemporary China.* Cambridge: Contemporary China Institute Publications, Cambridge University Press.

———. 1984. "New Peasant Family Forms in Rural China." *The Journal of Peasant Studies* 14 (4): 469–499.

———. 1986. "Domestic Service in China." *Economic and Political Weekly* 21 (6): 256–260.

———. 1994. *From Heaven to Earth: Images and Experiences of Development in China.* London: Routledge.

Dai Kejing and Paula R. Dempsey. 1998. "Working Sisters from Outside: Rural Chinese Household Workers in Beijing." *Current Research on Occupations and Professions* 10:11–29.

Davin, Delia. 1976. *Women-Work: Women and the Party in Revolutionary China.* Oxford: Oxford University Press.

———. 1998. "Gender and Migration in China." In *Village Inc.: Chinese Rural Society in the 1990s,* ed. Fleming Christiansen and Zhang Junzuo, 230–240. London: Curzon Press.

Donato, Katharine M., Donna Gabaccia, Jennifer Holdaway, Martin Manalansan IV, and Patricia R. Pessar. 2006. "A Glass Half Full? Gender in Migration Studies." *International Migration Review* 40 (1): 3–26.

Dutton, Michael. 1998. *Streetlife China*. Cambridge: Cambridge University Press.

Evans, Harriet. 2000. "Marketing Femininity: Images of the Modern Chinese Woman." In *China Beyond the Headlines*, ed. Timothy B. Weston and Lionel M. Jensen, 217–244. Lanham, MD: Rowman & Littlefield.

———. 2008. *The Subject of Gender: Daughters and Mothers in Urban China*. Lanham, MD: Rowman & Littlefield.

Evans, Harriet, and Stephanie Donald. 1999. *Picturing Power in the People's Republic of China*. Lanham, MD: Rowman & Littlefield.

Fan, C. Cindy. 2000. "Migration and Gender in China." In *China Review 2000*, ed. Chung-Ming Lau and Jianfa Shen, 423–454. Hong Kong: Chinese University Press.

———. 2004. "Out to the City and Back to the Village: The Experiences and Contributions of Rural Women Migrating from Sichuan and Anhui." In *On the Move: Women and Rural-to-Urban Migration in Contemporary China*, ed. Arianne M. Gaetano and Tamara Jacka, 177–206. New York: Columbia University Press.

———. 2007. *China on the Move: Migration, the State, and the Household*. New York: Routledge.

Fan, C. Cindy, and Youqin Huang. 1998. "Waves of Rural Brides: Female Marriage Migration in China." *Annals of the Association of America Geographers* 88 (2): 227–251.

Fan, C. Cindy, M. Sun, and S. Zheng. 2011. "Migration and Split Households: A Comparison of Sole, Couple, and Family Migrants in Beijing, China." *Environment and Planning A* 43: 2164–2185.

"Fanzhong de jiawu chengle tamen shiye shang de zhangai" [Onorous burden of housework is obstacle to career development]. 1985. *Zhongguo Funü Bao* [China Women's News]. 10 April, 10.

Farrer, James. 2002. *Opening Up: Youth Sex Culture and Market Reform in Shanghai*. Chicago: University of Chicago Press.

Faure, David, and Tao Tao Liu, eds. 2002. *Town and Country in China: Identity and Perception*. New York: Palgrave.

Fei Xiaotong. 1992 [1946]. *From the Soil: The Foundations of Chinese Society*. Trans. Gary G. Hamilton and Wang Zheng. Berkeley: University of California Press.

Felski, Rita. 1995. *The Gender of Modernity*. Cambridge, MA: Harvard University Press.

Feuerwerker, Yitsi Mei. 1998. *Ideology, Power, Text: Self-Representation and the Peasant "Other" in Modern Chinese Literature*. Stanford, CA: Stanford University Press.

Fong, Vanessa. 2004. *Only Hope: Coming of Age under China's One-Child Policy*. Stanford, CA: Stanford University Press.

Fraser, Nancy. 1989. *Unruly Practices: Power, Discourse, and Gender in Contemporary Social Theory*. Minneapolis: University of Minnesota Press.

Friedman, Sara L. 2000. "Spoken Pleasures and Dangerous Desires: Sexuality, Marriage and the State in Rural Southeastern China." *East Asia: An International Quarterly* 18 (4): 13–39.

Gaetano, Arianne M. 2010. "Single Women in Urban China and the 'Unmarried Crisis': Gender Resilience and Gender Transformation." Lund University Working Papers in Contemporary Asian Studies, no. 31.

Geertz, Clifford. 1973. *The Interpretation of Cultures*. New York: Basic Books.

Giddens, Anthony. 1991. *Modernity and Self-Identity: Self and Society in the Late Modern Age*. Stanford, CA: Stanford University Press.

Gilmartin, Christina K. 1995. *Engendering the Chinese Revolution: Radical Women, Communist Politics, and Mass Movements in the 1920s*. Berkeley, CA: University of California Press.

Goldman, Merle, and Roderick MacFarquhar. 1999. *The Paradox of China's Post-Mao Reforms*. Cambridge, MA: Harvard University Press.

Goldstein, Sidney, Zai Liang, and Alice Goldstein. 2000. "Migration, Gender, and Labor Force in Hubei Province, 1985–1990." In *Re-Drawing Boundaries: Work, Households, and Gender in China*, ed. Barbara Entwisle and Gail E. Henderson, 214–30. Berkeley, CA: University of California Press.

Gong Weibin. 1998. *Laodong li waichu jiuye yu nongcun shehui bianqian* [Labor migration and village social change]. Beijing: Cultural Relics Press.

Gottschaung, Suzanne. 2007. "Maternal Bodies, Breast-Feeding, and Consumer Desire in Urban China." *Medical Anthropology Quarterly* 21 (1): 64–80.

Greenhalgh, Susan. 1993. "The Peasantization of the One-Child Policy in Shaanxi." In *Chinese Families in the Post-Mao Era*, ed. Deborah Davis and Stevan Harrell, 219–250. Berkeley, CA: University of California Press.

Greenhalgh, Susan, and Jiali Li. 1995. "Engendering Reproductive Policy and Practice in Peasant China: For a Feminist Demography of Reproduction." *Signs: Journal of Women in Culture and Society* 20 (3): 601–641.

Greenhalgh, Susan, and Edward Winckler. 2005. *Governing China's Population: From Leninist to Neoliberal Biopolitics*. Stanford, CA: Stanford University Press.

Gries, Peter Hays, and Stanley Rosen, eds. 2004. *State and Society in 21st Century China: Crisis, Contention, and Legitimation*. New York: RoutledgeCurzon.

Griffiths, Michael B. 2010. "Lamb Buddha's Migrant Workers: Self-Assertion on China's Urban Fringe." *Journal of Current Chinese Affairs* 39 (20): 3–37.

Guang, Lei. 2003. "Rural Taste, Urban Fashions: The Cultural Politics of Rural/Urban Difference in Contemporary China." *Positions* 11 (3): 613–646.

Guang, Lei, and Fanmin Kong. 2010. "Rural Prejudice and Gender Discrimination in China's Urban Job Market." In *One Country, Two Societies: Rural-Urban Inequality in Contemporary China*, ed. Martin K. Whyte, 241–264. Cambridge, MA: Harvard University Press.

Guo Qiu. 1994. "Jiawu laodong shehuihua: zhongguo funu de dierci jiefang" [The Socialization of Domestic Labor: The Second Liberation of Chinese Women]. *Zhongguo Funü Bao* [China Women's News]. 21 September.

Halfacre, Keith H., and Paul J. Boyle. 1993. "The Challenge Facing Migration Research: The Case for a Biographical Approach." *Progress in Human Geography* 17.

Hall, Stuart. 1996. "Who Needs Identity?" In *Questions of Cultural Identity*, ed. Stuart Hall and Paul du Gay, 1–17. Thousand Oaks, CA: Sage.

Hannum, Emily, and Albert Park. 2007. *Education and Reform in China.* Routledge Studies in Asia's Transformations. New York: Routledge.

Hannum, Emily, Meiyan Wang, and Jennifer Adams. 2010. "Rural-Urban Disparities in Access to Primary and Secondary Education under Market Reforms." In *One Country, Two Societies: Rural-Urban Inequality in Contemporary China,* ed. Martin K. Whyte, 125–146. Cambridge, MA: Harvard University Press.

Hanser, Amy. 2008. *Service Encounters: Class, Gender, and the Market for Social Distinction in Urban China.* Stanford, CA: Stanford University Press.

Henderson, Gail E., Barbara Entwisle, Li Ying, Yang Mingliang, Xu Siyuan, and Zhai Fengying. 2000. "Re-Drawing the Boundaries of Work: Views on the Meaning of Work (*Gongzuo*)." In *Re-Drawing Boundaries: Work, Households, and Gender in China,* ed. Barbara Entwisle and Gail E. Henderson, 33–50. Berkeley, CA: University of California Press.

Hershatter, Gail. 1997. *Women in China's Long Twentieth Century.* Berkeley, CA: University of California Press.

———. 2000. "Local Meanings of Gender and Work in Rural Shaanxi in the 1950s." In *Re-Drawing Boundaries: Work, Households, and Gender in China,* ed. Barbara Entwisle and Gail E. Henderson, 79–96. Berkeley: University of California Press.

Hirsch, Eric. 2001. "When Was Modernity in Melanesia?" *Social Anthropology* 9 (2): 131–146.

Hirsch, Jennifer S., and Holly Wardlow, eds. 2006. *Modern Loves: The Anthropology of Romantic Courtship and Companionate Marriage.* Ann Arbor, MI: University of Michigan Press.

Hochschild, Arlie R. 2012 [1983]. *The Managed Heart: Commercialization of Human Feeling.* Berkeley, CA: University of California Press.

Hoffman, Lisa M. 2006. "Autonomous Choices and Patriotic Professionalism: On Governmentality in Late-Socialist China." *Economy and Society* 35 (4): 550–570.

Hondagneu-Sotelo. 2005. "Gendering Migration: Not for 'Feminists Only'—And Not Only in the Household." Working Paper #05-02f. Princeton University: The Center for Migration and Development Working Paper Series. Princeton, NJ.

Honig, Emily. 1985. "Socialist Revolution and Women's Liberation in China—A Review Article." *Journal of Asian Studies* 44 (2): 329–336.

———. 1986. *Sisters and Strangers: Women in the Shanghai Cotton Mills, 1919–1949.* Stanford, CA: Stanford University Press.

———. 2000. "'Iron Girls' Revisited: Gender and the Politics of Work in the Cultural Revolution, 1966–1978." In *Re-Drawing Boundaries: Work, Households, and Gender in China,* ed. Barbara Entwisle and Gail E. Henderson, 97–110. Berkeley: University of California Press.

Honig, Emily, and Gail Hershatter. 1988. *Personal Voices: Chinese Women in the 1980s.* Stanford, CA: Stanford University Press.

Hooper, Beverley. 1998. "Flower Vase and Housewife: Women and Consumerism in Post-Mao China." In *Gender and Power in Affluent Asia,* ed. Krishna Sen and Maila Stivens, 167–193. London: Routledge.

Hoy, Caroline. 1999. "Issues in the Fertility of Temporary Migrants in Beijing." In *Internal and International Migration: Chinese Perspectives*, ed. Frank N. Pieke and Hein Mallee, 134–155. Surrey: Curzon Press.

Hu, Hsin Chin. 1944. "The Chinese Concept of Face." *American Anthropologist* 46:45–64.

Huang Xiyi. 1992. "Changes in the Economic Status of Rural Women in the Transformation of Modern Chinese Society." *Social Sciences in China* (Spring): 83–105.

Hyde, Sandra T. 2007. *Eating Spring Rice: The Cultural Politics of AIDS in Southwest China.* Berkeley, CA: University of California Press.

Ikels, Charlotte. 2004. "Serving the Ancestors, Serving the State: Filial Piety and Death Ritual in Contemporary Guangzhou." In *Filial Piety: Practice and Discourse in Contemporary East Asia*, ed. Charlotte Ikels, 88–105. Stanford, CA: Stanford University Press.

Jacka, Tamara. 1997. *Women and Work in Rural China: Change and Continuity in an Era of Reform.* Cambridge: Cambridge University Press.

———. 2000. "'Other Chinas' China's Others: A Report on the First National Forum for the Protection of the Rights of Migrant Women Workers, June 16–18, 1999, Beijing." *New Formations* 40:128–137.

———. 2005. "Finding a Place: Negotiations of Modernization and Globalization among Rural Women in Beijing." *Critical Asian Studies* 37 (1): 51–74.

———. 2006. *Rural Women in Urban China: Gender, Migration, and Social Change.* Armonk, NY: M. E. Sharpe.

———. 2009. "Cultivating Citizens: *Suzhi* (Quality) Discourse in the PRC." *Positions: East Asia Cultures Critique* 17 (3): 523–535.

Jackson, Michael. 2005. *Existential Anthropology: Events, Exigencies, and Effects.* New York: Berghahn Books.

———. 2008. "The Shock of the New: On Migrant Imaginaries and Critical Transitions." *Ethnos* 73 (1): 57–72.

Jacobs, Andrew. 2011. "China Takes Aim at Rural Influx." *New York Times.* 30 August.

Jasper, James M. 1998. "The Emotions of Protest: Affective and Reactive Emotions in and around Social Movements." *Sociological Forum* 13 (3): 397–424.

Jiao, Priscilla. 2010. "The Great Wall of Beijing: Official Plans May Lock Down Whole City." *South China Morning Post.* 5 July.

Johnson, Kay Ann. 1983. *Women, the Family, and Peasant Revolution in China.* Chicago: University of Chicago Press.

Jones, Gavin. 2010. "Changing Marriage Patterns in Asia." Asia Research Institute Working Paper No. 131. National University of Singapore: Singapore.

Judd, Ellen R. 1989. "Niangjia: Chinese Women and Their Natal Families." *The Journal of Asian Studies* 48 (3): 525–544.

———. 1990. "'Men Are More Able': Rural Chinese Women's Conceptions of Gender and Agency." *Pacific Affairs* 63 (1): 40–62.

———. 1994. *Gender and Power in Rural North China.* Stanford, CA: Stanford University Press.

———. 2002. *The Chinese Women's Movement between State and Market.* Stanford, CA: Stanford University Press.

Jun Jing. 2004. "Meal Rotation and Filial Piety." In *Filial Piety: Practice and Discourse in Contemporary East Asia*, ed. Charlotte Ikels, 53–62. Stanford, CA: Stanford University Press.

Kabeer, Naila. 2000. *Bangladeshi Women Workers and Labour Market Decisions: The Power to Choose*. New Delhi: Vistaar Publications.

Kandiyoti, Deniz. 1988. "Bargaining with Patriarchy." *Gender and Society*, Special Issue to Honor Jessie Bernard 2 (3): 274–290.

Kearney, Michael. 1995 "The Local and the Global: The Anthropology of Globalization and Transnationalism." *Annual Review of Anthropology* 24:547–565.

Kipnis, Andrew B. 1997. *Producing Guanxi: Sentiment, Self and Subculture in a North China Village*. Durham, NC: Duke University Press.

———. 2001. "The Disturbing Educational Discipline of 'Peasants.'" *The China Journal* 46:1–24.

———. 2011. *Governing Educational Desire: Culture, Politics, and Schooling in China*. Chicago: University of Chicago Press.

Knight, John, Lina Song, and Jia Huaibin. 1999. "Chinese Rural Migrants in Urban Enterprises: Three Perspectives." *The Journal of Development Studies* 35(3): 73–104.

Ko, Dorothy. 1994. *Teachers of the Inner Chambers: Women and Culture in 17th-century China*. Stanford, CA: Stanford University Press.

Kwong, Julia. 2004. "Educating Migrant Children: Negotiations between the State and Civil Society." *The China Quarterly* 180:1073–1088.

Lai, Mingyan.1995. "Female but Not Woman: Gender in Chinese Socialist Texts." In *Forming and Reforming Identity*, ed. Carol Siegel and Ann Kibbey, 287–318. New York: New York University Press.

Larson, Wendy. 1998. *Women and Writing in Modern China*. Stanford, CA: Stanford University Press.

Lawson, Victoria A. 2000. "Arguments within Geographies of Movement: The Theoretical Potential of Migrants' Stories." *Progress in Human Geography* 24 (4): 173–189.

Lee, Anru. 2004. *In the Name of Harmony and Prosperity: Labor and Gender Politics in Taiwan's Economic Restructuring*. Albany, NY: SUNY Press.

Lee, Ching Kwan. 1998. *Gender and the South China Miracle: Two Worlds of Factory Women*. Berkeley: University of California Press.

———. 2007. *Against the Law: Labor Protests in China's Rustbelt and Sunbelt*. Berkeley, CA: University of California Press.

Li Limei and Li Si-ming. 2010. "The Impact of Variations in Urban Registration within Cities." In *One Country, Two Societies: Rural-Urban Inequality in Contemporary China*, ed. Martin King Whyte, 188–215. Cambridge, MA: Harvard University Press.

Li Shi and Luo Chuliang. 2010. "Reestimating the Income Gap between Urban and Rural Households in China." In *One Country, Two Societies: Rural-Urban Inequality in Contemporary China*, ed. Martin K. Whyte, 105–121. Cambridge, MA: Harvard University Press.

Lieberman, Sally Taylor. 1998. *The Mother and Narrative Politics in Modern China*. Charlottesville and London: University Press of Virginia.

Liu, Xin. 2000. *In One's Own Shadow: An Ethnographic Account of the Condition of Post-Reform Rural China*. Berkeley: University of California Press.

Lu, Hanchao. 2002. "Urban Superiority, Modernity, and Local Identity: A Think Piece on the Case of Shanghai." In *Town and Country in China: Identity and Perception*, ed. David Faure and Tao Tao Liu, 126–144. New York: Palgrave.

Lu, Hanlong. 2000. "To Be Relatively Comfortable in an Egalitarian Society." In *The Consumer Revolution in Urban China*, ed. Deborah Davis, 124–141. Berkeley and Los Angeles: University of California Press.

Ma, Eric, and Hau Ling "Helen" Cheng. 2005. "'Naked' Bodies: Experimenting with Intimate Relations among Migrant Workers in South China. *International Journal of Cultural Studies* 8 (3): 307–328.

Magnani, Elisabetta, and Rong Zhu. 2012. "Gender Wage Differentials among Rural-Urban Migrants in China." *Regional Science and Urban Economics* 42 (2012): 779–793.

Mahler, Sarah J., and Patricia Pessar. 2001. "Gendered Geographies of Power: Analyzing Gender across Transnational Spaces." *Identities: Global Studies in Culture and Power* 7 (4): 441–459.

———. 2006. "Gender Matters: Ethnographers Bring Gender from the Periphery toward the Core of Migration Studies." *International Migration Review* 40 (1): 27–63.

Mallee, Hein. 1996. "In Defense of Migration: Recent Chinese Studies on Rural Population Mobility." *China Information* 10 (3/4): 108–140.

Mann, Susan. 1997. *Precious Records: Women in China's Long Eighteenth Century*. Stanford, CA: Stanford University Press.

Mao, Zedong. 1965. *Selected Works of Mao Zedong*, vol. 1. Beijing: Foreign Language Press.

Mao Zhuoyan, Shen Maocheng, and Liu Yonggang. 2008. "Jiaqiang liudong funü jihua shengyu fuwu de jidian sikao" [How to Strenghten the Family Planning Services to Floating Women]. *Xibei Renkou* [Northwest Population] 3 (29): 116–120.

McHugh, Kevin E. 2000. "Inside, Outside, Upside Down, Backward, Forward, Round and Round: A Case for Ethnographic Studies in Migration." *Progress in Human Geography* 24 (1): 71–89.

Meisner, Maurice. 1999. *Mao's China and After: A History of the People's Republic*. New York: Free Press.

Mellerman, Mei-ling. 2008. *Gender and Rights Research Report on Chinese Female Migrant Domestic Workers*. Beijing: Migrant Women's Club and UNESCO.

Meng Xianfan. 1995. *Gaige dachao zhong de zhongguo funü* [Chinese women in the tide of reform]. Beijing: China Social Sciences Press.

"Migrant Workers and Their Children." 2013. *China Labour Bulletin*. 27 June. http://www.clb.org.hk/en/content/migrant-workers-and-their-children. Accessed May 1, 2014.

Miller, Eric T. 2004. "Filial Daughters, Filial Sons: Comparisons from North China." In *Filial Piety: Practice and Discourse in Contemporary East Asia*, ed. Charlotte Ikels, 34–52. Stanford, CA: Stanford University Press.

Mills, Mary Beth. 1999. *Thai Women in the Global Labor Force: Consuming Desires, Contested Selves*. New Brunswick, NJ: Rutgers University Press.

Milwertz, Cecilia N. 2000. "Organising Rural Women Migrants in Beijing." In *Women in the City: Visibility and Voice in Urban Space*, ed. Jane Darke, Sue Ledwith, and Roberta Woods, 174–188. New York: Palgrave MacMillan

"Moving on Up: The Government Unveils a New 'People-Centered' Plan for Urbanization." 2014. *The Economist*. 22 March.

Murphy, Rachel. 2004. "The Impact of Labor Migration on the Well-Being and Agency of Rural Chinese Women: Cultural and Economic Contexts and the Life Course." In *On the Move: Women and Rural-to-Urban Migration in Contemporary China*, ed. Arianne M. Gaetano and Tamara Jacka, 243–276. New York: Columbia University Press.

Naughton, Barry J. 2006. *The Chinese Economy: Transitions and Growth*. Cambridge, MA: MIT Press.

O'Donnell, Mary Ann. 1999. "Pathbreaking: Construction Gendered Nationalism in the Shenzhen Special Economic Zone." *Positions* 7 (2): 343–375.

O'Hanlon, Rosalind. 1988. "Recovering the Subject: Subaltern Studies and the Histories of Resistance in Colonial South Asia." *Modern Asian Studies* 22:189–224.

Oishi, Nana. 2005. *Women in Motion: Globalization, State Politics, and Labor Migration in Asia*. Stanford, CA: Stanford University Press.

Ong, Aihwa. 1999. *Flexible Citizenship: The Cultural Logics of Transnationality*. Durham, NC: Duke University Press.

Ortner, Sherry B. 1984. "Theory in Anthropology Since the Sixties." *Comparative Studies in Society and History* 26 (1): 126–166.

———. 1995. "Resistance and the Problem of Ethnographic Refusal." *Comparative Studies in Society and History* 37 (1): 173–193.

———. 1996. *Making Gender: The Politics and Erotics of Culture*. Boston: Beacon Press.

———. 2006. *Anthropology and Social Theory: Culture, Power, and the Acting Subject*. Durham, NC: Duke University Press.

Otis, Eileen M. 2011. *Markets and Bodies: Women, Service Work, and the Making of Inequality in China*. Stanford, CA: Stanford University Press.

Ozyegin, Gul. 2001. *Untidy Gender: Domestic Service in Turkey*. Philadelphia, PA: Temple University Press.

Parish, William L., and Martin King Whyte. 1978. *Village and Family in Contemporary China*. Chicago: University of Chicago Press.

Parker, Lyn. 2005. *The Agency of Women in Asia*. New York: Marshall Cavendish Academic.

Pedraza, Sylvia. 1991 "Women and Migration: The Social Consequences of Gender." *Annual Review of Sociology* 17:303–325.

Peng Peiyun. 1995. "Preface." In *Dangdai Zhongguo Funü Jiating Diwei Yanjiu* [Women's domestic status in contemporary China], ed. Sha Jicai. Tianjin: People's Press.

Pessar, Patricia, and Sarah J. Mahler. 2003. "Transnational Migration: Bringing Gender In." *International Migration Review* 37 (3): 812–846.

Phillips, Michael R., Xianyun Li, and Yanping Zhang. 2002. "Suicide Rates in China, 1995–99." *The Lancet* 359 (9309): 835–840.

Postiglione, Gerard A., ed. 2006a. *Education and Social Change in China: Inequality in a Market Economy*. Armonk, NY: M. E. Sharpe.

———. 2006b. "Schooling and Inequality in China." In *Education and Social Change in China: Inequality in a Market Economy*, ed. Gerard A. Postiglione, 3–24. Armonk, NY: M. E. Sharpe.

Poston, Dudley L. Jr., Eugenia Conde, and Bethany DeSalvo. 2011. "China's Unbalanced Sex Ratio at Birth: Millions of Excess Bachelors and Societal Implications. *Vulnerable Children and Youth Studies* 6 (4): 314–320.

Potter, Sulameith Heins, and Jack M. Potter. 1983. *China's Peasants: The Anthropology of a Revolution*. Cambridge: Cambridge University Press.

Program for the Development of Chinese Women [Zhongguo funü fazhan gangyao]. 1995–2000. *All-China Women's Federation Pamphlet*. (Adapted by State Council in 1995).

Pun Ngai. 1999. "Becoming *Dagongmei* (Working Girls): The Politics of Identity and Difference in Reform China." *The China Journal* 42:1–18.

———. 2003. "Subsumption or Consumption? The Phantom of Consumer Revolution in 'Globalizing' China." *Cultural Anthropology* 18 (4): 469–492.

———. 2005. *Made in China: Women Factory Workers in a Global Workplace*. Durham, NC: Duke University Press.

Pun Ngai and Lu Huilin. 2010. "Unfinished Proletarianization: Self, Anger, and Class Action among the Second Generation of Peasant-Workers in Present-Day China." *Modern China* 36 (5): 493–519.

Qiu, Peiyuan, Yang Yang, Juying Zhang, and Xiao Ma. 2011. "Rural-to-Urban Migration and Its Implication for New Cooperative Medical Scheme Coverage and Utilization in China." *BMC Public Health* 11:520. http://www.ncbi.nlm.nih.gov/pmc/articles/PMC3142513/.

Riley, Nancy E., and Robert W. Gardner. 1993. "Migration Decisions: The Role of Gender." In *Internal Migration of Women in Developing Countries: Proceedings of the UN Expert Meeting on the Feminization of Internal Migration* (Aguascalientes, Mexico, 22–25 October 1991), 195–206. New York: United Nations Department for Economic and Social Information and Policy Analysis.

Roberts, Kenneth, Rachel Connelly, Zhenming Xie, and Zhenzhen Zheng. 2004. "Patterns of Temporary Labor Migration of Rural Women from Anhui and Sichuan." *The China Journal* 52:49–70.

Rofel, Lisa. 1999. *Other Modernities: Gendered Yearnings in China after Socialism*. Berkeley: University of California Press.

———. 2007. *Desiring China: Experiments in Neoliberalism, Sexuality and Public Culture*. Durham, NC: Duke University Press.

Rollins, Judith. 1985. *Between Women: Domestics and Their Employers*. Philadelphia: Temple University Press.

Romero, Mary. 1992. *Maid in the USA*. New York: Routledge.

Rozelle, Scott, Li Guo, Minggao Shen, Amelia Hughart, and John Giles. 1999. "Leaving China's Farms: Survey Results of New Paths and Remaining Hurdles to Rural Migration." *China Quarterly* 58:367–393.

Salzinger, Leslie. 1991. "A Maid by Any Other Name: The Transformation of 'Dirty Work' by Central American Immigrants." In *Ethnography Unbound: Power and Resistance in the Modern Metropolis*, ed. Michael Buroway et al., 139–160. Berkeley: University of California Press.

Schein, Louisa. 1994. "The Consumption of Color and the Politics of White Skin in Post-Mao China." *Social Text* 41 (Winter): 141–164.

Scheper-Hughes, Nancy. 2008. "A Talent for Life: Reflections on Human Vulnerability and Resilience." *Ethnos* 73 (1): 25–56.

Scott, James. 1985. *Weapons of the Weak: Everyday Forms of Peasant Resistance*. New Haven, CT: Yale University Press.

Selden, Mark. 1993. "Family Strategies and Structures in Rural North China." In *Chinese Families in the Post-Mao Era*, ed. Deborah Davis and Stevan Harrell, 139–165. Berkeley, CA: University of California Press.

Selden, Mark, and Wu Jieh-min. 2011. "The Chinese State, Incomplete Proletarianization and Structures of Inequality in Two Epochs." *The Asia-Pacific Journal* 9 (5), no. 1. Available at www.japanfocus.org.

Shih, Shu-mei. 2001. *The Lure of the Modern: Writing Modernism in Semicolonial China, 1917–1937*. Berkeley: University of California Press.

Short, Susan. 2003. "Having Daughters, Having Sons: Sex Preference and Family Building under the One-Child Policy." Paper Presented at the Conference "Daughters' Worth Re-evaluated: Changing Intergenerational Relations and Expectations in Contemporary China," Fairbank Center, Harvard University, Cambridge, MA, April 5–6.

Sidel, Ruth. 1972. *Women and Childcare in China: A Firsthand Report*. New York: Hill and Wang.

Silvey, Rachel M. 2000. "Diasporic Subjects: Gender and Mobility in South Sulawesi." *Women's Studies International Forum* 23 (4): 501–515.

———. 2004. "Power, Difference, and Mobility: Feminist Advances in Migration Studies." *Progress in Human Geography* 28 (4): 1–17.

———. 2006. "Geographies of Gender and Migration: Spatializing Social Difference." *International Migration Review* 40 (1): 64–81.

Solinger, Dorothy. 1999. *Contesting Citizenship in China: Peasant Migrants, the State, and the Logic of the Market*. Berkeley: University of California Press.

Stacey, Judith. 1984. *Patriarchy and Socialist Revolution in China*. Berkeley, CA: University of California Press.

Stapleton, Kristin. 2000. *Civilizing Chengdu: Chinese Urban Reform, 1895–1937*. Cambridge, MA: Harvard University Press.

Summerfield, Gale. 1994. "Economic Reform and the Employment of Chinese Women." *Journal of Economic Issues* 28 (3): 715–732.

Sun, Wanning. 2004. "Indoctrination, Fetishization, and Compassion: Media Constructions of the Migrant Woman." In *On the Move: Women and Rural-to-Urban Migration in Contemporary China*, ed. Arianne M. Gaetano and Tamara Jacka, 109–128. New York: Columbia University Press.

———. 2009. *Maid in China: Media, Morality and the Cultural Politics of Boundaries*. New York: Routledge.

Tan, Lin, and Susan E. Short. 2004. "Living as Double Outsider: Migrant Women's Experiences of Marriage in a County-Level City." In *On the Move: Women and Rural-to-*

Urban Migration in Contemporary China, ed. Arianne M. Gaetano and Tamara Jacka, 151–174. New York: Columbia University Press.

Tan Shen. 2000. "The Relationship between Foreign Enterprises, Local Governments, and Women Migrant Workers in the Pearl River Delta." In *Rural Labor Flows in China*, ed. Loraine A. West and Yaohui Zhao, 292–309. Berkeley: Institute of East Asian Studies, University of California.

Tang Can. 1998. "Sexual Harassment: The Dual Status of and Discrimination against Female Migrant Workers in Urban Areas." *Social Sciences in China* 19 (3): 64–71.

Tang Can and Feng Xiaoshuang. 1996. "Lao baomu yu xiao baomu: Liang bei ren de shidai xinhen: Anhui Wuwei xian diaocha sanji" [Old maids and young maids: The travails of two generations: An account of an investigation in Wuwei County, Anhui]. *Orient* (June): 49–54.

Taylor, Philip. 2001. "Critical Views of Modernity from Vietnam." *Anthropology News* 9 (December): 8–10.

To, Sandy. 2013. "Understanding Sheng Nu ('Leftover Women'): The Phenomenon of Late Marriage among Chinese Professional Women." *Symbolic Interaction* 36 (1): 1–20.

Trager, Lillian. 1988. *The City Connection: Migration and Family Interdependence in the Philippines*. Ann Arbor, MI: University of Michigan Press.

Unger, Jonathan. 1982. *Education under Mao: Class and Competition in Canton Schools, 1960–1980*. New York: Columbia University Press.

Urry, John. 2007. *Mobilities*. Cambridge: Polity Press.

Wallis, Cara. 2013. *Technomobility in China: Young Migrant Women and Mobile Phones*. New York: New York University Press.

Wang, Fei-Ling. 2004. "Reformed Migration Control and New Targeted People: China's *Hukou* System in the 2000s." *China Quarterly* 177 (March): 115–132.

———. 2011. "China's Evolving Institutional Exclusion: The *Hukou* System and Its Transformation." In *The Institutional Dynamics of China's Great Transformation*, ed. Xiaoming Huang, 110–129. New York: Routledge.

Wang Feng and Zuo Xuejin. 1997. "Socialist Dualism and the Migration Process in China: The Case of Shanghai." Paper presented at the workshop on Rural Labor Migration in 1990s China, University of California, Irvine, 26 April.

Wang Huaxin. 1998. *Nongmin Jincheng Jiuye Zhinan* [Problems of farmers entering cities]. Beijing: China Agriculture Press.

Wang Zheng. 1999. *Chinese Women and the Enlightenment: Oral and Textual Histories*. Berkeley, CA: University of California Press.

———. 2000. "Gender, Employment, and Women's Resistance." In *Chinese Society: Change, Conflict, and Resistance*, ed. Elizabeth J. Perry and Mark Selden, 158–182. London: Routledge.

Wank, David L. 2000. "Cigarettes and Domination in Chinese Business Networks: Institutional Change during the Market Transition." In *The Consumer Revolution in Urban China*, ed. Deborah S. Davis, 268–286. Berkeley: University of California Press.

Wesoky, Sharon. 2001. *Chinese Feminism Faces Globalization*. New York: Routledge.

Whyte, Martin King. 1990. "Changes in Mate Choice in Chengdu." In *Chinese Society on the Eve of Tiananmen*, ed. D. Davis and E. Vogel, 181–213. Cambridge, MA: Harvard University Press.

———. 2000. "The Perils of Assessing Trends in Gender Inequality in China." In *Re-Drawing Boundaries: Work, Households, and Gender in China*, ed. Barbara Entwisle and Gail E. Henderson, 157–167. Berkeley: University of California Press.

———. 2010. "The Paradoxes of Rural-Urban Inequality in Contemporary China." In *One Country, Two Societies: Rural-Urban Inequality in Contemporary China*, ed. Martin King Whyte, 1–25. Cambridge, MA: Harvard University Press.

Willis, Katie, and Brenda S. A. Yeoh, eds. 2000. *Gender and Migration*. Northampton, MA: Elgar Reference.

Wolf, Diane Lauren. 1992. *Factory Daughters, Gender, Household Dynamics, and Rural Industrialization in Java*. Berkeley: University of California Press.

Wolf, Margery. 1972. *Women and the Family in Taiwan*. Stanford, CA: Stanford University Press.

———. 1985. *Revolution Postponed: Women in Contemporary China*. Stanford, CA: Stanford University Press.

Woon, Yuen-fong. 2000. "Filial or Rebellious Daughters? Dagongmei in the Pearl River Delta Region, South China, in the 1990s." *Asian and Pacific Migration Journal* 9 (2): 137–169.

The World Bank and the Development Research Center of the State Council, P. R. China. 2014. *Urban China: Toward Efficient, Inclusive, and Sustainable Urbanization*. Preliminary manuscript accessed on April 21, 2014, at www.worldbank.org. (Now available at https://openknowledge.worldbank.org/.)

Wright, Caroline. 1995. "Gender Awareness in Migration Theory: Synthesizing Actor and Structure in Southern Africa." *Development and Change* 26:771–791.

Wu Jieh-Min. 2010. "Rural Migrant Workers and China's Differential Citizenship: A Comparative Institutional Analysis." In *One Country, Two Societies: Rural-Urban Inequality in Contemporary China*, ed. Martin King Whyte, 55–81. Cambridge, MA: Harvard University Press.

Xin Meng. 2000. "Regional Wage Gap, Information Flow, and Rural-Urban Migration." In *Rural Labor Flows in China*, ed. Loraine A. West and Yaohui Zhao, 251–277. Berkeley: Institute of East Asian Studies, University of California Press.

Xu, Feng. 2000. *Women Migrant Workers in China's Economic Reform*. New York: St. Martin's Press.

Yan, Hairong. 2003a. "Spectralization of the Rural: Reinterpreting the Labor Mobility of Rural Young Women in Post-Mao China." *American Ethnologist* 30 (4): 578–596.

———. 2003b. "Neoliberal Governmentality and Neohumanism: Organizing *Suzhi*/Value Flow through Labor Recruitment Networks." *Cultural Anthropology* 18 (4): 493–523.

———. 2008. *New Masters, New Servants: Migration, Development, and Women Workers in China*. Durham, NC: Duke University Press.

Yan, Yunxiang. 1996. *The Flow of Gifts: Reciprocity and Social Networks in a Chinese Village*. Stanford, CA: Stanford University Press.

———. 2002. "Courtship, Love and Premarital Sex in a North China Village." *The China Journal* 48:29–53.

———. 2003. *Private Life under Socialism: Love, Intimacy, and Family Change in a Chinese Village, 1949–1999*. Stanford, CA: Stanford University Press.

———. 2006. "Girl Power: Young Women and the Waning of Patriarchy in Rural North China." *Ethnology* 45 (2): 105–123.

———. 2010. "The Chinese Path to Individualization." *The British Journal of Sociology* 61 (3): 489–512.

Yang Ji. 1994. "Housekeepers Help Others and Better Themselves." *Beijing Review* (December), 22–23.

Yang, Martin C. 1965. *A Chinese Village: Taitou, Shantung Province*. New York: Columbia University Press.

Yang, Mayfair Mei-hui. 1994. *Gifts, Favors, and Banquets: The Art of Social Relationships in China*. Ithaca, NY: Cornell University Press.

———. 1999. "From Gender Erasure to Gender Difference: State Feminism, Consumer Sexuality, and Women's Public Sphere in China." In *Spaces of Their Own: Women's Public Sphere in Transnational China*, ed. Mayfair Mei-hui Yang, 35–67. Minneapolis: University of Minnesota Press.

Yang, Xiushi, and Guomei Xia. 2008. "Temporary Migration and STD/HIV Risky Sexual Behavior: A Population-Based Analysis of Gender Differences in China." *Social Problems* 55 (3): 322–346.

Yip, Winnie. 2010. "Disparities in Health Care and Health Status: The Rural-Urban Gap and Beyond." In *One Country, Two Societies: Rural-Urban Inequality in Contemporary China*, ed. Martin K. Whyte, 147–165. Cambridge, MA: Harvard University Press.

Young, Jason. 2011. "China's Changing *Hukou* System: Institutional Objectives, Formal Arrangements, and Informal Practices." In *The Institutional Dynamics of China's Great Transformation*, ed. Xiaoming Huang. New York: Routledge.

Zai Liang and Yiu-por Chan. 2004. "Migration and Gender in China: An Origin-Destination Linked Approach." *Economic Development and Cultural Change* 52 (2): 423–443.

Zhang, Hong. 2004. "'Living Alone' and the Rural Elderly: Strategy and Agency in Post-Mao China." In *Filial Piety: Practice and Discourse in Contemporary East Asia*, ed. Charlotte Ikels, 63–87. Stanford, CA: Stanford University Press.

———. 2007. "China's New Rural Daughters Coming of Age: Downsizing the Family and Firing Up Cash-earning Power in the New Economy." *Signs* 32 (3): 671–698.

Zhang, Li. 2000. "The Interplay of Gender, Space and Work in China's Floating Population." In *Re-Drawing Boundaries: Work, Households, and Gender in China*, ed. Barbara Entwisle and Gail E. Henderson, 171–196. Berkeley: University of California Press.

———. 2001. *Strangers in the City: Reconfigurations of Space, Power, and Social Networks within China's Floating Population*. Stanford, CA: Stanford University Press.

———. 2010. *In Search of Paradise: Middle-class Living in a Chinese Metropolis*. Ithaca, NY: Cornell University Press.

Zhang, Li, and Aihwa Ong, eds. 2008. *Privatizing China: Socialism from Afar*. Ithaca, NY: Cornell University Press.

Zhang, Qian Forrest. 2011. "Rethinking the Rural-Urban Divide in China's New Stratification Order." *International Journal of China Studies* 2 (2): 327–344.

Zhang Zhen. 2000. "Mediating Time: The 'Rice Bowl of Youth' in Fin de Siècle Urban China." *Public Culture* 12 (1): 93–113.

Zhao Chonglin. 1996. "Jiejie tu Beijing le" [Elder sister has gone to Beijing]. *Nongjia Nü Baishitong* [Rural Women Knowing All] (February), 27.

Zhao Shukai. 2000. "Organizational Characteristics of Rural Labor Mobility in China." In *Rural Labor Flows in China*, ed. Loraine A. West and Yaohui Zhao, 231–250. Berkeley: Institute of East Asian Studies, University of California.

Zhao Weijie. 1995. "Economic Development and the Marriage Crisis in the Special Economic Zones of China." In *Women in Market Societies: Crisis and Opportunity*, ed. Barbara Einhorn and Eileen Janes Yeo, 206–216. Aldershot, UK: Edward Elgar.

Zheng, Tiantian. 2009. *Red Lights: The Lives of Sex Workers in Postsocialist China*. Minneapolis: University of Minnesota Press.

Zheng Zhenzhen, Yun Zhou, Lixin Zheng, Dongxia Zhao, Chaohua Lou, and Shuangling Zhao. 2001. "Sexual Behavior and Contraceptive Use among Unmarried Young Women Migrant Workers in Five Cities in China." *Reproductive Health Matters* 9 (17): 118–127.

Zhou, Kate. 1996. *How the Farmers Changed China*. Boulder, CO: Westview Press.

Zhou Xiao. 1989. "Virginity and Premarital Sex in Contemporary China." *Feminist Studies* 15 (2): 279–288.

Zhu, Jianfeng. 2010. "Mothering Expectant Mothers: Consumption, Production, and Two Motherhoods in Contemporary China." *Ethos* 38 (4): 406–421.

Index

abortion, 101, 114, 142n.12, 145n.4
abuse in domestic service, 63, 64, 69
agency: definition of, 6–7, 138n.8; use of,
  8–9, 28–29, 79, 128, 132. *See also*
  resistance
age of migrant population: family and, 100,
  101, 104, 105, 107, 110, 112, 117; work
  and, 1–3, 5, 6, 28, 43, 137n.3
agricultural economy, 19, 25, 33–35
All-China Women's Federation, 14, 26, 48,
  59, 138n.1, 138n.4, 143n.2
amah, 137n.1
amei, 65
anticrime campaigns, 20. *See also* safety
  concerns
apprentice system, 59, 116, 144n.4
authority, 59–64, 65–67. *See also* parental
  control

baomu, 1, 67, 137n.1
beauty constructs: inner quarters femininity,
  35, 50, 62, 141n.19; urban consumer
  culture and, 81, 86–88. *See also* identity
  and consumer culture
beauty industry, 85, 88, 93, 94
beepers, 85
Beijing as cultural center, 16, 83–84, 139n.6
Beijing Evening News, 138n.2
Beijing Labor Bureau, 14, 62, 64
Beijing Municipal Women's Federation, 14
Beijing Olympics, 20, 119
Berman, Marshall, 2–3
birth stories, 114, 117–118, 121, 122, 125
boredom as motivator, 30, 40, 42
Bossen, Laurel, 24

Bourdieu, Pierre, 7
bride wealth, 38–39, 111, 113
brothels, 94

cadre households, 17, 18, 55, 59, 107, 143n.4
capitalism. *See* consumer culture; market
  socialism
CCP. *See* Communist Party of China (CCP)
cell phones, 85
chambermaids. *See* hotel housekeeping
  industry
Changying: education and, 88, 128; family
  of, 105, 117–120, 125, 126; Qiaolian and,
  86, 109; on tradition, 20, 31, 32; work of,
  6, 57, 86
chengjia, 41
chengren gaokao, 89
Chen Village study, 34
childbirth: *hukou* and, 114, 117, 122–125;
  sex-selective practices in, 113, 142n.12,
  145n.4; state-controlled, 9, 19, 39, 109,
  140n.16, 142nn.11–12, 145n.1; stories of,
  114, 117–118, 121–122. *See also* pregnancy
child-brides abolition, 139n.10
childcare workers, 14, 49, 54
children: care of migrant, 115, 121, 122,
  124–125, 126, 141n.20; education of
  migrant, 6, 18, 138n.7, 141n.20, 143n.1;
  hukou and, 109, 124–125, 140n.13,
  145n.3. *See also* family planning
Chu, Julia Y., 33
civil servants. *See* cadre households
class and skin color, 35, 86
cleaning industry, 67–70, 71, 86. *See also*
  hotel housekeeping industry

ABOUT THE AUTHOR

ARIANNE M. GAETANO is assistant professor of anthropology and women's studies at Auburn University. She earned a PhD in anthropology from the University of Southern California in 2005 and subsequently held positions at the Asia Research Institute of the National University of Singapore and the Center for East and Southeast Asian Studies at Lund University in Sweden. Her publications include journal articles and book chapters, and she coedited *On the Move: Women and Rural-to-Urban Migration in Contemporary China* (Columbia University Press 2004) with Tamara Jacka.

Production Notes for

Gaetano / *Out to Work: Migration, Gender, and the Changing Lives of Rural Women in Contemporary China*

Cover design by Julie Matsuo-Chun

Text design by George Whipple with display type in Minion Pro Bold and text type in Minion Pro

Composition by Westchester Publishing Services

Printing and binding by Sheridan Books, Inc.

Printed on 55 lb. House White Hi-Bulk D37, 360 ppi.